Table of Contents

List of Contributors V

About the Guest Editor VII

Preface IX

Gerald Cradock
Who Owns Child Abuse?
Reprinted from: *Soc. Sci.* **2014**, 3(4), 854-870
http://www.mdpi.com/2076-0760/3/4/854 1

Celia H. Brackenridge and Daniel Rhind
Child Protection in Sport: Reflections on Thirty Years of Science and Activism
Reprinted from: *Soc. Sci.* **2014**, 3(3), 326-340
http://www.mdpi.com/2076-0760/3/3/326 18

Mike Hartill and Melanie Lang
"I Know People Think I'm a Complete Pain in the Neck": An Examination of the
Introduction of Child Protection and "Safeguarding" in English Sport from the Perspective
of National Governing Body Safeguarding Lead Officers
Reprinted from: *Soc. Sci.* **2014**, 3(4), 606-627
http://www.mdpi.com/2076-0760/3/4/606 34

Gretchen Kerr, Ashley Stirling and Ellen MacPherson
A Critical Examination of Child Protection Initiatives in Sport Contexts
Reprinted from: *Soc. Sci.* **2014**, 3(4), 742-757
http://www.mdpi.com/2076-0760/3/4/742 56

**Raphaël Fournier, Thibault Cholez, Matthieu Latapy, Isabelle Chrisment,
Clémence Magnien, Olivier Festor and Ivan Daniloff**
Pedophile Activity in Different P2P Systems
Reprinted from: *Soc. Sci.* **2014**, 3(3), 314-325
http://www.mdpi.com/2076-0760/3/3/314 72

Helen C. Whittle, Catherine E. Hamilton-Giachritsis and Anthony R. Beech
"Under His Spell": Victims' Perspectives of Being Groomed Online
Reprinted from: *Soc. Sci.* **2014**, 3(3), 404-426
http://www.mdpi.com/2076-0760/3/3/404 84

William Budiselik, Frances Crawford and Donna Chung
The Australian Royal Commission into Institutional Responses to Child Sexual Abuse:
Dreaming of Child Safe Organisations?
Reprinted from: *Soc. Sci.* **2014**, 3(3), 565-583
http://www.mdpi.com/2076-0760/3/3/565 108

Kathleen Coulborn Faller
Forty Years of Forensic Interviewing of Children Suspected of Sexual Abuse,
1974–2014: Historical Benchmarks
Reprinted from: *Soc. Sci.* **2015**, 4(1), 34-65
http://www.mdpi.com/2076-0760/4/1/34 128

Amy Risley
Protecting Children and Adolescents in Uruguay: Civil Society's Role in Policy Reform
Reprinted from: *Soc. Sci.* **2014**, 3(4), 705-725
http://www.mdpi.com/2076-0760/3/4/705 161

Julia Sloth-Nielsen
Regional Frameworks for Safeguarding Children: The Role of the African Committee of
Experts on the Rights and Welfare of the Child
Reprinted from: *Soc. Sci.* **2014**, 3(4), 948-961
http://www.mdpi.com/2076-0760/3/4/948 181

List of Contributors

Anthony R. Beech: School of Psychology, University of Birmingham, Edgbaston, Birmingham B15 2TT, UK

Celia H. Brackenridge: Centre for Sport, Health and Well-being, Heinz Wolff Building, Brunel University London, Uxbridge UB8 3PH, UK

William Budiselik: School of Occupational Therapy and Social Work, Curtin University, Western Australia 6102, Australia

Thibault Cholez: LORIA/INRIA Nancy-Grand Est, 615 Rue du Jardin Botanique, 54600 Villers-lès-Nancy, France

Isabelle Chrisment: LORIA/INRIA Nancy-Grand Est, 615 Rue du Jardin Botanique, 54600 Villers-lès-Nancy, France

Donna Chung: School of Occupational Therapy and Social Work, Curtin University, Western Australia 6102, Australia

Kathleen Coulborn Faller: School of Social Work, University of Michigan, 1080 S. University Ave, Ann Arbor, MI 48109-1106, USA

Gerald Cradock: Department of Sociology, Anthropology and Criminology, University of Windsor, 401 Sunset Ave., Windsor, ON N9B 3P4, Canada

Frances Crawford: School of Health, University of New England, New South Wales 2351, Australia

Ivan Daniloff: Sorbonne Universités, UPMC Univ Paris 06, UMR 7606, LIP6, F-75005 Paris, France; CNRS, UMR 7606, LIP6, F-75005 Paris, France

Olivier Festor: LORIA/INRIA Nancy-Grand Est, 615 Rue du Jardin Botanique, 54600 Villers-lès-Nancy, France

Raphaël Fournier: TI/Institut Galilée, Université Paris-Nord, 99 avenue JB Clément, 93430 Villetaneuse, France

Catherine E. Hamilton-Giachritsis: School of Psychology, University of Birmingham, Edgbaston, Birmingham B15 2TT, UK

Mike Hartill: Department of Sport & Physical Activity, Edge Hill University, St Helens Road, Ormskirk L39 4QP, UK

Gretchen Kerr: Faculty of Kinesiology and Physical Education, University of Toronto, 55 Harbord Street, Toronto, M5S 2W6, Canada

Melanie Lang: Department of Sport & Physical Activity, Edge Hill University, St Helens Road, Ormskirk L39 4QP, UK

Matthieu Latapy: Sorbonne Universités, UPMC Univ Paris 06, UMR 7606, LIP6, F-75005 Paris, France; CNRS, UMR 7606, LIP6, F-75005 Paris, France

Ellen MacPherson: Faculty of Kinesiology and Physical Education, University of Toronto, 55 Harbord Street, Toronto, M5S 2W6, Canada

Clémence Magnien: Sorbonne Universités, UPMC Univ Paris 06, UMR 7606, LIP6, F-75005 Paris, France; CNRS, UMR 7606, LIP6, F-75005 Paris, France

Daniel Rhind: Centre for Sport, Health and Well-being, Heinz Wolff Building, Brunel University London, Uxbridge UB8 3PH, UK

Amy Risley: Department of International Studies, Rhodes College, 2000 North Parkway, Memphis, TN 38112-1690, USA

Julia Sloth-Nielsen: Department of Public Law and Jurisprudence, University of the Western Cape, Bellville, Western Cape 7535, South Africa; Department of Child Law, University of Leiden, Leiden 2311, The Netherlands; African Committee of Experts on the Rights and Welfare of the Child, Addis Ababa, Ethiopia

Ashley Stirling: Faculty of Kinesiology and Physical Education, University of Toronto, 55 Harbord Street, Toronto, M5S 2W6, Canada

Helen C. Whittle: Child Exploitation and Online Protection Centre, London SW1V 2WG, UK; School of Psychology, University of Birmingham, Edgbaston, Birmingham B15 2TT, UK

About the Guest Editor

Nigel Parton is Professor in Applied Childhood Studies at the University of Huddersfield, England where he has worked for most of the last forty years. A social worker by background he has written and edited over twenty books and a hundred articles and chapters on the broad areas of child protection, child welfare and social work and in recent years has developed a particular interest in studying and comparing child protection policies and systems in different jurisdictions. Recent books include 'Child Protection: International Trends and Orientations' (edited with N Gilbert and M Skivenes. New York:Oxford University Press, 2011) and 'The Politics of Child Protection: Contemporary Developments and Future Directions' (Basingstoke; Palgrave/Macmillan, 2014).

Preface

Developments in Child Protection: Foreword(s) for Three Book Volumes

The last forty years has witnessed increasing public, political and media concern about the problem of child maltreatment and what to do about it. This is now evident in most jurisdictions and is receiving serious attention from many international and trans-national organisations. While the '(re)discovery' of the problem in the USA was particularly associated with the 'battered baby syndrome' this has now broadened to include: physical abuse, sexual abuse, neglect, emotional abuse, abuse on the internet, child trafficking, female genital mutilation, sexual exploitation and refers to all children and young people, not just babies. Similarly, the focus of attention has broadened from intra-familial abuse to abuse in a whole variety of settings including schools, day care centres, churches, youth and sports clubs and the wider community more generally. There has also been a broadening of concern from not simply protecting children and young people from serious harm to also attempting to prevent the impairment of their health and development and to ensure that they are able to grow up in circumstances which are consistent with the provision of safe and effective care so that all children can achieve the best outcomes.

In the process, the laws, policies, practices and systems which have been developed to try to identify and prevent child maltreatment have become much more wide-ranging and complex and have themselves been subject to continual criticism and review. A wide range of professionals and members of the community are all seen to have key roles to play in both protecting children and young people and also assessing and monitoring actual and potential perpetrators.

However, while these issues have been subject to often heated and high profile media and political debate, rarely have they received sustained analytic and research attention in the social sciences. It was in this context that the internet journal *Social Sciences,* in 2013, invited papers for publication in a *Special Issue* dedicated to the topic and these were published from July 2014 onwards. In the event thirty papers were accepted for publication—far and away the highest number of papers submitted and accepted previously for a *Special Issue* in the journal. Authors came from a range of countries including: Australia, Belgium, Canada, England, Ethiopia, France, Netherlands, New Zealand, Scotland, South Africa, Spain, and the USA. Sixteen of the thirty papers were based on original research, ten provided a policy analysis, two were based on particular practice developments, one was a literature review, and one provided a more theoretical/conceptual piece. Authors came from a wide range of disciplinary backgrounds including: sociology, history, social policy, sports science, psychology, social work, education, law and various branches of health and medicine. The focus of the papers was diverse, though they did tend to cluster around a number of themes and it is these that have provided the rationale for the organisation of the papers into the three published volumes; however, the process of organising and ordering the papers proved a particular challenge. There are ten papers in each volume.

Volume 1: Policy Changes and Challenges
Volume 1 takes as its central theme the ongoing and challenging issues which child protection agencies have to address and the policy and practice initiatives that are developed to try and address these. The volume includes papers on: the relationship between the decline in the rate of 'unnatural' deaths and the growth of concern about child abuse in the USA between 1940 and 2005; mandatory reporting; the balance between providing urgent intervention and meeting chronic need; risk and the Public Law Outline in England; the nature and implications of 'child centred' policies; the impact of intimate partner and family violence; the intended and unintended consequences of high profile child abuse scandals; developing multi-disciplinary team work in a health setting; and the possibilities of technology-based innovations in prevention programmes.

Volume 2: Issues in Child Welfare
Volume 2 is primarily concerned with how best to respond to maltreatment 'within' the family and hence has a range of papers which are much more concerned with the area of policy and practice more traditionally framed in terms of 'child welfare' and social work with children and families. It also includes a paper on how to respond to child maltreatment and neglect in a large hospital context.

Volume 3: Broadening Challenges in Child Protection
Volume 3 takes a somewhat broader brief and reflects many of the changes over the past twenty five years in terms of the broadening of concerns from maltreatment within the family to maltreatment in a variety of extra-familial contexts, including: sport, the internet, various institutional settings and is much more concerned with sexual abuse and the challenges for criminal justice and public protection.

Nigel Parton
Guest Editor

Who Owns Child Abuse?

Gerald Cradock

Abstract: Expectations of contemporary child protection apparatuses are strongly influenced by beliefs inherited from the nineteenth century child rescue movement. In particular, the belief that child abuse determination is obvious. However, this assumption fails to make a distinction between nineteenth century's emphasis on impoverished environments and the twentieth century introduction of the pathological child abuser. Moreover, the proliferation of kinds of child abuse, and the need to distinguish child abusers from non-abusers, means knowledge is now spread across an array of disciplines and professions, which necessarily destabilizes the definition of child abuse. The increasing exposure of alternate care systems as potentially abusive has similarly destabilized the old common sense solution to neglected children—namely removal. Finally, as uncertainty increases, and definitions become more divergent, the question of what child abuse is, and what should be done about it, becomes increasingly politicized.

Reprinted from *Soc. Sci.* Cite as: Cradock, G. Who Owns Child Abuse? *Soc. Sci.* **2014**, *3*, 854–870.

1. Introduction

Perhaps the most curious thing about child abuse is the degree to which its practical definition is usually treated as obvious even though its precise composition and boundaries are subject to chronic and intense disagreement. The problem is not so simple as whether one person's discipline is another person's child abuse, nor whether children's exposure to adult sexuality is child abuse or bad manners, nor even what the appropriate balance between "coddling" and "neglect" might be. To frame the problem in these binaries obscures the degree to which the understanding of child abuse is fundamentally epistemological. In other words, this view inevitably presumes child abuse has a reality independent of the varied discursive practices that constitute it. The presumption implies a consensus of what child abuse *really* is, what its effects are *known* to be, and what practical *solutions* should be applied even where there are deeply divided opinions.

Suggesting that knowledge of what is and what is not child abuse is problematic seems out-of-step with modern professional and lay knowledge about child abuse. Public perception, inevitably fueled by inquiries into child deaths and stoked by lurid and occasionally hysterical press coverage, tends to view the presence or absence of child abuse as obvious to anyone with eyes to see and ears to hear. Meanwhile, the copious studies linking certain parental behaviors and practices with poor intellectual and emotional outcomes for their children add the imprimatur of science to this impression. Law, too, especially as expressed in the reports of legally trained inquirers, tends to view individual cases of child abuse—and especially the child deaths that are inquiries' frequent objects—as uniformly avoidable with the proper application of widely available professional knowledge.

The view that there is a single and universal phenomenon designated by the term "child abuse" is fundamentally a modernist conception. It is a means of placing child abuse outside the confusions and complexities of history by positing a true description of a fixed reality [1]. To paraphrase the sociologist Norbert Elias, this manner of describing child abuse is a "retreat into the present" whereby current practices and discourses are projected as epistemological absolutes applicable at any time and in any place [4]. From this perspective, as civilization develops child abuse is increasingly discovered or revealed as our knowledge expands. However, historians of childhood—and others utilizing historical sociology—have repeatedly drawn attention to the developing status of childhood and the place of children within society more generally [4–6]. This development is often seen as a form of teleological progress, but is more accurately described as an aspect of a culturally specific moment; a pattern of conduct necessitated within historically specific social and cultural configurations. For example, a concept such as "fostering" has dramatically different meanings for the medieval period in contrast to our contemporary age. More significantly, behind this difference lay radically different notions of what is best for children, and what kinds of attachments children require.

This paper will make several relatively simple points: First, the "obviousness" of child abuse is not a reflection of the current state of knowledge, but rather a legacy inherited from the 19th century child rescue movement and the over-confidence of the "scientific charity" ideology that absorbed it. Second, new knowledge in the field of child abuse is more or less incoherent and therefore it is to be expected that child protection action will reflect that incoherency. Finally, child protective action is fundamentally political because of this broad range of definitions and specialist epistemologies. These observations are significant for anyone engaged in the child protection project, but most especially for the review mechanisms that have proliferated over the past several decades. If child abuse is a fixed property engaged in by a specific and pathological kind of human, then it is reasonable to believe child abuse can be eliminated by deploying a fixed set of techniques. However, if child abuse is not a fixed property but variable, not only through time but across knowledge domains, then it follows that proposed solutions are likely to vary according to the epistemological rules of each knowledge domain. In other words, there is no reason to suppose a consensus of what constitutes child abuse is possible, no matter how desirable it might be. In other words, calling for "oined-up" services, or single "child-centered" practices will always be thwarted by the incommensurability of varied knowledge constructions and their resultant practices.

---

[1] An anonymous reviewer remarked that this strongly constructionist position breaks down in the instances of severe harm both because the social consensus that it is wrong is likely to be very high, but also because the harm is embodied and therefore unequivocal. This is, of course, a thorny philosophical question to which I can only give brief reply. I argue that historically the social consensus has been highly variable and while there is no doubt children's physical suffering has been "real" throughout history it has not necessarily been a problem for society as a whole. Boswell's (1988) [1] history of child abandonment or de Mause's (1974) [2] account of the history of childhood supports this view. However, I would prefer to follow Hacking [3] by suggesting that to ask "is it real?" is to ask the wrong question. Instead, the salient question is: why do we now designate harm to children as "abuse", and why do we believe it is committed by persons categorized as "child abusers"?

2. Child Saving

The term "child saving" is generally associated with philanthropic movements of the nineteenth century whose principle interest was saving children from the depredations and vices of the newly industrialized cities of Europe and North America. In general, the objective of child savers was removal; ideally children would be removed from squalid urban conditions to healthful and wholesome rural surroundings where the endemic physical and moral diseases of city life would be cleansed in fresh country air and the salutary company of rural yeomanry (see for example: [7]).

The emphasis on removal is significant because it marks a break with prior childcare practices. Residential placement of impoverished children in homes specifically designed for children was unusual in Western Europe until the eighteenth and nineteenth centuries. By contrast, in the Byzantine Empire state-sponsored and private orphanages were a common occurrence beginning as early as the fifth century A.D. [8]. The *Ospedeli degli Innocenti* founded at Florence in the early fifteenth century was the first—or at least one of the first—purpose built orphanage in Western Europe [9]. London had an orphanage by the mid sixteenth century (notable because it was not directly tied to a specific parish) [10], and Paris opened an orphanage in the early seventeenth century [11]. The later appearance of orphanages in Western Europe may have been a consequence of monasteries' ability to receive (male) children as oblates, or perhaps because of the widespread and traditional use of fostering and abandonment. In any case, it seems likely that most foundling children died, were more or less indentured, or found themselves in the usual resorts of the destitute; almshouses, hospitals, and the like [2].

In contrast, by the beginning in the mid-eighteenth century there is a discernible shift in adult attitudes toward dependent children. First, child welfare institutions were increasingly child specific. Second, early orphanages such as Captain Coram's London Foundling Hospital became larger than their predecessors because, in principle, they sought to service all children in need [12]. Even so, by the mid nineteenth century orphanage populations were so large children were exported from Britain to the colonies by the tens of thousands. Second, orphanages were increasingly linked to the health of the nation. Destitute and neglected children were not simply the devil's workshop, but were indicative of the decline of the race, and in the case of Britain, a threat to Empire. Thus, for example, Coram's boys were set to work making rope and sails in anticipation of their future employment in Britain's vast imperial merchant marine.

At least for England, the need for universal orphanages was linked to the traditional Poor Laws, which were organized on the localism of the parish. Consequently, as parishes merged into urban areas, and the population became more mobile, ensuring the support of the poor—including children—by their home parish became increasingly difficult to enforce [13]. Certainly, by the mid-nineteenth century the combination of mass migration to the cities and uncertain employment had created an army of street urchins that overwhelmed traditional forms of charity. The result was the child-savers and other reformers of the urban poor.

These nineteenth century child savers were both similar to and different from those who had gone before. They were similar insofar as both iterations of philanthropy knew full well that "orphan" meant poor; not "without parent". Both understood that infants who entered orphanages usually died, and both reckoned a child's stay in an orphanage was limited to middle childhood because children were routinely apprenticed or placed in service around the age of ten or twelve years. As well, for the most part those who financially and administratively supported orphanages were motivated by religious and social status factors. The nineteenth century child savers, however, were markedly more zealous in their activity than their forebears. The Victorian philanthropist was not content to wait until approached for favor by destitute parents, but actively sought out the poor in their hovels. Further, these reformers saw themselves as buttressing the very foundations of society. They were not simply alleviating poverty through charity, but reforming and reorganizing society upon scientific principles. The anticipated result in the British Empire was the furthering of Imperial glory and the advancement of civilization, while in the United States child welfare was believed necessary for the survival of republican democracy.

Many explanations have been advanced as to why the nineteenth century evinced such deep concern for children. These include: a new muscular Christianity; the spread and dominance of a bourgeois family ethic; a sacralisation of childhood; the universalization of schools; the demographic transition; the rise of romanticism; and more. No doubt all of these are true to a degree, but from the point of view of historical sociology it seems this refiguring of childhood and adult responsibilities toward children is reflective of a vector of development stretching across centuries. In the classic work of Ariés [5] and Elias [14] our attention is drawn not only to differences in the structures and functions of historical social formations, but also the corresponding shifts in *sentiment* accompanying these changes. Of course, one should not overly romanticize general Victorian sentiment. No doubt those who went on "slumming" tours of London's East End were as likely drawn by the same impulse one might have for going to the zoo [15], but there is no denying many others were deeply moved. The novels of Dickens, the reporting of Jacob Riis, and the publicity photographs of Barnardo, were not mere cries in the wilderness. People were emotionally moved, and some were moved enough to become tirelessly active.

For these child savers, the problem was obvious. Neglected children either lived ragged and alone on the street, or inhabited dark and filthy tenements and hovels where violence and vice were rampant. Dr. Barnardo and his lamp, the New York Children's Aid Society agent, the lady "friendly visitor" from the Settlement House sought out children living in these conditions and cajoled, bribed, or outright abducted them to places of safety. With the exception of sexually abused girls and criminal boys the particular experiences of particular children were not of much interest to their saviors [7,16]. Child savers did not save children from categorized forms of abuse, but from a life of urban degradation and squalor. Nor did the child savers vary much in their remedial recommendation; children were to be *removed* to the country. By the turn of the twentieth century, even those few voices speaking in favor of institutional care through cottage style orphanages agreed such orphanages should be located in the country (See for example [17]).

Even as the twentieth century created the social worker along with her social casework skills, the self-evident-ness of children's plight persisted. Some children continued to be removed due to the effects of poverty, but poverty faded from the causation horizon. Rather, the social casework formula propagandized by Charlotte Whitten in Canada [18] and Mary Richmond [19] in the United States spoke to the need to moralize the poor rather than engaging in the indiscriminate charity they believed encouraged dependency and sloth. This is not to denigrate the enormous and widespread scientific project that accompanied the Child Study movement, the Juvenile Courts, the influence of psychoanalysis, and the promotion and dissemination of research-based knowledge by such organizations as the Children's Bureau in the United States. Children, it seemed, were suddenly at the center of a scientific industry. Yet for all that, social casework and its allied professions remained remarkably confident in its own moralizing activities and its ability to simply "know" when children were in need of removal. The new knowledge, no matter how carefully researched and publicized, was not so much incorporated as grafted onto an existing moral assuredness predicated upon the inherent superiority of the bourgeois family.

Such was the state of child protection for the first two-thirds of the twentieth century. Through radical improvements in infant and maternal care, infant mortality dropped sharply. New nutrition strategies such as the Canada Food Guide emphasized the importance of healthy practices underwritten by healthy baby contests at local fairs, and universalized public health and sanitation practices meant children were healthier throughout their lives [20,21]. Eventually, a point was reached where children's health was simply assumed and both parents and experts could turn their attention to whether children were happy and achieving their full potential. There were, however, some nagging worries. In the late 1940s radiographers began to notice that children's bones were being broken and healed in secret. While psychology and psychiatry worried about toilet training and attachment interruption, a small group of doctors began to wonder if even middle class parents were deliberately physically harming their children [22]. Finally, in 1962 Kempe and his colleagues published *The Battered-Child Syndrome* [23] and the world of childhood was revolutionized.

3. Child Abuse as Science

If the early child savers needed little besides the evidence of their own eyes to identify neglected children, their judgments with respect to the children's parents and other adults were equally morally straightforward. Children's ill treatment was caused by poverty, ignorance, and in the often-brazen anti-Catholic sentiment of Protestant child savers, by the ignorance of the priesthood [16]. In the eyes of some of the more broad-minded child savers poverty and ignorance may have excused neglect and vice, but generally speaking assessments of parents were framed within moral parameters. With the exception of Tardieu's mid nineteenth century work at Paris, there is no figure of *child abuser* as a pathological threat [24]. Whether in the diaries of CAS workers in New York, the textbooks written by Mary Richmond, or the deliberations of the White House conference on dependent children [15,19,25], parents are never described as pathologically disordered. Thus, when Hacking [26] describes the displacement of cruelty, neglect, and incest with the general term "child abuse" he is perhaps only half right. It wasn't that "child abuse" was a twentieth century discovery, but the child *abuser* in all his or her iterations, became a new explanation for the maltreatment of children.

Thus, when Kempe and his colleagues described the "battered-child syndrome" in 1962 (almost twenty years after radiologists had first described evidence of it), it was not the existence of the "syndrome" that created the ensuing moral panic, but the realization that it was *parents* from all social classes who were inflicting the battering. Kempe specifically described these parents as in need of medical supervision and psychiatric counseling. Those who maltreated children were no longer morally depraved or hopelessly impoverished; they were mentally ill and extremely dangerous.

As Nelson [27] has famously documented, the impact of Kempe's paper was both wide and deep. That is, Kempe didn't just put child abuse on the map; he arguably created an entire industry that rapidly spread from Denver to encompass the globe. By the end of the 1960s, the figure of the child abuser was as feared and endemic as "Reds under Beds" in the 1950s. And, just like the Reds, child abusers came in increasingly diverse and secretive forms. In the 1980s when sexual abuse was recognized not as "incest", "white slavery", or peculiar rural marriage practices, but as a specific form of sexual deviancy practiced by child abusers who were usually known to their victims, child protection workers were confronted with a whole new set of challenges. Largely ignorant of children's sexuality, and ill-equipped to manage the coordination of family and criminal matters, the child protection system was overwhelmed by allegations of present and past sexual abuse by parents, friends, institutions, and, finally, sadistic cults practicing "ritual abuse" [28].

With all of this attention to saving children from child abusers, the scientific world was equally overwhelmed. For example, the hard science of memory found itself questioned as therapists made claims about the mind's ability to recover unadulterated repressed memories [3]. But while the Recovered Memory movement fought desperate battles with their "False Memory Syndrome" opponents, other less emotive questions arose. Suddenly everything from baby's sleeping habits and parental smoking [29], the mysterious Munchausen's by Proxy Syndrome [30], and the problem of SIDS were drawn into the ambit of child abuse [31,32]. The term child abuse came to absorb virtually every possible way a child might be harmed, and in keeping with the characteristic drift of neoliberal regimes toward responsibilization, parents were increasingly scrutinized for error [33].

Thus, child abuse research continually produces correlative studies purporting to show connections between particular parental behaviors and poor later outcomes for children. This research, combined with a seemingly endless parade of scandals in child protection systems across the globe led to the incorporation of "risk" into child protection practice (See for example [34]). Specifically, the 1990s saw the widespread adoption of risk assessment tools into child protection practices. As I have discussed elsewhere, the adoption of risk assessments was not so much a utilization of scientific insight as a political strategy designed to blunt attacks on child protection systems and their functionaries [35]. The central characteristics of child protection risk assessments were their assumption that child abuse occurred within the family, and their emphasis on the characteristics of the potential adult *abuser* [2]. That said, one could also argue that the shift to risk thinking in child protection was away from specific persons in a specific situation and towards the search for risks in and of themselves. Hence, child protection began to slide into a world of almost pure abstraction wherein risks became more real than actual parents and children. The numbers generated by risk assessments purported to provide a scientific basis for decision-making and, moreover, the claim was always that these risk values were "research-based".

Precisely how "scientific" risk assessments truly are is open to debate. However, it is very clear that once child protection systems begin to think in terms of risks the universe of potential sources of child abuse becomes potentially endless—especially where risk of child abuse, and risk of harm, comes to mean more or less the same thing. In the kind of responsibilizing environment produced by neoliberal regimes there are no accidents; everyone is potentially at fault for their risk miscalculations [36]. Under such circumstances, determining child protection action is no longer a matter of common sense. The combination of ever multiplying sources of risk, and the ever more complex ways in which these risks are calculated and evaluated, suggest limitless possibilities for forms of child abuse.

4. Alternative Care as Iatrogenic Abuse

In the back alleys and tenements of the great Victorian cities the condition of children was so obviously abysmal that the only practical permanent solution appeared to be removal to places of safety. There were, of course, other forms of assistance available in the form of ragged schools, newsboy's hostels, and so forth, but the enormous growth of orphanages combined with large-scale child migration testified to the unflagging belief that removal, and ultimately country air, was the universal solution to the problem of urban child neglect [7,16].

Children removed to orphanages had notably mixed experiences. Unsurprisingly, by the beginning of the twentieth century a general consensus emerged claiming institutional care—especially congregate care—was generally harmful. Institutional care was said to produce listless, unimaginative, and docile children who would grow to be adults incapable of earning their own living or caring for themselves. Orphanages reacted by adopting cottage style living quarters that attempted to approximate normal family life, but even this style was considered a poor second choice to loving

---

[2] In North America, there is a specific genealogy of risk assessments waiting to be told. The assessment I am most familiar with is the one introduced in British Columbia. This was based on the New York State risk assessment and was itself the basis for the risk assessment adopted in Ontario. The British Columbian assessment was introduced with the assistance of Diana English who worked in Washington State. In previous research I have tried to work out exactly where risk assessments originated but without success. The concept of risk was originally used to identify risk populations but exactly when it jumped to identifying risk individuals is not clear but must have been sometime in the 1980s. One should also keep in mind that a backlash against pure risk assessment has resulted in a corresponding technology of "needs assessment". In Ontario, for example, both risk assessments and needs assessments exist side-by-side, although in my opinion whether there is any significant difference between the two is open to question. In any event, the politics of classification and quantifying of risk—or if you prefer, danger—was clearly revealed by the Laming Report's account of the death of Anna Climbié.

family care. There were dissenting voices—particularly from Catholic charities—but they were generally overruled.

In these early iterations of mass fostering it is remarkable how little effort was expended on finding out what happened to removed children. The New York Children's Aid Society did some follow up work in response to complaints from the Western States that New York's incorrigible children became the Midwest's juvenile and adult prison population [7,25], and inspections were carried out in Canada in response to complaints that orphans were being used as virtual slaves on Canadian farms, but by and large the efficacy of sending children West, and the superior care provided by family care, was taken for granted. Moreover, the movement of children was largely predicated upon a "clean break" philosophy. As ever, Victorian orphans were not without parents but permanent separation of children and parents was generally encouraged [37]. Despite this, children voluntarily placed by parents were never entirely out of the minds of their parents as correspondence between orphanages and parents attests [38]. For those children removed across continents and between continents, of course, such parental contact was effectively terminated.

In short, from the very beginning of the modernist child protection project the question of whether children were better off left in inadequate living circumstances, or starting life anew with foster or adoptive families was never entirely resolved. Model institutions such as the New York Orphanage on the Hudson suspected children in foster care were little more than cheap labor [17], while parents never ceased to see orphanages as stopgap measures who's main purpose was to help families through rough economic times. Jane Addams, for example, used the 1909 White House Conference as a platform to demand worker's compensation schemes to prevent children becoming dependent on charity or the state due to their fathers' industrial injuries [25].

The problem of alternative care for children tended to fade during the early decades of the twentieth century. Across the English-speaking world, orphanages closed or were repurposed. A growing welfare state alleviated much of the brutality of nineteenth century capitalism and consequently the street urchin disappeared. Those orphanages that survived were increasingly repurposed to service children suffering some sort of pathological condition. Orphanages ceased to be normative and, instead, became therapeutic [39]. Alternatively, orphanages were absorbed into a network of municipal social services as with Vancouver's first orphanage, which became—and remains to this day—a "Neighborhood House" [18]. The fostering and adoption concept remained, and at least in the U.S. became a major mechanism for families to survive the Great Depression, but orphanages were more or less terminated as a child welfare technology. The trend away from alternative care became a positive injunction with the post war acceptance of John Bowlby and Anna Freud's widely publicized and influential work on childhood attachment. According to this new truth regime, any separation of children from their attachment figures—normally understood as mothers—was itself harmful and should be avoided except for exceptional instances of neglect or abandonment [40].

When two decades later the Battered-Child Syndrome created the figure of the pathological child abuser the child protection system was placed in a quandary. Should children remain in the care of psychiatrically disturbed parents, or should they be removed? In Canada, the problem was particularly stark because the closure of Residential Schools for aboriginal children created a child care crisis for First Nations' settlements. The result was what became known as "the sixties scoop" when some First Nations lost virtually all their children to child protection authorities [41]. Without the now discredited mass institutional care provided by orphanages, child protection authorities sought to expand the fostering and adoptive systems to provide for the influx of children. However, by the end of the nineteen seventies this approach, too, had lost its appeal. It was increasingly obvious that children in foster care led a transient life drifting from one home to another, and that at least some foster parents were as abusive [42,43], if not more abusive, than the parents the children were supposedly being saved from.

In Canada, events such as the suicide of Richard Cardinal and other exposés in the press, called the entire concept of alternate care into disrepute [44]. As the growing body of inquiries and Court Judgements begun in the early nineteen seventies and continuing down to the present day demonstrate, not only were children being abused in their own families but they were also abused in the alternate care facilities and foster homes meant to protect them [3]. Despite the obvious fact that no amount of exhortation to better judgment, training, or education on the part of social workers was likely to increase the potential pool of foster parents living in an increasingly urbanized environment of two-earner families, variations of long term fostering or adoption became the clarion call of 1980s child welfare.

It is clear child protection apparatuses developed over the past two centuries have generated their own moral hazards. Put at its bluntest, the practice of child protection has become a source of child abuse because child protection activities have iatrogenic properties. Faced with this dilemma, child protection authorities are generally exhorted to engage in "preventative practice", which is usually understood as forms of increased surveillance and intervention.

5. Child Abuse: Event or Pattern?

The definition of child abuse within child protective practices tends to view child abuse as patterned and repetitive behavior on the part of a pathological child abuser. While it is true that child removals may occur as a consequence of acute and specific events, it is rare for those events to occur within an informational vacuum. By now given the constant call for professionals to be vigilant, the effect of mandatory reporting laws, and the general acceptance of high levels of surveillance and their accompanying risk calculi, it is unusual for an abused child to be completely unknown to authorities [45]. Indeed, a frequent complaint of inquiries into child protection scandals is that all the necessary information was known; it wasn't acted upon. It seems that in the practical world of child protection the question of whether a child is in need of protection is not a simple one-to-one correlation with a specific action classed as abuse, but rather a matter of thresholds of tolerance. For example, a single drunken party won't result in your child being

---

[3] With respect to institutional care there is now a network of scholars (to which I belong) who are concerned with both contemporary and historical abuse. This network is now composed of scholars from at least twelve different countries. From our seminars and the contributions to a book scheduled for publication in early 2015 it is clear that child abuse in institutions is both international in scope, and remarkably similar wherever it is found. A similar study for foster care would also be helpful. Suffice to say that newspaper accounts of children abused in foster care have been commonplace.

removed, but a pattern of drunkenness eventually will. A single slap across the buttocks of a two-year old is acceptable (in Canadian law), but a pattern of spankings is not. By contrast, sexual abuse is generally considered a "zero tolerance" form of abuse, but even here the boundaries between abusive behavior and inappropriate affection or poor judgment, are not always as obvious as one would hope. When, for example, the La leche league counsels mothers to breastfeed to as old as seven years, and acknowledges part of the attraction of this practice is its erotic overtones, is this child abuse [46]? Finally, who is to say when a familial sex abuser is "cured" or, perhaps more accurately, under sufficient self-control, they can resume a normal parental role?

The role of patterns plays out in much psychological research into the effects of child abuse. This body of research almost never refers to a single traumatic event but rather to patterns of harmful conduct. Insofar as child abuse *may* be defined as anything that causes harm to a child, these described patterns become the psychologists' definition of child abuse. More accurately, each of the many harmful patterns this literature describes is child abuse because they cause harm and therefore children ought to be protected from them. The immediate problem for child protection apparatuses is that no harmful pattern can be fully described by a psychological study. Harmful patterns must take place within a larger and often quite specific context, which at the very least will modulate the harmful pattern's effects and may even neutralize them. This problem is the fundamental sociological problem of understanding the relation of individuals to society at large, and then attempting to make universal and predictive statements about that relationship within a specific context.

Moreover, it is possible that while abusive behavior may be patterned, the actual harm done is caused by a specific incident. This is most obvious in the case of pediatric homicide where a child's death occurs as a result of a specific act of violence, and yet the larger context may be without positive evidence of previous child abuse. Such was the problem confronting the Canadian Goudge Inquiry in its consideration of wrongful convictions for child homicide [47]. Like the U.K. experience with the famous trio of wrongful convictions for child homicide, the Goudge Inquiry was prompted by the problem of determining cause of death in cases of apparent Shaken Baby Syndrome, short-fall injuries or Sudden Infant Death Syndrome [47]. In these instances, "cause of death" had significance in *both* the child protection and the criminal prosecution context. Further, both these contexts were reliant on knowledge and expert judgment generated outside their respective fields—namely medicine, and specifically pediatric forensic pathology. When the pathology turned out to be unreliable, both the child protection and criminal prosecution apparatuses were left without evidential foundation. For the prosecution apparatuses the result was wrongful convictions and incarcerations. For child protection, it meant child "wrongfully" removed and adopted because of those wrongful convictions. In the wake of these errors (and Lord Laming has similar advice for police officers with respect to doctors), it seems each knowledge regime has to operate according to its own standards and rules of establishing truth. Thus, while the child protection system is urged to find a singly language, its components are simultaneously advised not to trust truth generated outside their specialty. Significantly, the Goudge Inquiry specifically instructed coroners and pathologists to ignore patterned evidence suggesting child abuse and advised them to focus solely on the immediate circumstances when determining cause of death [48].

The instances highlighted by Goudge and the UK cases are not only about the specifics of diagnosing cause of death. Rather, they necessarily call into question approaches to child protection based upon contextual inference—that is to say, risk assessment. The Goudge Inquiry Report, and the *mea culpa* evidence given by leading international pathologists there, specifically criticizes cause of death diagnoses that apply general knowledge about child abuse causation to specific events, or apply prior prejudicial knowledge of the actors. It also implicitly denies diagnoses of exclusion; *i.e.*, if there is no other obvious cause child abuse is assumed. Instead, the consensus now insists upon positive knowledge meeting the "beyond reasonable doubt" standard for criminal evidence.

The problems associated with diagnosing cause of death in instances of short-fall injuries, Sudden Infant Death Syndrome, and Shaken Baby Syndrome, are dramatic both in their subject (child mortality) but also in their ability to shift the figure of the *child abuser* into the figure of the *wrongfully convicted*. While these instances focus our attention, they are but examples of a much larger problem of certainty in the child protection world. Where, for example, do we stand on Munchausen's by Proxy Syndrome? At one time, the medical discovery of this life-threatening psychiatric disease seemed a major victory for child protection, but in the wake of its main discoverers being disgraced—even if partially rehabilitated—the diagnosis is left in a curious kind of limbo [49]. The point is not whether these syndromes do or do not exist, but their sudden uncertainty clears the way for other claims under uncertain conditions. Do vaccinations cause autism? Does inscribing a swastika in ink on a child's arm cause the child to become a fascist? (And is that abuse?) Do sports involving head collisions necessarily cause brain disease? Is *Uncle Tom's Cabin* too racist for children to read?

No matter how tendentious these sources of child abuse may appear, they do at least make causal claims. That is, they claim exposure to a given circumstance or context is harmful. There is, however, still the difficulty of what is meant by *potential*. During the latter part of the twentieth century child abuse began to be couched in terms of an ideal childhood in which parents and/or the state were said to have responsibility for ensuring children reach their full potential. On the one hand, the goal was laudable insofar as it placed children's abilities and ambitions center stage. However, what was to be done about children who lived in situations where their significant adults actively discouraged children achieving their full potential, or didn't much care about their children's potential but were nonetheless adequate parents, or fundamentally disagreed with the child's belief in their own potential. Does, for example, a child's potential to be a great ice hockey player mean his or her parents should allow their child to risk his or her brain's future health?

This multiplication of potential forms and sources of harm to children has combined with exhortations—often contained within government inquiries—reminding professionals, quasi-professionals and the general public that child abuse is everyone's responsibility means the circle of experts has also expanded exponentially. As I have noted elsewhere [35], it is striking how inquiries into child fatalities in the 1970s saw social responsibility as resting exclusively with social work child protection apparatuses. It is equally striking that this is no longer the case. Inquiry reports such as the Gove Inquiry or the Laming Inquiry describe themselves as promoting a "child centered" philosophy, by which they mean the entire structure of government and civil society should pivot around the discovery and amelioration of child abuse [4].

In short, unlike the nineteenth century child savers who found children in need of protection in precisely the places and forms they expected—and indeed could not ignore—now the potential for harm can come from almost anywhere. Indeed, concern about the proliferation of sources of risk to children has found its way into both academic and popular literature. Complaints about coddled young adults who experience "failure to launch" are heard next to the hard sell of surveillance technologies for daycare and the home. The whole is exacerbated by the increasing tendency to responsibilize individual parents for their children's success or failure in an increasingly competitive world [50].

6. Conclusions: The Vanishing Point of Child Protection?

The most significant difference between nineteenth and twenty-first century child protection is that the sources and forms of children's vulnerability are no longer obvious. In addition, it is not obvious what the solution to cases of child abuse ought to be. The confidence of nineteenth century child savers has been badly shaken over the past several decades. In the mid-nineteenth century the victims of child neglect and the forms that neglect took were glaringly obvious to anyone who visited London's Eastside, New York's Five Corners, or their counterparts in any major city. Further, removal to orphanages and eventually the country was the universally sanctioned solution.

There were, of course, disputes amongst child rescuers about the particular children to be assisted, and the particular forms that assistance ought to take. Orphanages and charitable support typically distinguished between full orphans and half-orphans, religious affiliation, and the depth of moral depravity children were likely to express. However, these distinctions were not made on the basis of types or severity of child abuse—that was generally seen as generic—but rather by the moral standing of parents or the children themselves.

Disagreements over congregant care as against a cottage model, continuing contact between parents and "clean break" philosophy, and the nagging suspicion that children placed on farms might be little more than exploited labor flared up from time to time, but the basic faith in the technology of *removal* seldom wavered. The late twentieth century recognition that alternate care systems, either institutional or fostering based were also sources of harm to children (not to mention sources of liability) has brought removal as a solution under suspicion.

The crucial contribution of Kempe and his colleagues was to introduce the figure of the child abuser. This new figure was deliberately separated from a specific environment and therefore child

---

[4] As I write this the impact of the sexual exploitation scandal at Rotherham in the UK is making itself felt. What had formerly been cast by authorities as a problem of runaway or incorrigible adolescents is now recast as sexual exploitation and irresponsible multiculturalism. In former times, of course, it would have been cast as "white slavery". I do not mean to minimize the abuse these children experienced, but it is remarkable how they have acquired a new public profile. Something similar occurred in the wake of Ian Huntley's arrest and conviction for killing two adolescent girls. That Huntley had been a corrupting influence on adolescent girls was well known to both the police and child protection authorities, but it took the deaths to recast his behavior from abettor of minor delinquencies and suspected sexual impropriety to that of murderous intent.

protection workers could no longer assume children in need of help were confined to specific locations associated with poverty. Now, abusers were potentially everywhere including within alternate care systems. The result was a turn to risk technologies in the hope that scientific knowledge, appropriately ordered, would reveal child abusers through a global analysis of conduct and desire. Necessarily, no one discipline or profession could possibly know or predict all potential sources of harm and therefore child protection was increasingly cast in terms of global social effort. Knowledge of what child abuse is, and what should be done about it, was supposed to cross these "silos" of intellectual and professional effort.

The broadening of knowledge apparatuses responsible for detecting child abuse, and the increasing sophistication of research into harms perpetrated by child abusers and experienced by children mean the general consensus about what constitutes child abuse and what ought to be done about it is increasingly spread across knowledge domains. Who would have dreamed in the 1970s that a crucial specialty in child abuse research would be bio-mechanics? For that matter, it wasn't that long ago doctors refused to engage with child abuse at all, and if comments following the travails of Sir Roy Meadow are to be believed doctors may be withdrawing from child abuse research and treatment in alarming numbers.

While it may seem self-evident that drawing the entire array of social actors into the world of child protection is a good thing, such an ambition neglects the difficulties associated with multiple interpretations of what constitutes child abuse, and the multiple preferred methods for alleviating its consequences. Of course, complexity and multi-disciplinary interpretations are not, in themselves, problematic. Many contemporary scientific projects require intense collaboration across disciplines. Space flight, for example, would be unthinkable without such cooperation. However, a distinction between these projects and the demands placed on child protection authorities is precisely that nobody working on a complex aeronautics project would expect every discipline to know the same core knowledge, and have equally valid approaches to *all* possible issues arising. Rather, such multi-disciplinary projects have their various specialized knowledge bases *coordinated* by a project manager. No one would expect all of NASA's scientists to take equal responsibilities for *all* the functions of space flight. Why then is it often assumed that everyone involved with children is equally skilled at detecting and understanding child abuse?

The central problem facing child protection in the twenty-first century is not necessarily too little knowledge—and certainly not too little information—but how to manage the avalanche of empirical claims and theories available. More to the point, how are those charged with authority to undertake the most draconian child protection actions (child removals) to evaluate the myriad sources of information inundating their practice? Moreover, as the alternative care system is increasingly understood as inherently harmful, what alternative technologies of residential care can child protection call upon? It seems as if the sources and types of child abuse increase in inverse proportion to the availability of safe alternatives.

Insofar as the child protection project continues, it does so because most child abuse is relatively easy to determine; not because of great scientific advances, but because child protection action remains rooted in the obvious just as it always has. In the final analysis, this is simply to say that most child protective action remains normative; children are removed from parents not because there is a demonstrable scientifically valid proof of harm, but because certain adult conduct is sufficiently outside the norm to draw the full force of moral policing. Some things obviously are abuse, some things obviously are not abuse, and many things are neither or both. As ever, it is the latter cases that preoccupy child protection practitioners because it is there the most dangerous hazards are to be found. Here danger is understood as the combination of potentially catastrophic consequences with high levels of uncertainty.

It is the problem of coping with uncertainty that defines child protection action as fundamentally political. When child abuse was obvious, child protection practitioners proceeded with the confidence that they represented the general "common sense" of larger public tolerances and were, therefore, outside politics. However, as the commonality of sense becomes increasingly divergent, and as expert knowledge divides along disciplinary and administrative lines, the practical definition of child abuse becomes more uncertain. Of course, the problem of complexity and diversity is not unique to child protection. The emergence of "risk" in the analytic work of Ulrich Beck, Richard Ericson, and others points to difficulties created by multiple experts analyzing uncertain conditions from varied epistemological locations. Divergence of opinion is to be expected amongst experts, but this divergence of opinion is not always tolerable. In particular, controversy over uncertain definitions fuels political action. Thus, insofar as child protection practice takes place in an uncertain domain influenced by multiple knowledge regimes deployed by a wide variety of experts, it must be understood as *necessarily* political. As Ian Hacking [26] pointed out, controversies over child abuse are really controversies over the meaning and practice of "normal": and nothing is as superficially obvious or as political as defining a norm.

Nico Stehr [51] has remarked that social science scholars often erroneously use "complexity" and "unknowable" as synonyms. The present problem of knowledge regimes involved with child abuse is not one of complexity, but rather one of different epistemological domains grappling with evaluating human conduct. From this perspective, consensus on what constitutes child abuse, and what to do about it, can never be anything more than aspirational. Child abuse is not a coherent set of fixed or even relatively stable characteristics. Rather, it is an unstable and shifting discursive domain in which "harm" and "danger" to children are constantly negotiated and renegotiated within and across knowledge domains. This means there can be no "blueprint" or "master narrative" of child protection. And, this is not a bad thing. If child abuse had remained obvious, then there would be no need to change perceptions of what is, and is not, acceptable behavior toward children. Change, however, is always fraught—we do well to remember that none of us can predict what will count as the child abuse of the future.

Conflicts of Interest

The author declares no conflict of interest.

References

1. Boswell, John. *The Kindness of Strangers: The Abandonment of Children in Western Europe from Late Antiquity to the Renaissance.* New York: Vintage Books, 1988.

2. DeMause, Lloyd. "The Evolution of Childhood." In *The History of Childhood*. Edited by Lloyd de Mause. New York: The Psychohistory Press, 1974.
3. Hacking, Ian. *Rewriting the Soul: Multiple Personality and the Sciences of Memory*. Princeton: Princeton University Press, 1995.
4. Elias, Norbert. "The Retreat of Sociologists into the Present." *Theory, Culture and Society* 4 (1987): 223–47.
5. Ariés, Phillipe. *Centuries of Childhood: A Social History of Family Life*. Translated by Robert Baldrick. New York: Vantage Books, 1962.
6. Cunningham, Hugh, and Michael Morpurgo. *The Invention of Childhood*. London: BBC Books, 2006.
7. Brace, Charles Loring. *The Dangerous Classes of New York and Twenty Years Work among Them*, 3rd edition with addenda. Reprinted with original illustrations. Montclair: Patterson Smith, 1967 [1880].
8. Miller, Timothy S. *The Orphans of Byzantium: Child Welfare in the Christian Empire*. Washington, D.C.: The Catholic University of America Press, 2003.
9. Gavitt, Philip. *Charity and Children in Renaissance Florence: The Ospedale Degli Innocenti, 1410–1536*. Ann Arbor: University of Michigan Press, 1990.
10. Trollope, William. *A History of the Foundation of Christ's Hospital*. London: William Pickering, 1834. Available online: http://books.google.ca/books?id=xIHAAAAQAAJ&pg=PA101&lpg=PA101&dq=a+history+of+the+foundation+of+christ%27s+hospital&source=bl&ots=u5rdpY1vI2&sig=tDcdpiDTLntCaKTimAifqGOmr_I&hl=en&sa=X&ei=N4hSVIHbOYkyASBxYKICg&ved=0CDQQ6AEwAw#v=onepage&q=a%20history%20of%20the%20foundation%20of%20christ%27s%20hospital&f=false (accessed on 4 November 2014).
11. Fuchs, Rachel. *Abandoned Children: Foundlings and Child Welfare in Nineteenth-Century France*. Albany: State University of New York Press, 1984.
12. McClure, Ruth. *Coram's Children: The London Foundling Hospital in the Eighteenth Century*. New Haven and London: Yale University Press, 1981.
13. Longmate, Norman. *The Workhouse: A Social History*. London: Pimlico, 2003.
14. Elias, Norbert. *The Civilizing Process: Sociogenetic and Psychogenetic Investigations*, rev. ed. Translated by Edmund Jephcott. Edited by Eric Dunning, Johan Goudsblom and Stephen Mennell. Oxford: Blackwell Publishing, 2000.
15. Koven, Seth. *Slumming: Sexual and Social Politics in Victorian London*. Princeton and Oxford: Princeton University Press, 2004.
16. Mr. Smith. "Daily Journal." Original handwritten document. New York Children's Aid Society Archives, Series V, Sub-series V-1, vol. 45. Held by the New York Historical Society, New York, n.p., 1853.
17. Reeder, Rudolph R. *How Two Hundred Children Live and Learn*. Edited by Robert H. Bremner. New York: Arno Press, 1974 [1909].
18. Rooke, Patricia T., and R. L. Schnell. *Discarding the Asylum: From Child Rescue to the Welfare State in English Canada 1800–1950*. Lanham: University Press of America, 1983.

19. Richmond, Mary. *What is Social Casework: An Introductory Description.* New York: Russell Sage, 1956 [1922].
20. Smuts, Alice Boardman. *Science in the Service of Children, 1893–1935.* New Haven: Yale University Press, 2005.
21. Arnup, Katherine. *Education for Motherhood: Advice for Mothers in the Twentieth-Century Canada.* Toronto: University of Toronto Press, 1994.
22. Klienman, Paul K. "'Multiple Fractures in the Long Bones of Infants Suffering from Chronic Subdural Hematoma'—A Commentary." *American Journal of Roentenology* 187 (2006) 1403–04.
23. Kempe, C. Henry, Frederic N. Silverman, Brandt F. Steele, William Droemueller, and Henry K. Silver. "The Battered-Child Syndrome." *Journal of the American Medical Association* 181 (1962): 105–12.
24. Labbé, Jean. "Ambroise Tardieu: The Man and His Work on Child Maltreatment a Century before Kempe." *Child Abuse and Neglect* 29 (2005): 311–24.
25. Addams, Jane. "Modern Devices for Minimizing Dependency." In *Proceedings of the Conference on the Care of Dependent Children.* Washington, D.C.: Government Printing Office, 1909.
26. Hacking, Ian. "The Making and Molding of Child Abuse." *Critical Theory* 17 (1991): 253–87.
27. Nelson, Barbara J. *Making an Issue of Child Abuse: Political Agenda Setting for Social Problems.* Chicago and London: University of Chicago Press, 1984.
28. Observations about the lack of preparedness of child protection authorities for the landslide of sexual abuse disclosures during the 1980s comes from the author's own experience working in child protection through the 1980s and into the early 1990s. However, for more formal support see events surrounding the "Cleveland Affair" in the U.K. as well as accounts of panics over sex-abuse rings in the U.K. and North America.
29. Leach, Charlotte E. A., Peter S. Blair, Peter J. Fliming, Iain J. Smith, Martin Ward Platt, Peter J. Berry, Jean Golding, and the CESDI SUDI Research Group. "Epidemiology of SIDS and Unexplained Sudden Infant Deaths." *Pediatrics* 104 (1999): e43. Available online: http://pediatrics.aappublications.org/content/104/4/e43.full.pdf+html?sid=1562e4f6-7146-4dce-9b78-c8e65dde251e (accessed on 31 October 2014).
30. Southall, David P., Michael C. B. Plunkett, Martin W. Banks, Adrian F. Falkove, and Martin P. Samuels. "Covert Recording of Life-Threatening Child Abuse: Lessons for Child Protection." *Pediatrics* 100 (1997): 735–72.
31. Goudge, Stephen T. *Inquiry into Pediatric Forensic Pathology in Ontario.* Toronto: Ontario Ministry of the Attorney General, 2009. Available online: http//www.attoneygeneral.jus.gov.on.ca/inquiries/goudge/report/index.html (accessed on 30 September 2014).
32. *Regina and Sally Clark.* [2003] EWCA CRim 1020.
33. Rose, Nikolas. *Powers of Freedom: Reframing Political Thought.* Cambridge, UK: Cambridge University Press, 1999.
34. Gove, Thomas. *Report of the Gove Inquiry into Child Protection.* British Columbia: The Inquiry in British Columbia, 1995, vol. 2, p. 75.

35. Cradock, Gerald. "Risk, Morality, and Child Protection: Risk Calculation as Guides to Practice." *Science, Technology, and Human Values* 29 (2004): 314–31.
36. Ericson, Richard V., Aaron Doyle, and Dean Barry. *Insurance as Governance.* Toronto: University of Toronto Press, 2003.
37. For a more detailed account see: Cradock, Gerald. "'Friendless and Helpless': Orphanages as Institutional Response to Mass Migration." Paper presented at Youth Movements and Utopian Spaces, University of Nottingham, Nottingham, UK, 27 June 2013.
38. Dulberger, Judith A. *"Mother Donit Fore the Best": Correspondence of a Nineteenth-Century Orphan Asylum.* New York: Syracuse University Press, 1996.
39. Hacsi, Timothy A. "Orphanages as a National Institution: History and its Lessons." In *Home Away From Home: The Forgotten History of Orphanages.* Edited by Richard B. McKenzie. New York and London: Encounter Books, 2009, pp. 227–48.
40. Goldstein, Joseph, Anna Freud, and Albert J. Solnit. *Beyond the Best Interests of the Child*, new edition with epilogue. New York: Free Press, 1973.
41. For a comprehensive examination of Canada's use of Indian Residential Schools see the website of the recently completed Truth and Reconciliation Commission of Canada. Available online: http://www.trc.ca/websites/trcinstitution/index.php?p=3 (accessed on 11 June 2014).
42. There is a significant literature on alternate placement instability for children in state care. See for example: Fernandez, Elizabeth. *Significant Harm: Unraveling Child Protection Decisions and Substitute Care Careers of Children: Perspective of Child Welfare Workers and Biological Parents.* Adershot: Avebury, 1996.
43. In Canada, there is a growing body of case law concerning child abuse in alternate care. Two of the more famous cases are: C.A. *et al.* v. Critchley *et al.* 1998 CanLII 9129 (BC Ca). Available online: http://canlii.ca/t/ljwefc (accessed on 11 July 2014), and *K.L.B. v. British Columbia* (2003) SCC 51, 2 SCR 403.
44. Obomsawin, Alanis. *Richard Cardinal: Cry from a Diary of a Metis Child.* Ottawa: National Film Board of Canada, 1986.
45. Deukmedjian, John, E., and Gerald Cradock. "From Community to Public Safety Governance in Policing and Child Protection." *Canadian Review of Sociology* 45 (2008): 367–88.
46. For a scathing critique of the La Leche League see: Badinter, Elisabeth. *The Conflict: How Modern Motherhood Undermines the Status of Women.* Translated by Adrian Huntere. New York: Harpercollins Publishers, 2010.
47. *Regina and Sally Clark. Harris and others v R*, and *R. v Angela Cannings.*
48. For a more detailed analysis of the Goudge Inquiry see: Cradock, Gerald. "Thinking Goudge: Fatal Child Abuse and the Problem of Uncertainty." *Current Sociology* 59 (2010): 362–78.
49. Chadwick, David L., Henry F. Krous, and Desmond K. Runyan. "Meadow, Southall, and the General Medical Council of the United Kingdom." *Pediatrics* 117 (2006): 2247–51.
50. Donzelot, Jacques. *The Policing of Families.* Translated by Robert Hurley. Baltimore: Johns Hopkins University Press, 1977.
51. Stehr, Nico. "The Authority of Complexity." *British Journal of Sociology* 52 (2001): 313–30.

Child Protection in Sport: Reflections on Thirty Years of Science and Activism

Celia H. Brackenridge and Daniel Rhind

Abstract: This paper examines the responses of state and third sector agencies to the emergence of child abuse in sport since the mid-1980s. As with other social institutions such as the church, health and education, sport has both initiated its own child protection interventions and also responded to wider social and political influences. Sport has exemplified many of the changes identified in the brief for this special issue, such as the widening of definitional focus, increasing geographic scope and broadening of concerns to encompass health and welfare. The child protection agenda in sport was initially driven by sexual abuse scandals and has since embraced a range of additional harms to children, such as physical and psychological abuse, neglect and damaging hazing (initiation) rituals. Whereas in the 1990s, only a few sport organisations acknowledged or addressed child abuse and protection (notably, UK, Canada and Australia), there has since been rapid growth in interest in the issue internationally, with many agencies now taking an active role in prevention work. These agencies adopt different foci related to their overall mission and may be characterised broadly as sport-specific (focussing on abuse prevention in sport), children's rights organisations (focussing on child protection around sport events) and humanitarian organisations (focussing on child development and protection through sport). This article examines how these differences in organisational focus lead to very different child protection approaches and "solutions". It critiques the scientific approaches used thus far to inform activism and policy changes and ends by considering future challenges for athlete safeguarding and welfare.

Reprinted from *Soc. Sci.* Cite as: Brackenridge, C.H.; Rhind, D. Child Protection in Sport: Reflections on Thirty Years of Science and Activism. *Soc. Sci.* **2014**, *3*, 326–340.

1. Introduction

As with other social institutions, such as the church, health and education, sport has both initiated its own child protection interventions and also responded to wider social and political influences. The parameters of the debate about maltreatment in sport were originally narrowly focussed on sexual abuse [1,2]. However, as research enquiry into abuses of athletes has grown [3], the attention of sport managers and policy makers has gradually widened to include other types of non-accidental harm [4]. In addition, the geographic scope of child protection in sport has broadened away from its origins in "developed" nations, such as UK, Canada and Australia, to encompass children's rights work in emerging nations and sport development contexts [3]. The discursive emphasis on child protection in sport has also shifted over the years, from one concerned with individual perpetrators and victims to a wider interest in athlete health and welfare, human rights and integrity in sport [5]. This article suggests that sport qualifies as a social institution that shares many of the risk and protective features of other social institutions. It then examines in more detail the changes outlined above and considers how these have shaped the reputation of sport as an example of institutional child protection. Next, the article discusses globalisation and the competing interests in child protection of various international stakeholder groups. The article then critiques the scientific approaches used thus far to inform activism and policy changes in this field before concluding with some possible future challenges for child protection in sport.

2. Institutional Child Protection: The Place of Sport

Sport is defined here as a social or cultural institution or organisation rather than one confined to bricks and mortar and, thus, falls under the terms of institutional child abuse and protection addressed by such authors as Wolfe *et al.* and Gallagher [6–8]. To that extent, it is similar to other social institutions, such as religion (with its churches or mosques, for example) or education (with schools and colleges) in potentiating abuses of power relations. Additionally, just as organised religion and education have had to implement child protection, sport has also had to come to terms with abuse and abusers in its ranks and with ways of preventing and responding to such problems [9–11].

Studies in a range of countries have demonstrated that sport can provide a context in which abuse and non-accidental harm can take place, whether perpetrated by authority figures, such as coaches, or peer athletes, and at all competitive stages, from college to the elite level [12–14]. Studies have been conducted on sexual abuse and harassment in the USA, Australia, Canada and Denmark [15–19]. Summarising studies from ten European countries, Fasting reported sexual harassment prevalence in sport of 14%–73% and sexual abuse prevalence in sport of 2%–22% [20]. In the first prevalence study on young people's experiences of organised youth sport within UK, Alexander *et al.* administered retrospective questionnaires to over 6000 young people [21]. Although sport was viewed as positive for many young people, many had also suffered negative encounters. Participants reported experiencing emotional harm (75%), sexual harassment (29%), physical harm (24%), self-harm (10%) and sexual harm (3%). Despite these findings, there remains a lack of data on the prevalence of abuse in sport. Synthesising this body of research is made complicated because different definitions and conceptualisations of abuse have been utilized in the different studies in terms of whether reports of 'harassment' are also included and whether 'harm' rather than 'abuse' has been adopted. The lack of a standardised definition and associated measure of abuse in sport means that confident conclusions cannot yet be drawn regarding prevalence. Notwithstanding these reservations, it can be concluded that incidents of abuse do happen in sport, and hence, the issue merits consideration. Furthermore, it was reported that a total of 652 reported safeguarding cases, covering referrals for a range of issues from bullying to harassment to abuse, had been managed within organised sport in the UK throughout 2011 [22]. These data reinforce the reality that sport is by no means a problem-free environment.

Notwithstanding its origins in ancient civilisations, modern sport is generally acknowledged to have been codified around the time of the Industrial Revolution [23]. It has served a number of different social purposes, from education (through callisthenics, physical training, then physical education), to health, to leisure, to economic and social productivity. Sport, as it is known today, exists at different levels of intensity, from the elite/international or Olympic standard down to recreational and leisure involvement. Such is the cultural power of sport now that major international sport agencies have become a focus for social policy attention. Contrary to the adage that "sport and politics should not mix", prevalent in the 1950s and 1960s, sport has become a central but contested element of the political portfolio of both the "developed" and "developing" nations [24–26]. In the UK, for example, sport is not a statutory service, so it does not command the same attention in debates about service delivery and budgeting as do education, health, and so on. However, it has become highly valued culturally, especially since the London 2012 Olympic and Paralympic Games. Borrowing from Townsend's notion of the Fifth Social Service (social work), it has even been suggested that sport might now be regarded as the Sixth Social Service [27,28].

Along with the commercial and cultural growth of organised sport have come demands for sport to adopt the same standards of equity and diversity expected of other major social institutions, such as education and health [24]. Notwithstanding struggles and reversals, race, gender and sexuality, disability and other social inclusion themes have gradually become mainstreamed within most sport organisations [29–32]. Child protection and safeguarding are arguably the latest of these themes that are beginning to make their mark on both policy and practice in sport [33].

3. Changes in the Child Protection Agenda since the 1980s

The institution of sport was, at one time, a cultural and political island, defined as separate and free from the rest of society, with a kind of Cinderella status [34]. The historic institutional blindness of sport to child abuses led to an almost complete absence of prevention measures. By the 1980s, there were many reported cases of sexual, physical and emotional abuse in sport, but very few were publicised and virtually no studies had been conducted [2]. At the start of the 1990s, some scientific studies were beginning to emerge in the research literature, and a few pioneers began to develop child protection policies and training programmes and interventions [35–37].

Child abuse and exploitation in sport gradually emerged as a theme of interest in the centres of sporting power, and this led to changes, such as policy discussions and public statements by politicians [38–40]. By the new millennium, some progress had been made in persuading the power brokers in sport that something should be done about child protection, and the 2000s saw major growth in science, activism and prevention policy development. In 2000, the Bratislava Conference of Ministers of Sport described the issue as "… a new and sensitive subject" that had "… long been hidden under the table", and a delegate commented at a 2001 CDDS conference of 26 European countries "I feel sorry for you English ... We don't have this problem in Belarus". By 2012, however, the European Commission had funded a collaborative review of research and policy initiatives covering: Belgium, Cyprus, the Czech Republic, Denmark, France, Germany, Greece, the Netherlands, Norway, Slovenia, Spain and UK [41].

Although initially driven by sexual abuse scandals, the child protection 'movement' in sport has since embraced a range of additional harms to children, such as physical and psychological abuse, neglect and damaging hazing (initiation) rituals. The definitional focus of the child protection movement has thus widened considerably in concert with the growing evidence base for these harms [42]. At the same time, the geographic scope of the issues has broadened to encompass the Global South, the Far East and other corners of the sporting landscape [43,44].

Parton argues that approaches to child protection in the UK have shifted with ideological and political trends over the past forty years or so [45]. Over this time, government guidance has grown in detail and in prescriptiveness and the focus of concern has widened, from baby battering, to non-accidental injury, to child abuse, to the safeguarding and promotion of child welfare [45]. Each shift in approach has been related to the political ideology and priorities of the party in power. In 2001, Brackenridge outlined eight different potential frameworks for policy on sexual exploitation in sport (Table 1) ([2], p. 191).

Table 1. Frameworks for policy on sexual exploitation in sport.

Policy Approach	Description
Child protection	Narrowly focussed on prevention and recognition of types of child abuse (sexual, physical, emotional and neglect) and on referral
Duty of care	Focussed on children and emphasising legal duties *in loco parentis*
Child welfare	Focussed on children, but emphasising broader concerns, including social, environmental and educational opportunities, peer group relations and ensuring that the child thrives overall
Anti-harassment	Focussed on athlete protection from sexual harassment and bullying, with particular controls on authority figures
Athlete welfare	Wider concerns for the overall health and well-being of athletes that encompass freedom from exploitation and the development of athlete autonomy
Equity/equal opportunities	Focussed on compliance with national equal opportunities law and employment standards. Often underpins liberal aspirations for qual/fair treatment
Quality assurance	Risk management systems that embed sexual safety within the overall operation of the organisation; regularly monitored and evaluated
Ethics/human rights	Broadly focussed on moral standards and guidelines within the context of international law

At that time, very few countries, UK included, had actually developed prevention policies of any kind in the context of sport. Looking back over the intervening thirteen years, it is possible to trace how these frameworks, and others, have been adopted or adapted by national and international sport agencies. In the UK, for example, the focus has shifted beyond simply child protection and abuse prevention, largely addressed through mass education and training programmes for coaches, sport scientists and other stakeholders [46], to the imposition of mandatory safeguarding standards for all national sport governing bodies [47], to the inclusion of children's rights and broader conceptions of athlete welfare [5].

4. Child Protection and Globalisation in Sport

Since organised sport is a feature of the global economy [48], inevitably, child protection in sport is a part of the associated global flows in sport, whether in events management, scientific enquiry or policy development. In the mid-1990s, only a few sport organisations acknowledged or addressed child abuse and protection, notably in UK, Canada and Australia. Since then, the welfare and protection of the child athlete has assumed growing significance, as the scale of international sport has expanded. Child rights have, at last, begun to impinge on sport in ways that were previously unthinkable [42]. Rights advocates, for example, have now found a voice in some of the world's most important sporting organisations, from the International Olympic Committee down to national governing bodies [49,50]. This has happened both as a result of research work within sport (see Section 2 above) and pressure from outside sport (such as, for example, the New Labour government requirements for business modernisation and for compliance with best practice in social inclusion) ([24], pp. 8–46; [51]). Sport has been traditionally resistant to incursions from equity and rights advocates and has had a tense relationship with groups pressing for a better deal for women, blacks and minorities, LGBTQ and disabled athletes. In some parts of the world, it is dangerous for anyone who challenges the status quo in sport [52,53]. At the same time, it is important to recognise that significant advances have been made and that models of good practice are available in some countries that can perhaps stimulate positive social change elsewhere. Such models include policies and programmes for: Member Protection (overseen by the Australian Sports Commission) [54], Safe Sport (overseen by the U.S. Olympic Committee) [55], Respect In Sport (originally introduced via the Red Cross in Canada) [56], athlete safety (promoted by Safe4Athletes, an NGO in the USA) [57] and race and gender equity (overseen by UK Sport) [58].

Article 19 of the 1989 UN Convention on the Rights of the Child asserts that all children have the right to be protected from violence, calling on States Parties to take all appropriate measures for the protection of children, including while in the care of others. Frequently, sport is used as a mechanism for repairing broken communities after human conflicts or natural disasters. Leading proponents include: Right To Play [59]; the British Council through their Dreams and Teams programme [60]; and International Inspiration, an offshoot of the London 2012 Olympic and Paralympic Games legacy [61]. However, sport itself is by no means neutral when it comes to the safety and welfare of the child. In 2007, this issue was recognised as a gap in the provisions of UNICEF who subsequently developed a strategy for enhancing child protective measures in sport [42]. These measures included: strengthening child protection systems around and within sport organisations; increasing awareness and strengthening the protective role of parents, teachers, coaches and other caregivers, as well as the media; developing and implementing standards for the protection and well-being of child athletes; implementing sport for development and other international programmes and initiatives; and improving data collection and research to develop an evidence base.

Future developments in this field are likely to explore how the different research and policy interests in sport and international development might coalesce. One especially relevant initiative in this regard is the launch of a set of *International Standards for Safeguarding and Protecting Children in Sport* that were first publicised by UNICEF's Child Protection through the Sport Working Group at the 2012 Beyond Sport Summit in London [62]. This work on piloting international safeguarding standards in sport compliments ongoing work being done by UNICEF and others in development and humanitarian environments, attempting to make sport a safer place for children. A project funded by the Child Abuse Programme of Oak Foundation in 2013, for example, focused particularly on the two major sporting events taking place in Brazil: the 2014 FIFA football (soccer) World Cup and the 2016 Summer Olympic Games [63]. Oak's rationale was to build collaborations with agencies, such as the IOC and FIFA, in order to advance its aspirations as a major international advocate for child protection. Further, their aim to have child protection mandated as an element of event bidding processes by these two powerful world bodies was intended to provide a strong example for other sport organisations to follow.

5. Mapping Organisational Missions for Athlete Protection and Safeguarding

In their review of factors related to institutional abuse, Wolfe and his colleagues emphasised how important organisational mission was and how this could influence willingness to disclose abuse, commitment to abusive authority figures, and so on [6]. It is therefore important to try to understand how the various missions of those involved in safeguarding children in sport might affect the efficacy of their work and where the boundaries might lie between them. By doing this, gaps, overlaps and contradictions might emerge that can inform future prevention practices.

Each of the major stakeholder groups associated with children and sport has different interests related to their different missions (see Figure 1). Arguably, the sport agencies, including the IOC and the international federations of sport, such as FIFA, have a mission based on performance enhancement and commercial success, *i.e.*, the development of sport [28,64–68]. Within this core business, child protection, where it is recognised, subserves performance objectives.

The child protection agencies, including UNICEF [69] and Save the Children [70], have missions based on children's rights, protection and social justice. Many of these organisations have adopted sport programmes, because they see sport as a useful vehicle for achieving these objectives. They are entirely focussed on the child and his or her welfare and, thus, not interested in sport performance outcomes.

The international development agencies, including government development ministries and the UN peacekeeping operations, have missions based on peace-building and post-disaster development [71,72]. Again, their objectives are usefully met through an array of sport programmes. The term commonly adopted to describe this approach is "sport for development" or S4D. An S4D project is defined as any initiative, project, programme, multi-stakeholder initiative, campaign or other activity that uses sport as a tool to reach development or humanitarian objectives [73]. By definition, therefore, the humanitarian objectives of S4D programmes trump the sport development ones.

Because of these differences in mission, political tensions can arise when any one organisational group attempts to pressure another to deviate from or augment its mission. For example, where a sport federation engages in humanitarian schemes without observing cultural sensitivities it may cut across the values and principles of local agencies and/or humanitarian groups. Equally, if a development body attempts to influence the regulation of sport it may receive short shrift from sport managers who deem this as encroaching on their expertise and concerns.

Potential "mission tensions" can arise within collaborative S4D programmes, depending on which organisation is the main "sponsor". Where the lead agency is from a sport background, then child protection interests may well be absent or minimal. For example, it is possible for football organisations to use S4D programmes as thinly-veiled opportunities to recruit and develop sporting talent in so-called "football farms" in South Africa [74]. Where the lead agency in an S4D project comes from a development or child protection background, however, such as UNICEF or the NSPCC, it is much more likely that child protection interests will be both recognised and promoted systemically.

Figure 1. Conceptual map of organisational missions.

[Venn diagram with three overlapping circles:
- **International development** — Mission: Peace-building and development *through* sport
- **Sport** — Mission: Development *of* sport. Child protection *in* sport
- **Child protection** — Mission: Children's rights, protection and social justice *around* and *through* sport]

Remedies to these tensions include cross-sector partnerships (corporate/government/NGO), inter-agency collaborations and open dialogue and negotiation between the different vested interests. There are encouraging signs that such mechanisms are beginning to help embed child protection and safeguarding in the international sport delivery system. Examples include the interagency steering group responsible for the International Safeguarding Standards project [75] and a multi-disciplinary forum on 'Harnessing the Power of Sport to Address Gender-Based Violence' organised by the Sport for Development and Peace International Working Group [76].

6. Social Science, Activism and Power Relations

Good science provides the evidence that informs good policy, yet scientific enquiry is also subject to the vagaries of social construction, political pressure and epistemological fashions [77]. Parton notes that "child welfare only becomes an issue when women's voices are being heard strongly" ([45], p. 14). Similarly, child protection emerged as an area of social scientific enquiry within sport science through feminist and pro-feminist interests in the early to mid-1980s [78]. At that time, women's sport was struggling to be accepted as a legitimate concern by mainstream feminism, which defined it as a cultural institution made by and for men. Feminists sought to disrupt the gender order of the day, which, to them, logically eschewed sport. Women's sport advocates also struggled for acceptance among the male power elites who controlled almost all positions of authority [79]. Child abuse in sport became used as a mechanism to draw attention to and, eventually, to prompt policy responses by the major sporting bodies. As described elsewhere ([2], Ch. 9) the pattern of official response to child abuse in sport was usually a prolonged period of denial, followed by one or more celebrated cases in the media exposing high profile coach abusers and/or high profile athlete victims, followed by moral panic [80,81], followed by consolidated efforts to develop and implement codes of practice, education and training, registration and vetting and other prevention schemes—what Critcher would describe as 'moral regulation' [82]. In UK, this included the carrot and stick approach of mandating safeguarding standards among the governing bodies of sport as a condition of annual funding.

Many of the earliest research studies of sexual abuse and harassment in sport focussed on the interpersonal dynamics: who did what to whom, when, how and why [83]? Relationships between the coach, athlete and parent were thus the main object of research [17,19,84–86]. This narrow focus on the subject defined sexual abuse as a consequence of interpersonal and relational dynamics, thus situating sport as a kind of surrogate family. This type of research drew extensively on the psychopathology literature, such as that on sex offender profiling and typologies. This particular stream of sport science work had important consequences for activism and prevention which became equally narrowly focussed on interventions to change individual behaviours and led to a proliferation of interventions, such as: policy statements, codes of practice for coaches, parents and officials, coach education workshops, prohibitions on driving, being alone with or even touching young athletes and preoccupation with vetting procedures and criminal record checks. Arguably, this drew attention away from the socio-cultural drivers of sex abuse in sport: capitalist obsession with performance quantification and winning, reinforcement of gender and authority hierarches that privileged the status quo and the global spread of neo-colonialism through major sporting events [23].

A second, slightly wider perspective on child abuse in sport defined sport as a workplace and drew from sexual harassment research in employment settings [87,88]. However, this approach also had limited consequences for prevention. Despite examining organisational culture in sport as a component of an abusive environment it led to protective interventions based on human resource solutions, such as recruitment and induction procedures, education and training. These interventions focussed mainly on "getting the right people in sport" (an individual approach) rather than "getting sport right" (a systems approach). We would argue that systemic organisational elements, such as an ethical climate and measures to achieve transparency, good governance and accountability in sport, are likely to lead to more sustainable prevention and, ultimately, safer sport for all.

Importantly, we acknowledge that no instance of abuse can be divorced from its socio-cultural context: equally, multi- and inter-disciplinary explanations of abuse and abuse prevention would seem desirable. It is our judgement that sociological approaches to these issues have much to add to the current literature and the policies it informs. To this extent, we welcome recent analyses of swimming coaches' perceptions of surveillance, using Foucault, and male athlete subjection to sexual abuse, using Bourdieu [89,90].

7. Conclusions and Future Prospects for Institutional Safeguarding and Athlete Welfare

There is clearly no single solution to the problem of child abuse or to its prevention. Some would argue that effectiveness lies in addressing the behavioural parameters of abuse through education, training and support or advocacy to strengthen personal awareness or resistance [91]. Whilst such approaches may be necessary, however, they are not sufficient. No social institution, sport included, can afford to ignore the wider social conditions within which such problems arise.

When challenging apartheid in South Africa, Bishop Desmond Tutu and the South African Non-Racial Olympic Committee (SANROC) famously declared "There can be no non-racial sport in a racist society" [92]. In a similar intersectional vein, there can be no safe sport in an unsafe society: expecting sport to be held to a higher standard than the political, social and cultural environment in which it operates is a forlorn hope. As Parton argues, child welfare and protection in any given country is closely related to the overall welfare regime and political and policy context of that country [45]. For this reason, sport administrators need to work closely with specialists in ethics, human rights, public health and child welfare if safety for young athletes is ever to be achieved and maintained [93–96].

Social scientists and activists need to work together to generate and disseminate the knowledge base that underpins safeguarding and athlete welfare in sport. That knowledge base is arguably very thin when compared with the scientific evidence available on doping, exercise physiology and other psycho-physical aspects of sport. However, without strong science the efforts of child protection advocates are likely to be undermined and challenged by those whose vested interests construct and preserve the status quo.

It is tempting to argue that we might be reaching a kind of tipping point in sport where athlete welfare and personal development are becoming central concerns for sport administrators, coaches and other stakeholders. If so, then our obsession with "humans doing" is at last being matched by concern for "human beings" [97]. Then, there could be an equalisation of authority relations in sport that, in itself, reduces the opportunities for non-accidental harms to athletes. This humanitarian shift in sport may remain elusive unless it can be proven to advance the core mission of sport. If that happens, there might be a realisation that welfare enhances, rather than inhibits, performance success. For now, the dominant discourse in sport is still performance success and, to that extent, and if change is to be achieved, human rights advocates will need to find a performance rationale for their cause.

Acknowledgments

Thanks to Sandra Kirby and two anonymous reviewers for their valuable comments on an earlier version of this manuscript.

Author Contributions

Brackenridge drafted the article with conceptual and empirical inputs from Rhind. Editing was shared.

Abbreviations

CDDS: Council of Europe Committee for the Development of Sport;
FIFA: Federation of International Football Associations;
IOC: International Olympic Committee;
LBGTQ: lesbian, gay, bisexual, transgender and queer;
NGO: non-governmental organisations;
NSPCC: National Society for the Prevention of Cruelty to Children;
scUK: sports coach U.K.;

S4D: sport for development;
UN: United Nations;
UNICEF: United Nations Children's Fund.

Conflicts of Interest

The authors declare no conflict of interest.

References

1. Kirby, Sandra, and Lorraine Greaves. "Foul play: Sexual abuse and harassment in sport." Paper presented at the Pre-Olympic Scientific Congress, Dallas, TX, USA, 11–14 July 1996.
2. Brackenridge, Celia. *Spoilsports: Understanding and Preventing Sexual Exploitation in Sport*. London: Routledge, 2001.
3. Lang, Melanie, and Michael Hartill, eds. *Safeguarding, Child Protection and Abuse in Sport: International Perspectives in Research, Policy and Practice*. London: Routledge, 2014.
4. Brackenridge, Celia, and Daniel Rhind, eds. *Researching and Enhancing Athlete Welfare: Proceedings of the 2nd International Symposium of the Brunel International Research Network for Athlete Welfare (BIRNAW) 2013*. Uxbridge: Brunel University Press, 2014. Available online: http://www.brunel.ac.uk/sse/sport-sciences/research/bcshaw/birnaw (accessed on 8 May 2014).
5. Brackenridge, Celia, Tess Kay, and Daniel Rhind, eds. *Sport, Children's Rights and Violence Prevention: A Sourcebook on Global Issues and Local Programmes*. London: Brunel University Press, 2012. Available online: http://www.brunel.ac.uk/sse/sport-sciences/research/bcshaw/birnaw (accessed on 8 May 2014).
6. Wolfe, David A., Peter G. Jaffe, Jennifer L. Jetté, and Samantha E. Poisson. "Child Abuse in Community Institutions and Organizations: Improving Public and Professional Understanding." Report prepared for the Law Commission of Canada, Ottawa, Canada, September 2001. Available online: www.lfcc.on.ca/institutional.pdf (accessed on 8 May 2014).
7. Wolfe, David A., Peter G. Jaffe, Jennifer L. Jetté, and Samantha E. Poisson. "The impact of child abuse in community institutions and organizations: Advancing professional and scientific understanding." *Clinical Psychology: Science and Practice* 10 (2006): 179–91.
8. Gallagher, Bernard. "The extent and nature of known cases of institutional child sexual abuse." *British Journal of Social Work* 30 (2000): 795–817.
9. Gonsiorek, John C., ed. *Breach of Trust: Sexual Exploitation by Health Care Professionals and Clergy*. London: Sage, 1995.
10. Australian Royal Commission into Institutional Responses to Child Sex Abuse. *The Royal Commission Interim Report*. Sydney: Commonwealth of Australia, 2014, vol. 1. Available online: http://www.childabuseroyalcommission.gov.au/about-us/reports/interim-report-volume-1-final-020714_lr_web (accessed on 5 July 2014).

11. Department for Education (DfE). *Working Together to Safeguard Children: A Guide to Inter-Agency Working to Safeguard and Promote the Welfare of Children*. London: DfE, 2013.
12. Fasting, Kari, Celia Brackenridge, Karen Miller, and Don Sabo. "Participation in college sports and protection from sexual victimization." *International Journal of Sport and Exercise Psychology* 1 (2008): 427–41. doi:10.1080/1612197X.2008.9671883.
13. Vanden Auweele, Yves, Joke Opdenacker, Tine Vertommen, Filip Boen, Leon Van Niekerk, Kristine De Martelaer, and Bert De Cuyper. "Unwanted sexual experiences in sport: Perceptions and reported prevalence among Flemish female student-athletes." *International Journal of Sport and Exercise Psychology* 6 (2008): 354–65.
14. Fasting, Kari, Celia Brackenridge, and Jorunn Sundgot-Borgen. "Prevalence of sexual harassment among Norwegian female elite athletes in relation to sport type." *International Review for the Sociology of Sport* 39 (2004): 373–86. doi:10.1177/1012690204049804.
15. Volkwein, Karin, Frauke Schnell, Dennis Sherwood, and Anne Livezey. "Sexual harassment in sport: Perceptions and experiences of American female student-athletes." *International Review for the Sociology of Sport* 23 (1997): 283–95.
16. Starr, Katherine. "Safe4Athletes Survey Results." Available online: http://safe4athletes.org/blog (accessed on 17 July 2014).
17. Leahy, Trisha, Grace Pretty, and GershonTenenbaum. "Prevalence of sexual abuse in organised competitive sport in Australia." *Journal of Sexual Aggression* 8 (2002): 16–35.
18. Kirby, Sandra, Lorraine Greaves, and Olena Hanvisky. *The Dome of Silence: Sexual Harassment and Abuse in Sport*. London: Zed Books Ltd., 2000.
19. Toftegaard-Nielsen, Jan. "The forbidden zone: Intimacy, sexual relations and misconduct in the relationship between coaches and athletes." *International Review for the Sociology of Sport* 36 (2001): 165–82.
20. Fasting, Kari. "What do we know about sexual harassment and abuse in sport in Europe." Keynote speech presented at The European conference "Safer, better, stronger! Prevention of Sexual Harassment and Abuse in Sport", Berlin, Germany, 20–21 November 2012.
21. Alexander, Kate, Ann Stafford, and Ruth Lewis. *The Experiences of Children Participating in Organized Sport in the UK*. London: NSPCC, 2011.
22. Rhind, Daniel, Jamie McDermott, Emma Lambert, and Irena Koleva. "A review of safeguarding cases in sport." doi:10.1002/car.2306. Available online: http://onlinelibrary.wiley.com/doi/10.1002/car.2306/abstract (accessed on 17 July 2014).
23. Guttman, Allan. *From Ritual to Record: The Nature of Modern Sports*. New York: Columbia University Press, 1978.
24. Coalter, Fred. *A Wider Role for Sport: Who's Keeping the Score?* Abingdon: Routledge, 2007.
25. Coalter, Fred. "The politics of sport-for-development: Limited focus programmes and broad gauge problems?" *International Review for the Sociology of Sport* 45 (2010): 295–314.
26. Coalter, Fred. *Sport for Development: What Game are we Playing?* Abingdon: Routledge, 2013.
27. Townsend, Peter. *The Fifth Social Service: A Critical Analysis of the Seebohm Proposals*. London: The Fabian Society, 1970.

28. Brackenridge, Celia, Andy Pitchford, Kate Russell, and Gareth Nutt. *Child Welfare in Football: An Exploration of Children's Welfare in the Modern Game.* London: Routledge, 2007, p. 205.
29. Hylton, Kevin. *"Race" and Sport: Critical Race Theory.* London: Routledge, 2009.
30. Hargreaves, Jennifer. *Heroines of Sport: The Politics of Difference and Identity.* London: Routledge, 2000.
31. Cunningham, George B., ed. *Sexual Orientation and Gender Identity in Sport: Essays from Activists, Coaches and Scholars.* Texas: Texas A&M University Centre for Sport Management Research and Education, 2012.
32. Rolfe, Danielle, Karen Yoshida, Rebecca Renwick, and Carrie Bailey. "Balancing safety and autonomy: Structural and social barriers affecting the exercise participation of women with disabilities in community recreation and fitness facilities." *Qualitative Research in Sport, Exercise and Health* 4 (2012): 265–83.
33. Brackenridge, Celia, and Hamish Telfer. "Child protection and sport development." In *Handbook of Sport Development.* Edited by Barrie Houlihan and Mike Green. London: Routledge, 2011, pp. 451–63.
34. Gruneau, Rick. *Class, Sports and Social Development*, 2nd ed. Champaign: Human Kinetics, 1999.
35. National Coaching Foundation/NSPCC. *Protecting Children from Abuse: A Guide for Everyone Involved in Children's Sport.* Leeds: NCF, 1996.
36. Cense, Marianne. *Red Card or Carte Blanche. Risk Factors for Sexual Harassment and Sexual Abuse in Sport.* Arnhem: Netherlands Olympic Committee and Netherlands Sports Federation and Transact, 1997.
37. Malkin, Kris, Lynne Johnston, and Celia Brackenridge. "A critical evaluation of training needs for child protection in UK sport." *Managing Leisure—An International Journal* 5 (2000): 151–60.
38. Committee for the Development of Sport. "Provisional Resolution on the Prevention of Sexual Harassment and Abuse of Women and Children in Sport." Strasbourg: CDDS (99) 86, 30 November 1999. This draft resolution was prepared in advance of the Bratislava Conference of Ministers [39].
39. Committee for the Development of Sport. "Sexual harassment and abuse in sport especially the case of women, children and Youth." Resolution 3/2000, Secretary General's Report of the 9th Conference of Ministers responsible for Sport, Bratislava, Slovakia, 30–31 May 2000. Available online: http://www.coe.int/t/dg4/sport/resources/texts/spres00.3_en.asp (accessed on 11 May 2014).
40. Committee for the Development of Sport. "The Protection of Children, Young People and Women in Sport: How to guarantee human dignity and equal rights for these groups." Seminar Report, Hanasaari, Espoo, Finland, 14–16 September 2001.
41. Chroni, Stilani, Kari Fasting, Michael Hartill, Nadia Knorre, Montse Martin, Maria Papaestathiou, Daniel Rhind, Bettina Rulofs, Jan Toftegaard Stoeckel, Tine Vertommen, *et al. Prevention of Sexual and Gender Harassment and Abuse in Sports: Initiatives in Europe and Beyond.* Frankfurt am Main: Deutsche Sportjugend, 2012.

42. Brackenridge, Celia, Kari Fasting, Sandra Kirby, and Trisha Leahy. *Protecting Children from Violence in Sport: A Review with a Focus on Industrialized Countries*. Florence: UNICEF Innocenti Research Centre, 2010.
43. For example, South Africa: Leon Van Niekerk. "Protecting athletes from sexual harassment and abuse in South Africa." In *Safeguarding, Child Protection and Abuse in Sport: International Perspectives in Research, Policy and Practice*. Edited by Mel Lang and Michael Hartill. London: Routledge, 2014.
44. For example, the Republic of Korea: National Human Rights Commission of the Republic of Korea. *Guidelines: Human Rights in Sports*. Seoul: NHRC, 2011.
45. Parton, Nigel. *The Politics of Child Protection: Contemporary Developments and Future Directions*. Basingstoke: Palgrave Macmillan, 2014.
46. Sportscoach UK, and National Society for the Prevention of Cruelty to Children. *Safeguarding and Protecting Children: A Guide for Sportspeople*. Leeds: scUK, 2013.
47. Child Protection in Sport Unit. "Sports Safeguarding Children Initiative: Mid-project Progress Report." Available online: https://thecpsu.org.uk/news/2013/october/sports-safeguarding-children-initiative-report/ (accessed on 17 July 2014).
48. Maguire, Joe. "Sport and globalisation." Available online: http://sportanddev.org/en/learnmore/?uNewsID=86 (accessed on 5 July 2014).
49. International Olympic Committee. "Consensus Statement on Sexual Harassment and Abuse." 8 February 2007. Available online: http://www.olympic.org/medical-commission?tab=statements (accessed on 8 May 2014).
50. International Olympic Committee. "Sexual harassment and abuse in sport." Online prevention materials, 2010. Available online: http://sha.olympic.org/ (accessed on 8 May 2014).
51. The process of incorporating sport within the political agenda was accelerated under the UK's New Labour government, as explained by Fred Coalter [24].
52. Armstrong, Gary. *Football in Africa: Conflict, Conciliation and Community*. London: Palgrave, 2003.
53. Sugden, John, and Alan Tomlinson. "Digging the dirt and staying clean: Retrieving the investigative tradition for a critical sociology of sport." *International Review for the Sociology of Sport* 34 (1999): 385–97.
54. Australian Sports Commission. "National Member Protection Policy Template." Available online: http://www.ausport.gov.au/supporting/integrity_in_sport/resources/national_member_protection_policy_template (accessed on 8 July 2014).
55. US Olympic Committee. Available online: http://safesport.org/what-is-safesport/the-usoc-program/ (accessed on 8 July 2014).
56. Respect in Sport. Available online: http://respectinsport.com/ (accessed on 8 July 2014).
57. Safe4Athletes. "4 clubs: Model Policy." Available online: http://safe4athletes.org/4-clubs/model-policy (accessed on 8 July 2014).
58. Sport England. "Equality and diversity." Available online: http://www.sportengland.org/support__advice/equality_and_diversity.aspx (accessed on 8 July 2014).
59. Right to Play. Website: http://www.righttoplay.com (accessed on 17 July 2014).

60. British Council. "What's happening where?" Available online: http://www.britishcouncil.org/dreams-whats-happening-where_old.htm (accessed on 17 July 2014).
61. International Inspiration. "Protecting and safeguarding children." Available online: http://www.internationalinspiration.org/protecting-and-safeguarding-children (accessed on 8 May 2014).
62. Reynard, Stephen. "Child safeguarding at the 2013 Beyond Sport Summit." 16 September 2013. Available online: http://www.sportanddev.org/?6078/Child-safeguarding-at-the-2013-Beyond-Sport-Summit (accessed on 17 July 2014).
63. Brackenridge, Celia, Sarah Palmer-Felgate, Daniel Rhind, Laura Hills, Tess Kay, Anne Tiivas, Lucy Faulkner, and Iain Lindsay. *Child Exploitation and the FIFA World Cup: A Review of Risks and Protective Interventions.* London: Brunel University, 2013. Available online: http://www.brunel.ac.uk/__data/assets/pdf_file/0008/316745/Child-Protection-and-the-FIFA-World-Cup-FINAL.pdf (accessed on 8 July 2014).
64. Despite claims for being guided by strong values and ethics, such organisations are widely acknowledged to prioritise commercial and athletic performance above these. For critiques see references [28,65–68].
65. Jennings, Andrew. *The New Lords of the Rings: Olympic Corruption and How to Buy Gold Medals.* London: Simon and Schuster, 1996.
66. Whannel, Gary A. *Culture, Politics and Sport: Blowing the Whistle Revisited.* London: Routledge, 2008.
67. Sugden, John, and Alan Tomlinson. *FIFA and the Context for World Football.* Cambridge, UK: Polity, 1998.
68. Jennings, Andrew. *Foul! The Secret World of FIFA: Bribes, Vote Riggings and Ticket Scandals.* London: HarperSport, 2006. Available online: http://www.sportanddev.org (accessed on 8 May 2014).
69. United Nations Children's' Fund. "UNICEF's mission statement." Available online: http://www.unicef.org/about/who/index_mission.html (accessed on 17 July 2014).
70. Save The Children. "Our vision, mission and values." Available online: http://www.savethechildren.net/about-us/our-vision-mission-and-values (accessed on 17 July 2014).
71. United Nations. "What is peacekeeping?" Available online: http://www.un.org/en/peacekeeping/operations/peacekeeping.shtml (accessed on 17 July 2014).
72. Department for International Development. Available online: https://www.gov.uk/government/organisations/department-for-international-development (accessed on 17 July 2014).
73. SportandDev.org. "About this platform." Available online: http://www.sportanddev.org/en/learnmore/safeguarding/history_of_safeguarding/ (accessed on 8 July 2014).
74. Armstrong, Gary. "Warriors and good hope: The pioneering soccer franchise of Ajax Cape Town." *Politique Africaine* 118 (2010): 43–62.

75. NSPCC Child Protection in Sport Unit. "International move to safeguard children in sport." 5 June 2013. Available online: http://www.sportanddev.org/en/connect/myinfo.cfm?5705/Move-to-protect-children-in-sport (accessed on 17 July 2014).
76. United Nations. "Harnessing the Power of Sport to Address Gender-Based Violence discussed at the United Nations in Geneva." Available online: http://www.un.org/wcm/content/site/sport/home/template/news_item.jsp?cid=41918 (accessed on 8 July 2014).
77. Dickson, David. *The New Politics of Science*. Chicago: University of Chicago Press, 1988.
78. Brackenridge, Celia. "Women and children first? Child abuse and child protection in sport." *Sport in Society* 7 (2004): 322–37.
79. White, Anita, and Celia Brackenridge. "Who rules sport? Gender divisions in the power structure of British sport from 1960." *International Review for Sociology of Sport* 20 (1985): 95–107.
80. Cohen, Stanley. *Folk Devils and Moral Panics: The Creation of the Mods and Rockers*. London: MacGibbon and Kee, 1972.
81. Thompson, Keith. *Moral Panics*. London: Routledge, 1998.
82. Critcher, Chas. "Widening the focus: Moral panics as moral regulation." *British Journal of Criminology* 49 (2009): 17–34.
83. The work of Sandra Kirby and her colleagues in Canada was an important exception: see Kirby, Sandra, *The Dome of Silence: Sexual Harassment and Abuse in Sport* [18].
84. Crosset, Todd. "Male coach/female athlete relationships." Paper presented at the First International Conference for Sport Sciences, Sole, Norway, 15–16 November 1986.
85. Brackenridge, Celia. "'He owned me basically...': Women's experience of sexual abuse in sport." *International Review for the Sociology of Sport* 32 (1997): 115–30.
86. Brackenridge, Celia. "Healthy Sport for healthy girls? The role of parents in preventing sexual abuse in sport." *Sport, Education and Society* 3 (1998): 59–78.
87. Russell, Diana E.H. *Sexual Exploitation: Rape, Child Sexual Abuse, and Workplace Harassment.* London: SAGE, 1984, vol. 155.
88. Stockdale, Janet. *Sexual Harassment in the Workplace: Perspectives, Frontiers and Response Strategies*. London: SAGE, 1996, vol. 5.
89. Lang, Mel. "Surveillance and conformity in competitive youth swimming." *Sport, Education and Society* 15 (2010): 19–37.
90. Hartill, Michael. "The *sexual abuse of boys* in organized *male* sports." *Men and Masculinities* 12 (2009): 225–49.
91. See examples in Kaufman, Keith L. *The Prevention of Sexual Violence: A Practitioner's Sourcebook*. Holyoke: NEARI Press, 2010.
92. Reddy, Enuga S. "Sports and the Liberation Struggle: A tribute to Sam Ramsamy and others who fought apartheid sport." Available online: http://scnc.ukzn.ac.za/doc/SPORT/SPORTRAM.htm (accessed on 8 May 2014).
93. McNamee, Mike. "Ethics and sport." Available online: http://philosophyofsport.org.uk/resources/ethics-sport/ (accessed on 22 May 2014).

94. United Nations Office on Sport for Development and Peace. "Sport for development and peace: The UN system in action." Available online: http://www.un.org/wcm/content/site/sport/home/resourcecenter/resolutions/pid/19433 (accessed on 22 May 2014).
95. Laws, D. Richard. "Sexual offending as a public health problem: A North American perspective." *Journal of Sexual Aggression* 5 (2000): 30–44.
96. Kaufman, Keith, Michelle Barber, Heather Mosher, and Megan Carter. "Reconceptualising child sexual abuse as a public health concern." In *Preventing Violence in Relationships: Interventions across the Life Span.* Edited by Paul A. Schewe. Monsey: Criminal Justice Press, 2002, pp. 101–44.
97. Ingham, Alan G., Bryan Blissmer, and Kristin Wells Davidson. "The expendable prolympic self: Going beyond the boundaries of the sociology and psychology of sport." *Sociology of Sport Journal* 16 (1999): 236–68.

"I Know People Think I'm a Complete Pain in the Neck": An Examination of the Introduction of Child Protection and "Safeguarding" in English Sport from the Perspective of National Governing Body Safeguarding Lead Officers

Mike Hartill and Melanie Lang

Abstract: Child protection in sport emerged at the start of the 21st century amidst headlines about coaches raping, sexually assaulting and abusing children. Against this backdrop, in 2001 the UK government established an independent agency, the English Child Protection in Sport Unit (CPSU), which introduced national child protection standards for sports organizations. This included the requirement to appoint national "safeguarding lead officers". Utilizing the theoretical framework of sociologist Pierre Bourdieu, this paper considers the impact of "safeguarding and child protection" (SCP) within the English sports community through the experiences of those who have been at the vanguard of its implementation in the early years of its establishment within sport. Utilizing data from qualitative interviews with nine national safeguarding lead officers (SLOs), the paper discusses the challenges experienced by SLOs and critically appraises the relation between them (their *habitus*) and the prevailing logic (*capital*) within their sporting *fields*. We discuss the extent to which SLOs have been supported by their organizations and conclude with a consideration of the degree to which national governing bodies of sport (NGBs) have been invested in SCP.

Reprinted from *Soc. Sci.* Cite as: Hartill, M.; Lang, M. "I Know People Think I'm a Complete Pain in the Neck": An Examination of the Introduction of Child Protection and "Safeguarding" in English Sport from the Perspective of National Governing Body Safeguarding Lead Officers. *Soc. Sci.* **2014**, *3*, 606–627.

1. Introduction

Of the 63.1 million inhabitants of the UK, around 14 million are under 18 years [1] and almost 82% of these are involved in some form of competitive sport [2]. Despite these numbers, the traditional autonomy of the sports sector has made the government reluctant to intervene in sport, resulting in "a legacy of traditionalism and resistance to change" ([3], p. 10), including making sport slower than other institutions to adopt social reforms for child welfare. Consequently, measures to safeguard children in sport remain relatively recent additions to the British and international sport policy agenda [4].

In insisting that safeguarding children is *everyone's* responsibility, Every Child Matters [5] and its related legislation, The Children Act 2004, marked the beginning of change for sport. The Children Act 2004 makes clear that all sectors of society, including sport, have a responsibility for safeguarding and protecting children, and voluntary- and private-sector organizations, including those in sport, are required to have safeguarding measures in place.

Within sport, recognition of the need for safeguarding and protecting children was brought into stark relief when, in 1995, Olympic swimming coach Paul Hickson was convicted of fifteen charges of rape and sexual assault on teenage swimmers under his care [3]. At the time, most national governing bodies of sport (NGBs)—the organizations responsible for managing sport—had no strategy in place to safeguard and protect their millions of members. One of the first initiatives within sport following the Hickson case was the creation in 2001 of the Child Protection in Sport Unit (CPSU), the first government-backed agency with responsibility for safeguarding and child protection in sport [6].

In 2002, the CPSU introduced a set of standards for child protection for NGBs to work towards as a condition of receipt of government funding, the Standards for Safeguarding and Protecting Children in Sport [7,8][1]. The Standards are intended to:

> ...provide a framework for all those involved in sport to help them create a safe sporting environment for children and young people and protect them from harm ([8], p. 1).

The Standards focus on preventing and protecting children from abuse and managing suspected cases of abuse as well as broader safeguarding concerns, with NGBs required to audit their current position against one of three levels–Preliminary, Intermediary or Advanced [9]. According to the CPSU [9], 40 of 46 Sport England-funded NGBs have achieved the Advanced Level of the Standards. To help NGBs implement each of the 10 Standards, criteria is provided for each Standard. Standard 2: Procedures and Systems requires NGBs to have a "designated person/s", a named person "of sufficient seniority and support to carry out the role ... who is/are responsible for the implementation of the child protection policy" ([8], p. 6) both at club/facility (local) level and at NGB (national) level. At club- and regional-levels, these individuals are often known as "welfare officers", "child protection officers" or "children's officers", while at the NGB level they are referred to as national Safeguarding Lead Officers or SLOs [8].

SLOs have operational responsibility for managing, embedding and championing SCP within their NGB. Their role involves a range of duties including SCP policy development, monitoring and evaluation; managing recruitment and criminal history checks; developing and delivering SCP training and resources; providing SCP guidance to NGB members; and assessing and managing cases of abuse. More than a decade after the introduction of these roles, however, and despite the importance of those in these positions to ensuring children's welfare in sport, little is known about the experiences of individuals occupying these designated roles. While limited research has explored the experiences of designated individuals at the club level [10,11], to the best of our knowledge no studies have investigated the experiences of national SLOs for sport. Given the centrality of the SLO to the process and politics of establishing child protection and (latterly) safeguarding within British sport, this paper explores the experiences and perspectives of some of these individuals.

---

[1] The complete list of 10 Standards is: (1) Policy; (2) Procedures and Systems; (3) Prevention; (4) Codes of Practice and Behaviour; (5) Equity; (6) Communication; (7) Education and Training; (8) Access to Advice and Support; (9) Implementation and Monitoring; (10) Influencing.

2. Social Science and the Study of Child Protection in Sport

The relationship between social science and the recognition of child abuse in sport is significant. In the 1980s Celia Brackenridge, a feminist social scientist, publicly raised the issue of sexual harassment and abuse in sport [12]. Brackenridge [3,13,14] developed a critique of psychological theories of sexual violence. She offered a gendered account of male violence towards women and children within a sports system underpinned by hetero-patriarchal ideology that celebrated masculine privilege and sexualized the feminine. Brackenridge's work built on and contributed to broader critiques of the social spaces provided for women and children within sport [15–19]. On the basis of the abuse she uncovered, she argued for the development and introduction of SCP policies within sport.

In one of the only studies of its kind, Brackenridge was commissioned by the Football Association (FA)–by far the wealthiest NGB in English sport–to evaluate the impact of their child protection strategy on various stakeholders within football [20]. The work was supportive of the FA's efforts but questioned the extent to which SCP was accepted amongst all stakeholders. More recently, Piper and colleagues [21], based on the perspectives of sports coaches who have been subject to new policy developments, argue that the "intrusion" of SCP into sport (and of the CPSU) has caused adults to be fearful of working with (and especially touching) children and has, therefore, had a damaging impact on adult-child relations within sport. Others have drawn attention to the absence of independent research evaluation for the national programme of policy implementation led, since 2001, by the CPSU [22]. The English model has, however, received considerable support from other countries seeking to replicate this approach.

Nevertheless, research attention has tended to focus on sports cultures at the expense of investigating the SCP policy context and the impact of the rapid developments in this field. Indeed, the investigation of SCP in sport has largely been overlooked by social scientists within and beyond sport, and many researchers investigating abuse and exploitation in sport have ignored the conceptual tools and approaches available from within social theory. In addition, sport as a field of enquiry is often situated outside of mainstream social science. This paper attempts to contribute to a growing body of literature that has begun to address this (see [3,23–28]). In particular, through the perspectives of SLOs, we explore the relationship between individual SLOs and their organization. In doing so, we align ourselves with a Bourdieusian epistemology, which we now briefly outline.

3. Methodology

Pierre Bourdieu's "philosophy is condensed in a small number of fundamental concepts–*habitus, field, capital*–and its cornerstone is the two-way relationship between objective structures (those of social *fields*) and incorporated structures (those of the *habitus*)" ([29], p. vii). Unlike other major social theorists (see [30,31]), Bourdieu wrote specifically on sport (see [32,33]) and explicitly designated it a "relatively autonomous" cultural field ([34], p. 118).

For Bourdieu ([33], p. 72), whilst "there are general laws of fields ... a field defines itself by defining specific stakes and interests ... irreducible to the stakes and interests specific to other fields". Bourdieu ([33], p. 72) notes that "for a field to function, there have to be stakes and people prepared to play the game, endowed with the habitus that implies knowledge and recognition of the immanent laws of the field, the stakes." Thus, *fields* are characterized by "struggles" over "the monopoly of the legitimate violence (specific authority) which is characteristic of the field" ([33], p. 73). Therefore, adapting Grenfell and James ([35], p. 161), understanding sport as a field:

> ... is to see it as a structured space of forces and struggles into which individuals along with their habitus-specific dispositions enter ... the outcome of this encounter ... is the product of the interaction between them.

According to McNay ([36], p. 57), "[t]he idea of the field potentially yields a differentiated and dynamic model of power relations where each field has its own historicity and logic which may reinforce or conflict with those of other fields". Orthodoxy within any field is defended and conserved by those who monopolize the specific *capital* that characterizes a field. Hence, Brackenridge ([37], p. 265) observes that "most of the major sport organizations are run by self-selecting (male) oligarchies who are reluctant to give up their power".

Thus, Bourdieu theorizes social action from a position whereby historical social structures "inhabit" the individual, and it is on this basis that individual action is generated, but not determined. The habitus, then, is "the organizing principle of their action", the "*modus operandi* informing all thought and action (including thought of action)" ([38], p. 18), whilst the *habitus* is the concept Bourdieu uses to articulate the "generative principles or schemes which underlie practices":

> ... when individuals act, they always do so in specific social contexts or settings. Hence particular practices or perceptions should be seen, not as the product of the habitus as such, but as the product of the *relation between* the habitus, on the one hand, and the specific social contexts or "fields" within which individuals act, on the other ([39], p. 14).

Thus, thinking in terms of habitus and field "is to *think relationally*" ([40], p. 96): "Involvement in a field shapes the habitus that, in turn, shapes the actions that reproduce the field" ([41], p. 87).

Bourdieu's notion of *capital* and its accumulation are key to understanding the operations of fields and the actions of individuals and groups within them. Bourdieu's *capital* principally refers to the logic of a field, that is, what is counted as legitimate and valuable, and what is not. Bourdieu argues that within each field:

> Symbolic capital is any property (any form of capital whether physical, economic, cultural or social) when it is perceived by social agents endowed with categories of perception which cause them to know it and recognize it, to give it value ([29], p. 47).

Therefore, whilst Bourdieu [29] emphasizes that the social universe is such that all agents attribute, at least implicitly, a monetary value to their labour or time, *capital* can refer to any number of things (practices, traditions, locations) that are recognized and valued by social agents acting within the field. Bourdieu adopts a sporting analogy—"the feel for the game" (see [29])—to express the relation between *habitus* and *field*. Therefore, any consideration of social action must appreciate the normative logic or *capital*, specific to a *field*, as an appreciation for this field-specific capital is essential for "successful" action within any field.

The emergence of "child protection" within sport can clearly be construed as a meeting of *fields* with distinct, arguably very different logics of practice. This notion seems evident in the words of the first director of the CPSU, shortly after its establishment:

> ... those within and outside sport need to recognize that the significant changes in culture and practice that are required will take both time and resources. There are still some within sport who are resistant to change: those involved in promoting this work need to adopt an approach that will ensure change occurs at an appropriate pace ([6], p. 141).

It is with an interest in these "changes in culture and practice", and how they are navigated and negotiated, that has guided this investigation. Bourdieu's theoretical framework provides both the epistemological foundations for our methodological approach as well as the conceptual tools to "think through" our findings.

The Study

For Bourdieu, empirical research is essential for comprehending the relationship between *capital*, *field* and *habitus*. In selecting an appropriate method, Bourdieu advocated a pragmatic approach based on "the definition of the object and the practical conditions of data collection" ([40], p. 226). In particular, interviews offer:

> ... the respondent an absolutely exceptional situation for communication, freed from the usual constraints (particularly of time) that weigh on most everyday interchanges, and opening up alternatives which prompt or authorize the articulation of worries, needs or wishes discovered through this very articulation, the researcher helps create the conditions for an extra-ordinary discourse, which might never have been spoken, but which was already there, merely awaiting the conditions for its actualization ([42], p. 614).

Providing SLOs with an anonymous space within which they could articulate their views at length was deemed crucial if the research was to uncover something of the *relations* at play in the delivery of SCP in English sport. A conversational style was adopted whereby SLOs led the conversation and we prompted and encouraged them for further detail or asked questions to attempt to "see" the role of SLO through their eyes [43,44]. Interviews explored issues such as SLOs' perceptions of their role, the culture and organization of SLOs' NGB regards safeguarding, and safeguarding policy implementation in SLOs' organization. In attempting to identify "what particular structure of the habitus is in play here" ([45], p. 61), our intention is to enable a voicing of the experiences of SLOs to identify issues they consider critical.

The research was approved by the authors' university ethics committee and participants were offered anonymity; pseudonyms are used for participants, NGBs and all other identifying features. Access to potential participants was facilitated by the CPSU. In total, 40 SLOs from across 24 NGBs were introduced to the project by the first author during an SLO Support Forum—regular meetings scheduled by the CPSU to support SLOs. The CPSU provided the contact details of SLOs willing to be approached for the study.

As the SLOs were located across the country, interviews were conducted by telephone and, with their consent, recorded using a digital telephone recording cable and Dictaphone. Telephone interviews allow the possibility of cheaply accessing participants who would otherwise be difficult to reach in person, and they can generate data comparable in quality to that attained by face-to-face methods and increase participants' perceptions of anonymity [44,46]. Nine SLOs from eight NGBs were interviewed, with interviews lasting between 30 min and three hours. Participants had been in the SLO post between two and more than 10 years. Only two of the eight participating NGBs had appointed a man to the role of SLO.

Interviews were transcribed and data subjected to inductive analysis [47]. This involved reading and re-reading the text to become immersed in "the details and specifics of the data to discover important patterns, themes, and interrelationships" ([48], p. 362). Simultaneously, segments of text were coded into themes to facilitate analysis of text based on specific themes and to enable relationships between themes to be identified, including contradictory points and new categories. Through this process, themes became increasingly refined. Guided by our "relational" approach, we then focused on those areas which particularly identified the dynamic between *habitus* (of the SLOs) and *field*. As the position of SLO is occupied by a very small number of individuals, some contextual detail from the interview data has necessarily been excluded to protect their identities. We now present these themes, accompanied by initial commentary, before explicitly applying a Bourdieusian lens to further draw out our interpretation of these findings and the meanings within them.

4. Findings

4.1. Priorities, Resources and Responsibilities

SLOs raised a number of concerns around the manner in which SCP fitted into their organization's "core" business. The positioning of SCP within the organization's structure was a key concern, as was the resourcing of SCP and the priority it was given in terms of SLOs' workloads.

Responsibility for SCP may be situated within one of many different NGB departments, for example, within education, coach development, community sport development, legal and compliance, *etc.* The positioning of SCP within the organization's governance structure was identified by some as a crucial factor in effecting change as it impacted significantly on the extent to which an SLO's line manager could exert influence on senior executives and, thus, on the opportunities available to promote SCP at senior management level:

> SLO5: …the important thing to me really is where my line manager fits in terms of the whole organization, not necessarily where I fit. My line manager now is Head of [area] and is from the senior management team and that's the most important thing … that means that I can influence at senior management level.

The SLOs were acutely aware of the need to achieve a high profile within their organization. The underlying concern was that senior executives do not sufficiently value SCP or that they view it as less important than other areas:

> SLO2: The safeguarding team have recently been moved from [area] [to] Legal and Governance … I think this is better for safeguarding … I think we have definitely got a higher profile there, and I think that they are a bit more accepting of us, now we are in Legal and Governance.

The degree to which NGBs "accept" SCP, and the problems associated with whether or not SCP is considered a legitimate area within the development of sport, will be discussed further below.

While Sport England recently provided the CPSU with £1 million in funding over two years to develop and embed safeguarding and child protection in sport [49], NGBs are not required to set aside a minimum amount for this in the way they do for other operating costs, such as for sports coaching. Consequently, not only do resources for SCP vary according to the financial health of an NGB, they are also dependent upon the value that senior executives place on that area amidst other (funding-contingent) dimensions of their remit:

> SLO4: The larger NGBs … they've got money to throw at it. They normally have a permanent Lead Officer in place who has got maybe half a dozen staff around the regions, and they in turn have got one or two staff within the region. They've got a structure. Not everybody's as fortunate, unfortunately. … the bigger NGBs, they've got money to throw at child protection and we don't. It's as simple as that. We can only do what we can do.

SLOs from larger NGBs were primarily concerned with the absence of dedicated funding from Sport England for SCP:

> SLO3: There's no specific funding for safeguarding within the planning process. There will be a budget allocated to my area, I'm a budget holder, but there isn't … it's not allocated from any of the funding bodies specifically for safeguarding. So I would put a plan together to say 'this is how much we would need to deliver the safeguarding functions' and I then would kind of fight it out with everybody else.

> SLO7: … it concerns me that there is no money ring-fenced with the funding from Sport England. You know we get this funding but none of it is ring-fenced in regards to safeguarding … and I know there are other sports that have said this as well. If governing body's boards were advised that they have got to give X amount to safeguarding, they would probably take more notice of it.

Clearly, the resources available to an NGB are a significant factor in determining the extent of the SCP structure that can be established within a sport and the degree of SCP support that can be provided for that sports community. For some SLOs, the lack of specifically targeted funding raises the concern that essential resources are diverted to other areas considered higher priority.

The majority of SLOs in our sample expressed a clear commitment not just to the SLO responsibilities and the protection of children from abuse, but also to the broader principles of child welfare and children's rights. However, it is also evident that, as in our sample, many SLOs have responsibility for areas beyond SCP, for example, "doping" and "equity", and consequently SCP is only a subsidiary aspect of their role:

> SLO4: The main part of my role is club development, which includes club accreditation, which obviously includes child protection … child protection sits with those two areas. So, it might probably be around 20% of my role. … Really it's a bolt-on part of my job rather than a fundamental part.

> SLO6: If you asked me now [to take on the LO role] I would say no … but that's not to say I don't want to do the role because of what it involves, it's because it doesn't really fit in with my [additional role] now. … In an ideal world I would have moved that lead officer role onto someone else, but that hasn't been able to happen yet.

Clearly there is a concern here about the extent to which an official with designated responsibility for SCP is able to properly fulfill all aspects of the role amidst competing priorities. Where safeguarding is annexed to more "substantive" responsibilities, it seems important to question the extent to which a sport's external statements about how seriously it takes child welfare match the reality "on the ground". In the following section, we consider this in greater depth.

4.2. Organizational Resistance/Inertia

The initial refusal to accept that sportspeople (sexually) abuse children and the resistance to the introduction of SCP policy in sport is documented by Brackenridge [3]. All of the SLOs identified this resistance within their organizations:

> SLO2: … when I first joined there was a huge sort of push away from it … "this is ridiculous! We have managed all our lives without this, we don't need this! … this is all just political correctness gone mad!"

> SLO3: I don't think they understood it. I don't think it was seen as being particularly important. The difficulty was, I think in early days there was this feeling of "this doesn't happen in our sport." I think there was definitely a feeling of "this doesn't happen enough [to justify changes]."

> SLO7: I am advised that safeguarding is on the board meetings [but] I am yet to see it on any of the minutes. … my head of department is representative of safeguarding on the board. Unfortunately, I have never had him approach me and ask me for any data or details or anything about cases to feed back into the board, never, so it is quite disappointing.

A result of this organizational resistance to SCP was that some SLOs found themselves in the position of not only promoting SCP within their community-level sports clubs, but having to persuade their NGBs' internal departments of the value and legitimacy of SCP, and, therefore, of the SLO position:

> SLO3: I don't think they [senior management] really knew what to do with it. To me there wasn't really a willingness to … I needed their weight to say to the organization "this is important, you need to do it". … it was very isolating because anything that needed doing, I had to do and there was absolutely no team work involved … I think you have to be extremely, extremely determined and thick-skinned to be able to do it,

and driven to do the job. I don't think you can do this without the organization buying in, because it's not a one-person job. If it's genuinely going to work within the organization, it's got to be owned and driven by more than one person ... ultimately you need the executive team to do it because they are the decision makers–ultimately they drive the message. If they say it's important, then the organization sees it as important.

Senior managers have considerable influence on the culture of an organization [50] and their "buy-in" is clearly important if SCP is to be truly accepted, valued and adequately resourced. However, SLOs suggested gaining top-level support was a challenge and some felt their senior management had little genuine interest in SCP:

SLO7: ... sometimes you just feel "are you going to listen or what? Would you just like me to go away?" Cos that is the impression you get sometimes. [I] can never get in front of the CEO to put things forward, they just don't want to know—"I pay you to do the job, just do it".

SLO5: I think higher up the organization, they still kind of leave it up to the safeguarding department. There's still that whole, not understanding that everyone plays a part ... Like the [CPSU] safeguarding conference, I think there were very few CEOs there. I obviously started to go and they [NGB CEOs] said, "I think it's more for you." I said, "it is, but it'll be so good if you're there" but it was never going to happen.

The notion that child protection or safeguarding "is everyone's responsibility" has been a persistent message from child welfare advocates and organizations, such as the CPSU. Thus, the objective is to "embed" safeguarding principles and policies within sport, so that they play a meaningful rather than superficial role within an organization's culture. Indeed, the extent of support for SCP within an organization's leadership influences the culture [51]. However, these responses indicate that SCP in sport may be conceptualized as belonging solely to the safeguarding team (or more likely to the individual SLO). Where understanding of SCP amongst leadership is low, as it certainly has been within sport, the SLO role may, in fact, provide an opportunity for leaders to construct SCP as an area of expertise and the SLO as *the* "expert". We return to this issue below.

However, some SLOs discussed how initial resistance from within their organization had, over time, given way to greater, if somewhat begrudging, acceptance of the need for SCP:

SLO2: ... over the years I think people have recognized that we need to do something about it and they have become more accepting of it ... We still have to fight a little bit but nowhere near as bad as it used to be.

SLO6: ...whereas initially it was, "umm, why are we doing this? Why is this on the agenda?" to an understanding now of it—to them it presents a risk to the organization, you know, and umm, equally the importance of it. I think no one can ever deny the importance of child protection, it's just how much–for them it might get in the way of doing other business ... because it's always "not in my back yard". ... I think them understanding the number of cases we are dealing with, which I think has shocked them [management], that you know it is this sort like, "it doesn't happen, well, OK it does", and you know, people didn't used to wear seatbelts but now they do and they just accept it, and it's just that change of attitude … and eventually it's part of what we do. … the board have now got an increased interest in it and we report to them every meeting on where we are with it.

The indication here is that an NGBs' "understanding" refers not to a recognition of children's rights or the broader safeguarding agenda, but to a realization of the risk posed to the "business" and its reputation by the number of cases being reported. In some instances, SLOs felt compelled to emphasize the financial advantages of implementing safeguarding policy in order to "encourage" greater engagement by senior management:

SLO5: We have to be able to drive it and challenge a lot. And also stand by your guns. And also do it for the right reasons. Sometimes I had to resort to the whole, "you know what, if we don't do this, as a governing body, we won't get more take-off funding." It annoys me that you have to do it that way because my first selling message would always be you do it for the right reasons, because 28% of our memberships are juniors so we need to treat them in a responsible and appropriate manner … it frustrates me.

Whilst there is some sense of gradual change, SLOs seemed to have been positioned as "outsiders" within their own organization, the bearers of "bad news" and faced with ambivalence, reluctance, inertia and opposition.

4.3. A Complex and Specialist Role

The SLO role is both wide ranging in its remit and specialist in nature, yet there are no formal qualifications for or prior training to become a designated officer within sport, so SLOs enter their role from a variety of backgrounds and with a variety of different experiences and understandings of child welfare–in some cases the SLOs in this study had come from professional lives where they had gained experience of the statutory sector, such as the police, the legal profession, education, while others had not. As a result, the level of understanding of the SLOs' responsibilities varied at the point of entry into the role, leading them to note the challenges associated with the specialist nature of their role, particularly the required knowledge of statutory-sector legislation:

SLO3: … as a lead officer with a non-statutory background, I found that extremely challenging. … I still think dealing with cases within governing bodies … is quite difficult because they're all different and they'll all bring up different things … it's a very specialist area because it's verging on statutory and you have to kind of work out how you fit with statutory, how your organization deals with that. … the complexity of dealing with the statutory sector and dealing with individuals and their families and everything else … that was a massive, massive learning curve.

SLO9: I feel that, you know after four years I am pretty much to grips with the whole thing except when, when suddenly I get the legislation in front of me and I'm like "ooh, actually no that doesn't say what we have always thought it was saying for the last four years".

Some SLOs clearly lacked confidence in carrying out their duties, particularly when it meant dealing with external partners who they constructed as "experts" in child welfare compared to themselves:

> SLO5: I have ... contact with a child protection consultant who we pay ... and originally when I first started, if we had a case I would say, "can you ring the local authority and get the information?" or "can you ring the police?", and he would say, "no actually, *you* can—these are the pertinent questions", and I'd only been to actually one, as we call it, inter-agency meeting and I admit I was terrified, because I was thinking I hope they don't think that I'm a massive expert. [emphasis added].

A core part of the SLO's duties involves managing cases of child abuse, dealing with abusers and working with internal and external partners. In this sense, SLOs occupy positions of considerable responsibility, and the stress and emotional impact of the role is not to be underestimated. Child protection social workers suffer from higher levels of work-related stress than the national average, which has been linked to increased levels of staff turnover [52]. While the SLO's role is markedly different from social workers', the impact of managing allegations of abuse, especially in an environment where SLOs feel they are unsupported, must be acknowledged. Some SLO's reported a lack of emotional support, even isolation:

> SLO3: ... For me [I've learned the job] through fairly awful experience I have to say. I hope the sector has learnt to support people better, but I'm not sure that is the case. ... it's that we learn from the experience that some lead officers have had, in terms of the isolation of the role, because I think that role can be very isolating ... we need to make sure that it is more than just one person's responsibility ... it needs specialist support, not everybody can deal with that stuff. And actually I think people shouldn't be asked to deal with that stuff without having those support functions in place. It's a huge responsibility dealing with cases. I think a lot of early lead officers went through that and a lot of them fell by the way side as a result ... It's too much without the right support.

> SLO2: ... I will admit to you that 3, 4, or 5 years ago I would say that no, I didn't have the personal support that I needed, and that was when we did have cases that weren't very nice, and I did struggle with that, you know, going home and thinking about what had actually taken place. And also I didn't have anybody to bounce ideas off or even say "look this is really upsetting, read this". I had to keep it all within myself.

These participants begin to reveal the emotional impact that this role may take on an individual in terms of the strain of dealing with cases of child abuse, but which is then exacerbated by the specialist nature of the role and the lack of understanding and support available, leading to anxiety and feelings of isolation. With limited other people within their NGB who understand their role and the emotional impact of it, SLOs highlighted the importance of connecting with other SLOs for support:

> SLO3: I think that's the opportunity to meet with other people doing the same roles and I think lead officers need to meet with other lead officers because it's a kind of quite unique position and I think talking to other people who are having the same experiences

is really important because I think that helps the isolation. And I think just people knowing that people understand what you're doing and your challenges is quite reassuring sometimes.

Given the specialist nature of the SLO role, training is essential. However, while the responsibilities of SLOs are, in the words of one participant, "verging on statutory", SLOs receive significantly less training than their statutory counterparts to prepare them for the rigours of their role; SLO's receive two-day "specialist safeguarding training" known as *Time to Listen*, which is specifically designed for people with lead responsibility for safeguarding or safe recruitment [53]. SLO's commented on the extent to which this was able to prepare them for the complexity of managing cases of abuse:

> SLO3: I did [attend CPSU training for SLOs] but that in no way prepares you for the ins and outs of case management. ... *Time to Listen* is good training but it's not until you get into cases and how your organization deals with it that you kind of really get into the nitty-gritty of what dealing with cases is all about.

As designated people responsible for managing NGBs' child welfare responsibilities, SLOs are central to safeguarding and protecting children and young people in sport, yet, they require no formal child welfare qualifications and receive minimal training (and limited emotional support). This raises questions about the value attributed to SCP in sport and the support offered to those with operational responsibility for this area.

4.4. Constructions of Safeguarding and Child Protection in Sport

The way in which SCP is interpreted or constructed within the governing structures of sport has implications for how it is understood and managed and, concomitantly, the extent to which the SLO role is valued, prioritized and supported. It is evident that the SLOs in this study all had to battle against a narrow, risk-based, legalistic construction of their role:

> SLO8: Everything has to do with risk. Safeguarding is risk. When you write the child protection policies and guidelines, it's about cutting down the risk. ... you always get a lot ... "they're going to sue us." If you've not got your guidelines down, you're wide open.

> SLO9: ...the sort of relationship with our legal team hasn't always been perhaps the easiest. It's, you know, they are very aware that it is a big, high-risk area.

In the new age of insecurity characterized by risk consciousness [54], SCP is understood in terms of the risk it represents to an NGB. It is well over a decade since Brackenridge ([3], p. 182) noted that "even where policy development is now underway, it is all too often based upon fear rather than any genuine commitment to social justice, equity or human rights". All of the participants indicated, explicitly or implicitly, that SCP is of interest to NGBs principally, or only, to the extent that it may pose a threat to the organization's "core" business and, therefore, must be dealt with. Consequently, SCP was identified as a "dangerous" area. SLOs suggested some NGB members were daunted by SCP and, consequently, preferred to avoid dealing with it:

SLO5: I think people are fearful of child protection, so yeah there were reluctant people leading on the Standards Framework [new national initiative] ... I remember, it must have taken virtually a day to do a press release about, I think it was CRB checks ... there was some news story and I remember it took them all day to get the wording [of the press release] right, and I was thinking this is just because this person–no disrespect because they knew it—they were so worried about getting the wording right ... it could have been done in minutes.

Following high-profile media coverage of the apparent mishandling of child abuse cases by social work and medical professionals over the past three decades, sport NGB personnel cannot fail to have been aware of the consequences of "getting it wrong" where child protection is concerned. Thus, in a sector where very little experience or knowledge exists [3], unsurprisingly NGBs constructed SCP through negative and reactive frames. In most cases, this clashed with SLOs' broader agenda for child welfare in their sport:

SLO3: I think there's still a little bit of "you deal with the scary stuff and the horrible side of things" rather than being seen as a positive enhancement. I'd like to get to that stage where it's seen as a positive rather than just a person that sorts out the horrible stuff. I think the difficulty in safeguarding is quite often what you're trying to do is presented as being an issue. So it's kind of not seen as being important because it's preventative. You're doing things so that things don't go wrong—you know you're getting consent forms in place and making sure that people have been CRB checked—and they're kind of not seen as being ... it's quite difficult to explain that. People don't understand the value in planning and preparation that a lot of safeguarding is.

SLO5: ... I've always said to people, you know, "safeguarding, child protection, it's not just about a child that may be in distress, it's a much broader thing". I've done a lot with the organization as a whole in terms of, you know, the wider perspective, like how long the children are playing in tournaments and at what age should children be playing with adults.

The CPSU itself was established at a time when sexual abuse cases in sport had begun to emerge in significant numbers, accompanied by foreboding headlines in the national media. For example, according to Steven Downes in *The Observer*:

Youngsters in Britain face a growing danger of being sexually abused by their sports coaches ... this special report ... asks how we can best protect children from *the menace that may lurk at the poolside and in the changing rooms* ([55], emphasis added).

The introduction of a specialist unit focused on "child protection in sport" at a time when media narratives about predatory sex abusers in sport had recently emerged no doubt contributed to the dominance of a protection-focused discourse within NGBs, where compliance with national legislation on matters such as criminal history checks was equated with "the best interests of the child". It was into this climate that the first mandatory lead officers for *safeguarding* were established in 2003:

SLO1: I would say… [sigh] more compliance at the top level, that's how they see it. "Right, well, safeguarding, it's probably a lot of money. Have we got to do it?" "Yes, we have to do it, this is why we have to do it." "Right, well, we want to do it well and it fits in with our image, yeah, so that's fine, we can deal with that because it fits in." So the motives from the top are more compliance rather than belief, I would say.

Thus, the difficulty of establishing a broader safeguarding agenda, underpinned by a children's rights agenda, which goes beyond attempts to protect children from "the menace that may lurk at the poolside and in the changing rooms" [55], has, then, been a key feature of the experiences of the first SLOs within English sport.

5. Discussion

Our investigation has been guided by Bourdieu's epistemology which seeks "connections between individual subjectivities and the generating principles acting on them in the fields through which they pass in their life trajectories" ([35], p. 180). Through an investigation of the experiences and perspectives of those designated with "lead responsibility" for implementing "safeguarding", we have attempted to excavate the logic that has underpinned the early construction of "child protection" within English sport. In this final section we consider our findings through Bourdieu's conceptual framework.

Whilst none of the SLOs would describe themselves as child protection "experts", their role is explicitly defined as having responsibility for this area. In a field where there was a considerable knowledge vacuum around "child protection/safeguarding", in introducing a "designated person … who is responsible for the implementation of the child protection policy" ([8], p. 6) at the NGB level, it is perhaps unsurprising that SLOs were depicted as experts in this by their organizations. At one level this may be construed simply as a convenient means of senior management dealing with (whilst distancing themselves from) the "problem" of SCP. However, such a conclusion appears partial and superficial.

CEOs and executive committee members undoubtedly represent powerful expressions of what is most valued within the sporting field. Indeed, the greater the investment within a field, the greater the complicity between field and habitus: "The habitus is what enables the institution to attain full realization" ([56], p. 57). Although it is beyond the parameters of this study to properly investigate, the habitus of CEOs, presidents, board members, senior management and other officials within specific sporting fields are, arguably, the most developed representations of the field "made flesh" ([56], p. 57).

Conversely, SLOs are required to be simultaneously invested in both the field of "child protection/safeguarding" *and* the field of "sport". The individual habitus of each SLO, which led them to apply for, accept and maintain the role of designated "safeguarding lead", appeared to place them, to varying degrees, in conflict with the dominant logic of the field. Arguably, this misalignment leads to the frustration, anxiety and isolation our participants report. Thus, SLOs indicate a "belief" in safeguarding, but a simultaneous lack of investment—and lack of belief—from the field, in them.

Thus, SLOs' lack of (material and personal) organizational support can be seen as the product of their relation (or their role's relation) to the symbolic capital dominant within the sporting field.

Developing this further, it may be argued that the generative logic or principle of the sporting field is "performance"—that is, the successful domination of others (and others' bodies) through one's own corporeal/athletic endeavor. This is not the same as saying individual CEOs are purely focused on medals, *etc.*, nevertheless, material and symbolic resources (*capital*) within the field are organized according to this principle and distributed to those who are closest to this objective of corporeal domination. Therefore, it is possible to observe across sporting fields a complex infrastructure of supporting mechanisms, communities and agencies (including NGBs) wholly geared towards this principle, neatly captured by the Olympic slogan "*citius, altius, fortius*" (faster, higher, stronger).

If the child protection field can be momentarily encapsulated through the slogan "the welfare of the child is paramount" [57], the experiences of the SLOs in this study suggest that what is valued most by dominant agents within the administration of sport is (at least potentially) substantively different from that which is most valued within the field of child protection—for example, as one SLO noted, SCP was perceived as getting "in the way of doing other business". Indeed, beyond the "performance principle" even other areas that may be construed as part of sports" "social agenda" appear to be viewed with greater enthusiasm than the troublesome area of "safeguarding":

> SLO: "That's all happy-clappy stuff that we can publicize everywhere–look how good and wonderful we are". Well, I never get to see my CEO or Chair because they're not interested. If I did it wrong, or there was a big case, that'd be different. They'd want to see me then. But for [equal opportunities] it's like … "we've got another photo opportunity here."

Therefore, as an agent of the sporting field an SLO is required to promote (even enforce) practice that is accorded little value within that field. In such circumstances, a personal investment in SCP is crucial to SLOs remaining motivated to do the role and, hence, to SLO retention:

> SLO5: I really wanted to do this … I believe in it so much and I think it's absolutely the right thing to do.

> SLO3: I know people think I'm a complete pain in the neck. I'm the one who's, "hang on a minute, have we thought about the whatever" and that's the–you know, I would love to get to a stage where I'm not seen as the one that's the pain in the neck. … I really think the work's important. I really genuinely believe. I don't think I'd still be here if I didn't genuinely believe.

According to McNay ([36], p. 72) "a complex dynamic [exists] between the symbolic and the material, where the logic of the field may reinforce or displace the tendencies of the habitus. It is this tension that is generative of agency". "Displacement" is perhaps an apt expression for the experiences reported by some of our SLOs, who found themselves isolated and at odds with their senior management despite being heavily invested in their role. Nevertheless, through this tension it is also possible to observe the ways in which SLOs struggled against the pervading construction of their role (that is, in SLO3's words, "being about the scary, horrible side of things"). For example, SLOs reported (reluctantly) adopting "scare" tactics (principally around loss of resources and reputation) to convince senior management to engage with and commit support to SCP beyond the absolute minimum. In other words, and perhaps according to the degree to which they were personally invested in the child protection/safeguarding field, SLOs found creative ways in which to navigate and negotiate their role within their sporting field. Given the emotional pressures and anxieties that go with the role, it is hardly surprising that they report the need to be "thick-skinned".

It is clear, therefore, that the task of the SLO is considerable—indeed no less, perhaps, than to alter the underlying structure of the collective habitus that dominates within their particular sporting field. This was intuitively appreciated by our participants:

> SLO5: We have to be able to drive it, and challenge a lot. And also stand by your guns … I just wanted to be able to sort of change hearts and minds … it's cultural stuff, it's a slow burner … sowing the seeds and then coming back and trying to change people along a bit more.

The commitment to their role provides an important message for agencies recruiting individuals to such positions. Given the anxiety and tension that seems inherent in the SLO role, coupled with the organizational indifference and/or resistance that appears to accompany it (especially in the early years of introducing SCP in sport), the personal disposition and emotional resources—the *habitus*—that an individual must bring to the role should not be underestimated. This was illustrated succinctly by one of our participants who clearly provided a vital counter-balance to the discourse of compliance to minimum standards:

> SLO3: [Senior management said] "we're seen as being a good governing body and you're now suggesting we're not!" And I was sort of like, "I'm just saying that there's more to it than having a policy."

Clearly, for sport agencies who are serious about the introduction of SCP into their communities, it would be anticipated that considerably greater investment (of all forms of *capital*) is contributed to this endeavour than that reported by some of our participants. However, it must be recognized that NGBs—whilst constituted here as individual fields within which the politics of SCP in sport are played out—are also fields *within* fields. They are semi-autonomous fields, thus, whilst distinct, also subject to the influence of other fields. Therefore, they are also engaged in struggles over *capital* (e.g., funding, media coverage, public recognition) and these various struggles are clearly factors in the manner in which SCP is constructed within each sport. Thus, we observe that the discussion we present here is based on the views of just (a relatively small sample of) a single group within English governing bodies of sport. A fuller picture would incorporate the views of other key stakeholder groups, for example, department heads, senior management and CEOs, as well as other stakeholders within and without the NGB. Furthermore, this paper has mostly focused on the relation between the SLO and their management within the NGB. However, the interviews also revealed other relationships and these require separate analyses. Therefore, we frame this discussion merely as a contribution to the overall picture of the politics of child protection in English sport during the past decade, but not the totality of it. That said, we would reiterate that these individuals were particularly well placed to offer an important insight into this process and we would encourage other researchers to consider similar investigations.

If NGBs want to overcome (or avoid a return to) "inertial opposition" to SCP ([3], p. 185) organizational understanding and support for the SLO role is crucial. Our analysis suggests that SCP needs to be led, with vigour, from the top. Unless those agents with high volumes of cultural capital within each sporting field (not confined to the leadership of NGBs but certainly including them) respond positively and proactively to the children's rights agenda that underpins "safeguarding"—a fundamental aspect of which is the right to be protected from abuse and exploitation—the implementation of SCP within sport will be piecemeal, stifled and inadequate.

The invisible nature of much safeguarding work and the challenges of evidencing the benefits of this work to the sports community are not easily resolved and depend in large part on leadership being convinced that there is a discernible benefit to the organization. Thus, the evolution in safeguarding policy is not always evident in safeguarding *practice* and child protection often remains the key focus of many practitioners.

Paradoxically, the SLO role itself may have encouraged NGBs to annexe SCP from its core business rather than integrating it. This may well be reinforced by the specialist (typically three-hour) "safeguarding and child protection" "training" programmes sports personnel are required to undertake, offered (or rather *sold*) by various agencies and often required as a condition of accreditation (e.g., *ClubMark*). Compliance with official "minimum operating standards" clearly says little, if anything, about the extent to which individual dispositions are transformed, yet the number of people trained in SCP are often prioritized by sports agencies as "hard" evidence of cultural change. If SCP is to be truly integrated into sporting cultural practices, coach education needs to be substantively reconfigured around the principles and tenets of children's rights.

6. Conclusions

High-level efforts to address the abuse of children within sport contexts are evident and ongoing: for example, a recent Enlarged Partial Agreement on Sport (EPAS) conference highlighted the issue of child abuse in sport at a pan-European level [58]; the German Sport Youth, ENGSO Youth, and the SPORTUNION Austria have recently implemented European collaborations aimed at tackling sexual violence in sport; the European Commission has emphasized "the fight against sexual violence and harassment in sport" within its funding priorities for 2014–2020 [59]; and the United Nations Office for Sport for Development and Peace has also designated "child protection" as a key theme within its programme, "encouraging" member states to "implement plans to prevent the exploitation and abuse of children and youth in sport contexts" [60]. Such high-level plans are important, however, based on the analysis presented here, we suggest that for the implementation of "child protection in sport" to be meaningful (rather than superficial), organizations must demonstrate much greater investment, belief, in the philosophy of children's rights than was encountered by the SLOs interviewed here.

A broader safeguarding agenda clearly requires much greater organizational investment, illustrated by the substantial "Framework for Maintaining and Embedding Safeguarding for Children In and Through Sport" recently introduced by the CPSU [61]. Following full compliance with the national standards [7,8], this new *Framework* comprises 11 elements, the first of which is "organizational commitment to safeguarding" which requires that "leaders ensure that safeguarding principles underpin all areas of activity" and that they "monitor and evaluate the implementation" of the principles [61]. This is reinforced in a recent report: "Everyone from senior managers in national governing bodies, county sports partnerships and local authorities to clubs, coaches, parents and young people need to take ownership of this agenda" ([9], p. 4). We suggest that what the new "Sports Safeguarding Children Initiative" is in fact calling for, in Bourdieu's terms, is a transformation of the *sporting habitus*, or rather a disruption of the synchronicity between *habitus* and *field* as it is currently configured within the field of sports. Arguably, this has been the mission of the CPSU since its inception over a decade ago.

Thus, it is through destabilizing the inertia or "hysteresis" of the *sporting habitus* that "increased possibilities may arise for critical reflection on previously habituated forms of action" ([62], p. 196). This has surely been the role of the SLO in English/British sport. However, as Bourdieu ([29], p. 122) argues, "rupture cannot result from a simple awakening of consciousness; the transformation of dispositions cannot occur without a prior or concomitant transformation of the objective structures of which they are the product". This seems to provide some general support for the objective of Sport England and the NSPCC to transform (via the CPSU) the structures of the English (and British) sporting fields. However, according to our findings, within English sport, the destabilizing task required for social transformation–the transformation of dispositions—appears to have been highly dependent upon the fortitude of a small number of individuals and their willingness and capacity to challenge the inertia within the structures of their own organizations. In our opinion, whether there has in fact been a widespread transformation of dispositions is yet to be determined.

Acknowledgments

The authors would like to thank the three anonymous reviewers and the editors. In addition, the authors gratefully acknowledge the transcription services provided by postgraduate students Divyata Sohal and Jessica Thom, coordinated by Daniel Rhind (Brunel University).

Author Contributions

This research was conceived by the first author. Both authors contributed equally to the research design, data collection, analysis and writing up. Both authors read and approved the final manuscript.

Conflicts of Interest

The authors declare no conflict of interest.

References

1. Office for National Statistics. *2011 Census: Population Estimates for the UK, 27 January 2011*. London: Office for National Statistics, 2012. Available online: http://www.ons.gov.uk/ons/rel/census/2011-census/population-and-household-estimates-for-the-united-kingdom/stb-2011-census--population-estimates-for-the-united-kingdom.html (accessed on 4 July 2014).
2. Department for Culture, Media and Sport. *Taking Part October 2011 to September 2012 Supplementary Child Report*. London: Department for Culture, Media and Sport, 2013. Available online: https://www.gov.uk/government/publications/taking-part-october-2011-to-september-2012-supplementary-child-report--2 (accessed on 4 July 2014).
3. Celia Brackenridge. *Spoilsports: Understanding and Preventing Sexual Exploitation in Sport*, 1st ed. London: Routledge, 2001.
4. Melanie Lang, and Mike Hartill. "Safeguarding and Child Protection in Sport in England." In *Safeguarding, Child Protection and Abuse in Sport: International Perspectives in Research, Policy and Practice*, 1st ed. Edited by Melanie Lang and Mike Hartill. London: Routledge, 2014, pp. 13–22.
5. Department for Education and Skills. *Every Child Matters: Change for Children*. London: Her Majesty's Stationary Office, 2003. Available online: http://webarchive.nationalarchives.gov.uk/20130401151715/http://www.education.gov.uk/publications/eOrderingDownload/DFES10812004.pdf (accessed on 21 December 2013).
6. Steve Boocock. "The Child Protection in Sport Unit." In *Sexual Harassment and Abuse in Sport: International Research and Policy Perspectives*, 1st ed. Edited by Celia Brackenridge, Kari Fasting. London: Whiting & Birch, 2002, pp. 133–43.
7. Child Protection in Sport Unit. *Standards for Safeguarding and Protecting Children in Sport*, 1st ed. Leicester: Child Protection in Sport Unit, 2003.
8. Child Protection in Sport Unit. *Standards for Safeguarding and Protecting Children in Sport*, 2nd ed. Leicester: Child Protection in Sport Unit, 2006. Available online: https://thecpsu.org.uk/resource-library/2013/standards-for-safeguarding-and-protecting-children-in-sport/ (accessed on 16 July 2014).
9. Child Protection in Sport Unit. *Sports Safeguarding Children Initiative: Mid-Project Progress Report*. Leicester: Child Protection in Sport Unit, 2013.
10. Mike Hartill, and Philip Prescott. "Serious business or 'any other business'? Safeguarding and child protection policy in British rugby league." *Child Abuse Review* 16 (2007): 237–51.
11. Mike Hartill, Melanie Lang, and Nicholas Ashley. *Safeguarding and Child Protection in Rugby League: A Research Evaluation*. Ormskirk: Edge Hill University Press, 2014.
12. Celia H. Brackenridge. "Problem? What Problem? Thoughts on a Professional Code of Practice for Coaches." Paper presented at the Annual Conference of the British Association of National Coaches, Bristol, 16 December 1986.
13. Celia H. Brackenridge. "Sexual Abuse of Children in Sport: A Comparative Exploration of Research Methodologies and Professional Practice." Paper presented at the Pre-Olympic Scientific Congress, Malaga, Spain, 14–19 July 1992.

14. Celia H. Brackenridge. "Fair play or fair game: Child sexual abuse in sport organizations." *International Review for the Sociology of Sport* 29 (1994): 287–99.
15. Jon Timothy Curry. "Fraternal bonding in the locker room: A pro-feminist analysis of talk about competition and women." *Sociology of Sport Journal* 8 (1991): 119–35.
16. Peter Donnelly. "Who's Fair Game? Sport, Sexual Harassment and Abuse." In *Sport and Gender in Canada*, 1st ed. Edited by Phillip White, Kevin Young. Oxford: Oxford University Press, 1999.
17. Kari Fasting, Celia H. Brackenridge and Kristin Walseth. "Coping with sexual harassment in sport: Experiences of elite female athletes." *Journal of Sexual Aggression* 8 (2002): 16–36.
18. Jennifer Hargreaves. *Sporting Females: Critical Issues in the History and Sociology of Women's Sport*, 1st ed. London: Routledge, 1994.
19. Helen Lenskyj. "Unsafe at home base: women's experiences of sexual harassment in university sport and physical education." *Women in Sport and Physical Activity Journal* 1 (1992): 19–33.
20. Celia H. Brackenridge, Andy Pitchford, Kate Russell, and Gareth Nutt. *Child Welfare in Football: An Exploration of Children's Welfare in the Modern Game*, 1st ed. London: Routledge, 2007.
21. Heather Piper, Dean Garratt, and Bill Taylor. "Child abuse, child protection, and defensive 'touch' in PE teaching and sports coaching." *Sport, Education and Society* 18 (2013): 583–98.
22. Mike Hartill, and Jimmy O'Gorman. "Evaluation in Safeguarding and Child Protection in Sport." In *Safeguarding, Child Protection and Abuse in Sport: International Perspectives in Research, Policy and Practice*, 1st ed. Edited by Melanie Lang and Mike Hartill. London: Routledge, 2014, pp. 181–91.
23. Celia Brackenridge. "He owned me basically…: Women's experience of sexual abuse in sport." *International Review for the Sociology of Sport* 32 (1997): 115–30.
24. Mike Hartill. "The sexual abuse of boys in organized sports." *Men and Masculinities* 12 (2009): 225–49.
25. Melanie Lang. "Surveillance and conformity in competitive youth swimming." *Sport, Education and Society* 15 (2010): 19–37.
26. Dean Garratt, Heather Piper, and Bill Taylor. "Safeguarding sports coaching: Foucault, genealogy and critique." *Sport, Education and Society* 18 (2013): 615–29.
27. Mike Hartill. "Suffering in Gratitude: Sport and the Sexually Abused Male Child." In *The Routledge Handbook of Sport, Gender and Sexuality*, 1st ed. Edited by Jennifer Hargreaves and Eric Anderson. London: Routledge, 2014.
28. Melanie Lang. "Touchy subject: A Foucauldian analysis of coaches' perceptions of adult-child touch in youth swimming." *Sociology of Sport Journal*, 2014, in press. Available online: http://repository.edgehill.ac.uk/5958/ (accessed on 12 September 2014).
29. Pierre Bourdieu. *Practical Reason: On the Theory of Action*. Cambridge: Polity Press, 1998.
30. Richard *Giulianotti. Sport and Modern Social Theorists*, 1st ed. London: Palgrave, 2004.
31. Richard *Giulianotti. Sport: A Critical Sociology*, 1st ed. London: Polity Press, 2005.
32. Pierre Bourdieu. "Programme for a Sociology of Sport." In *In Other Words: Essays towards a Reflexive Sociology*. Cambridge: Polity Press, 1990, pp. 156–67.

33. Pierre Bourdieu. "How Can One be a Sportsman?" In *Sociology in Question*. London: Sage, 1993, pp. 117–31.
34. Pierre Bourdieu. *Sociology in Question*. London: Sage, 1993.
35. Michael Grenfell, and David James. *Bourdieu and Education: Acts of Practical Theory*. London: Falmer, 1998.
36. Lois McNay. *Gender and Agency: Reconfiguring the Subject in Feminist and Social Theory*. Cambridge: Polity, 2000.
37. Celia Brackenridge. "Men Loving Men Hating Women: The Crisis of Masculinity and Violence to Women in Sport." In *Gender and Sport: A Reader*, 1st ed. Edited by Sheila Scraton and Anne Flintoff. London: Routledge, 2002, pp. 255–70.
38. Pierre Bourdieu. *Outline of a Theory of Practice*. Cambridge: Cambridge University Press, 1977.
39. John B. Thompson. "Editor's Introduction." In *Language and Symbolic Power*. Edited by Pierre Bourdieu. Cambridge: Polity Press, 1991, pp. 1–31.
40. Pierre Bourdieu, and Wacquant, Loic. *An Invitation to Reflexive Sociology*. Cambridge: Polity Press, 1992.
41. Nick Crossley. "The phenomenological habitus and its construction." *Theory and Society* 30 (2001): 81–120.
42. Pierre Bourdieu. "Understanding." In *The Weight of the World: Social Suffering in Contemporary Society*. Edited by Pierre Bourdieu. Cambridge: Polity Press, 1999, pp. 607–26.
43. Colin Robson. *Real World Research*, 3rd ed. London: Sage, 2011.
44. Judith E. Sturges, and Kathleen J. Hanrahan. "Comparing telephone and face-to-face qualitative interviewing: A research note." *Qualitative Research* 4 (2004): 107–18.
45. Karl Maton. *"Habitus" in Pierre Bourdieu: Key Concepts*, 2nd ed. Edited by Michael Grenfell. Durham: Acumen, 2012, pp. 48–64.
46. Thomas K. Greenfield, Lorraine T. Midanik, and John D. Rogers. "Effects of telephone *versus* face-to-face interview modes on reports of alcohol consumption." *Addiction* 95 (2000): 277–84.
47. Preissle J. Goertz, and Diane M. LeCompte. *Ethnography and Qualitative Design in Educational Research*, 2nd ed. New York: Academic Press, 1993.
48. Robert B. Johnson, and Larry B. Christensen. *Educational Research: Quantitative, Qualitative, and Mixed Approaches*, 1st ed. London: Sage, 2012.
49. Sport England. "Sport England Boots Funding to Allow More Young People to Enjoy Sport in a Safe Environment." *Sport England*, 10 January 2013. Available online: http:www.sportengland.org/media-centre/news/2013/january/10/sport-england-boosts-funding-to-help-more-young-people-enjoy-sport-in-a-safe-environment (accessed on 15 July 2013).
50. Bob Lonne, Nigel Parton, Jane Thomson, and Maria Harries. *Reforming Child Protection*, 1st ed. London: Routledge, 2009.
51. Adrian Barton, and Penelope Welbourne. "Context and its significance in identifying 'what works' in child protection." *Child Abuse Review* 14 (2005): 177–94.
52. Lloyd Chris, Robert King, and Lesley I. Chenoweth. "Social work, stress and burnout: A review." *Journal of Mental Health* 11 (2002): 255–65.

53. Child Protection in Sport Unit. "Specialist Safeguarding Training." Available online: https://thecpsu.org.uk/training-events/specialist-safeguarding-training/ (accessed on 26 June 2014).
54. Beck Ulrich. *Risk Society: Towards a New Modernity*, 1st ed. London: Sage, 1992.
55. Steven Downes. "Every parents' nightmare." *Observer Sport Monthly*, 7 April 2002. Available online: http://www.observer.theguardian.com/print/0,,4386620-103977,00.html (accessed on 4 January 2014).
56. Pierre Bourdieu. *The Logic of Practice*. Cambridge: Polity Press, 1990.
57. United Nations General Assembly. "Convention on the Rights of the Child." Available online: http://www.refworld.org/cgi-bin/texis/vtx/rwmain?docid=3ae6b38f0 (accessed on 15 March 2013).
58. Council of Europe. "Enlarged Partial Agreement on Sport (EPAS)." Available online: http://www.coe.int/t/dg4/epas/News/News_2013_Budapest_Conf_EN.asp (accessed on 21 December 2013).
59. European Commission. "EU Conference on Gender Equality in Sport." Available online: http://ec.europa.eu/sport/news/20131129_en.htm (accessed on 21 December 2013).
60. United Nations Office on Sport for Development and Peace. "Child Protection in Sport." Available online: http://www.un.org/wcm/content/site/sport/home/unplayers/memberstates/sdp_iwg_thematicwgs/pid/6412 (accessed on 5 January 2014).
61. Child Protection in Sport Unit. *The Framework for Maintaining and Embedding Safeguarding for Children In and Through Sport*, 1st ed. Leicester: Child Protection in Sport Unit, 2012.
62. Lisa Adkins. "Reflexivity: Freedom or habit of gender?" In *Feminism after Bourdieu*, 1st ed. Edited by Lisa Adkins and Beverley Skeggs. Oxford: Blackwell, 2004, pp. 191–210.

A Critical Examination of Child Protection Initiatives in Sport Contexts

Gretchen Kerr, Ashley Stirling and Ellen MacPherson

Abstract: With the broadening of focus on child maltreatment beyond intra-familial settings, there is growing awareness of occurrences of maltreatment within the sport context. Millions of children participate in organized sport annually, and despite a tendency to view sport as a context by which to enhance the overall health and development of children, it is also a context in which children are vulnerable to experiences of maltreatment. The well-documented power ascribed to coaches, the unregulated nature of sport and a "win-at-all-costs" approach contribute to a setting that many propose is conducive to maltreatment. A number of high profile cases of sexual abuse of athletes across several countries in the 1990s prompted sport organizations to respond with the development of child protection measures. This study examined seven child protection in sport initiatives in terms of the extent to which they originated from research, had content that was consistent with scholarly work and were evaluated empirically. The findings indicated that these initiatives were not empirically derived nor evaluated. Recommendations are made to more closely align research with these initiatives in order to protect children and to promote a safe and growth-enhancing experience for young participants in sport.

Reprinted from *Soc. Sci.* Cite as: Kerr, G.; Stirling, A.; MacPherson, E. A Critical Examination of Child Protection Initiatives in Sport Contexts. *Soc. Sci.* **2014**, *3*, 742–757.

1. Introduction

The last forty years has been characterized with an enhanced focus on the welfare of children. In Westernized societies, in particular, a cultural shift has occurred in which youth are given special status apart from that of adults, one that is reflected in more child-centered educational practices, distinct legal status and structural mechanisms to protect the welfare of young people when the family structure breaks down [1]. Furthermore, there has been a shift in focus from protecting young people from harm to addressing ways to enhance the overall health and development of young people. As a result, considerable attention has been devoted to optimizing parenting methods, and importantly, this focus has extended beyond the family to a variety of child-populated contexts, including education, day care, sport and recreation settings.

Sport has historically been viewed as an important and beneficial arena for the growth and development of young people. A substantial body of literature supports such benefits as the development of physical strength and coordination, self-esteem, perseverance, teamwork and leadership, as a result of participation in organized sport [2,3]. In fact, sport tends to be viewed as being "innately good" [4] and a context that parents look to as a vehicle by which to enhance the overall health and development of their children. The fact that millions of children participate in organized sport every year is in part a testament to parents' beliefs that this context is a positive one for young people. In Canada, the United States and the United Kingdom, for example, between 45% and 75% of youth participate in organized sport [5–7].

In spite of predominantly positive views of sport, concerns about the competitive nature of sport for young people, including the resultant "win-at-all-costs" approach and high rates of injury, have been expressed for some time [8]. These concerns appear to have fallen on deaf ears, however, until the 1990s, when in several Westernized countries, a number of high-profile cases of sexual abuse of athletes by their coaches emerged. In Canada, for example, a television program called "Crossing the Line" documented examples of sexual abuse by male coaches of female athletes in volleyball, swimming and rowing teams. Also in the mid-1990s, a celebrated Canadian men's hockey coach, Graham James, named coach of the year, was charged and later convicted of numerous counts of sexual abuse; since that time, other athletes have also disclosed their experiences of abuse at the hands of James [9]. Also in the 1990s, former British Olympic Swimming coach, Paul Hickson, was charged with sexual abuse of his former athletes [4]; similarly, Australian triathlon coach, Brett Sutton, was also charged with sexual offences against a former athlete [10]. With the media scrutiny and very public exposure of these cases of harm in sport, those in the sport community could no longer blindly accept sport as a "moral oasis" or innately good for young people. In fact, sport organizations experienced pressure to be seen to be doing something about the safety and abuse of athletes. The result was the implementation of various athlete protection measures, including policies, educational programs and advocacy initiatives.

While the development of these initiatives is a positive reflection of societal views on the importance of addressing issues of child protection in sport, in order for these measures to be most effective, it is paramount that they are empirically informed and evaluated. The passion that is aroused in response to cases of child athlete maltreatment has understandably led to the development of preventative measures; however, if these measure are not grounded in theory and empirical data, they are unlikely to be effective in a sustained way. It has now been approximately twenty years since the first of such measures emerged in sport, and to-date, there has been an absence of analysis and systematic evaluation of these initiatives.

The purpose of the current study, therefore, was to critically review seven child protection initiatives in the context of organized sports with a focus on the extent to which these initiatives have been empirically informed and evaluated and whether the content included in these initiatives is congruent with scholarly work.

It is important to critically examine child protection initiatives in sport for several reasons. As mentioned earlier, sport is highly populated by young people and is seen as an important avenue for their overall health and development. In spite of this prevailing positive ideology of sport, various forms of maltreatment of young athletes have been documented. Since the high-profile media cases of sexual abuse in sport emerged in the 1990s, research on sexual abuse in particular has burgeoned. Although prevalence data are relatively unreliable due to differences in definitions of sexual abuse and harassment and under-reporting, findings from studies conducted in Denmark, Australia, Norway and Canada reveal that between 2% and 42% of athletes have reported experiences of inappropriate sexual conduct, including sexual assault, by their coaches [11–14]. Research on emotionally abusive experiences has emerged more recently, indicating that this form of maltreatment is the most commonly one experienced by athletes [15,16]. Although physical abuse and neglect in sport have not been investigated empirically, numerous anecdotal cases exist and include death of athletes as a result of the withdrawal of water during intense training in very hot temperatures [17]. Given the long-lasting effects that child maltreatment can have on mental health, including depression, anxiety and post-traumatic stress disorder, even into late adulthood [18,19], the pursuit of effective preventative measures is warranted.

An examination of child protection in sport initiatives is also critical given the well-documented and unique characteristics of the sport environment itself that enhance children's vulnerabilities to maltreatment by coaches in particular. As an example, the unquestioned power and authority ascribed to coaches by athletes, reflected in their references to coaches as a "parent" or "God-like" figure [4,20], enhances the power differential between coaches and athletes; this power and its misuse are fundamental to all forms of child maltreatment. The sport environment itself, with opportunities for the coach to be alone with an athlete during training and travelling, enhances vulnerabilities for maltreatment to occur [4]. Although one might assume that parents play a role in protecting their children from maltreatment, it appears instead that parents are often socialized into the sport culture in such a way as to relinquish control over their children to the coach [21]. Finally, the well-documented over-emphasis on winning and performance outcomes means that young athletes' wellbeing is often neglected by the adults in positions of authority [22,23].

Lastly, a critique of child protection in sport initiatives is necessary because of the self-regulated nature of sport. Historically, sport has been autonomous, unregulated, self-policing and dominated by a large un-scrutinized workforce [4,22]. In some countries, such as the USA, sport outside of the formal education system is provided almost entirely through volunteers. In other countries, such as Canada and the U.K., some state funding is provided for identified levels of sport, but other levels depend entirely upon volunteers. As an example, in Canada, over 40% of children between five and 14 years of age play soccer, and over 20% of this age group participate in minor league hockey; the coaches for these children's sport are almost exclusively volunteers [5]. Having such a volunteer base raises questions and concerns about whether or not these individuals have been scrutinized for previous incidences of maltreatment and have a minimal standard of training and education relative to child development and child protection issues. Interestingly, while one might expect that sport organizations in receipt of state funding would have higher obligations for accountability, this is not always the case. A recent study of Canadian national sport organizations that receive state funding indicates that the majority of these organizations fail to meet the requisite standards with respect to child protection to receive such funding [24].

The autonomous, unregulated nature of sport organizations also means that they are not monitored and evaluated by neutral, third-party bodies and, thus, are not necessarily held accountable. As David ([22], p. 229) wrote: "... in practice, due to the tradition of self-policing, paternalism, a fierce resistance to independent criticism and a refusal to accept that sport is not always "pure" and free from society's problems, the principles of accountability and scrutiny are still inadequately respected by the sporting world, or at best looked upon with suspicion." Sport organizations have an important role in responding to concerns about maltreatment of young people, but the ability of any organization to respond responsibly and effectively to issues of child protection depend in large part on the quality of the protective measures in place.

In an effort to scrutinize the empirical bases of child protection in sport initiatives, the following research questions were posed: (i) To what extent did the initiatives originate from research on athlete maltreatment? (ii) Is the content of the initiatives informed by and consistent with scholarly literature? (iii) Have the initiatives been evaluated empirically? Not only will this critique of child protection practices in sport potentially benefit sport practitioners and young athletes, but also the advancement of research and practice in complementary fields.

2. Sample

A total of seven athlete protection initiatives from four countries were examined, including: *Play by the Rules* from Australia, *Speak Out* and *Respect in Sport* from Canada, *Safe4Athletes* and *Safe to Compete* from the United States of America and the *Child Protection in Sport Unit* and *Children First* from the United Kingdom. These initiatives were selected on the basis of the following inclusion criteria: prioritized awareness-raising of child maltreatment and protection in sport; provided access to information and resources to facilitate sport organizations' abilities to prevent and/or intervene in cases of athlete maltreatment; and finally, available in the English language.

3. Data Collection and Analysis

A web-based analysis was chosen as the method for investigation, as it is recognized as a valuable avenue for exploring content and key messages. Further, for child protection resources to be of use to members of the sport community, they should be accessible, and the website is now the most frequent first point-of-contact for information about organizations and programs [25].

Data collection began by searching the web for any initiative matching the inclusion criteria cited above. The purpose of the web-based analysis was to assess the extent to which the content of the various athlete protection initiatives was empirically grounded and reflected current scholarly knowledge with respect to child maltreatment in sport. Recognizing that numerous forms of maltreatment can occur in sport, including, as a few examples, abuse, harassment, bullying, institutional maltreatment and child labor [26], the focus of this study was on the content covered by the athlete protection initiatives on relational child maltreatment (*i.e.*, sexual abuse, physical abuse, emotional abuse, neglect). Accordingly, the webpage information and all attached documentation covered by the initiatives on relational child maltreatment were reviewed in full.

Relational maltreatment refers to maltreatment that occurs within a critical relationship, one in which the child is dependent upon the adult for a sense of trust, security and fulfillment of needs [27]. Relational child maltreatment was chosen as the focus of the current study, as the vast majority of the related research in sport addresses abuses within the coach-athlete relationship, which in many cases can be classified as a critical relationship [26]. As athletes move up the competitive ladder in sport, they often spend more time with their coaches than with their parents; furthermore, athletes depend upon the coach for his or her expertise and access to necessary resources, and therefore, this qualify as a critical relationship [20]. This focus on relational maltreatment is also consistent with the foci of the media cases and scrutiny, which presumably speared the inception of child protection measures in sport.

Data recorded on the various athlete protection initiatives were then analyzed inductively, and the content was organized into main themes and summary tables. More specifically, data on the origins of the initiative and resources provided were examined. The current study assessed whether the child protection in sport initiatives identified all four forms of relational maltreatment: sexual abuse, physical abuse, emotional abuse and neglect [28]. Further, the ways in which the initiatives defined and provided examples of each form of child abuse were compared against those cited in the scholarly literature. A generally accepted definition of sexual abuse is: "any sexual interaction with person(s) of any age that is perpetuated: (1) against the victim's will; (2) without consent; or (3) in an aggressive, exploitative, manipulative, or threatening manner" [29]. Physical abuse is typically defined as: the infliction of physical harm on a child by a parent or caregiver [30]. Emotional abuse is referred to as patterns of non-physical harmful interactions, while neglect is a lack of reasonable care [31]. Any mention of contextual or descriptive information about the individual forms of child abuse were compared with existing literature, as well as procedures recommended for prevention and intervention. Information pertaining to contextual influences on vulnerability to maltreatment and whether or not the various initiatives have been evaluated empirically were also examined.

The final step in this phase of research was to run a descriptive analysis of the content described.

4. Results

To reiterate, the main research concerns for this study were to examine the extent to which: (i) the initiatives originated from research on athlete maltreatment; (ii) the content of the initiatives was congruent with scholarly literature; and (iii) the initiatives were evaluated empirically.

4.1. Origins of Initiatives

Four of the seven initiatives were reportedly developed in response to highly publicized cases of athlete maltreatment and, more specifically, cases of sexual abuse; two others resulted from the organization's recognition of the need to address athlete protection as part of their risk management responsibilities. Only one emerged from research following from a conference involving youth sport organizations, sport scientists, maltreatment consultants and other stakeholders involved in the prevention and intervention of maltreatment. Four of the initiatives were launched by sport organizations, while three were originated by organizations or individuals independent of any specific sport organization. Despite the lack of research as the stimulus for the development of the initiatives, five of the seven initiatives included empirical evidence on maltreatment in sport on the websites; two of these cited several sources of empirical information, while the other two referenced minimal research findings.

4.2. Descriptive Characteristics

A broad description of the athlete protection initiatives is important for providing a context for the evaluation. Each initiative stated a clear purpose and goals, although the degree of detail provided varied substantially across programs. All referred in some way to addressing and reducing harm experienced by children in sport; inherent in these goals was a focus on raising awareness of issues of abuse and child protection in sport. All of the initiatives, except for one, stated an intent to raise awareness regarding various forms of athlete maltreatment; the exception was an initiative explicitly aimed at sexual abuse alone. For all of the initiatives, the intended audiences included administrators, coaches, parents and athletes involved in organized sport. All of the initiatives engaged in modes of promotion and information dissemination, such as e-bulletins, posters, conference presentations, flyers and newsletters. Only three, however, promoted themselves through Facebook and/or Twitter. Most of the websites have a welcoming first page that is visually pleasing and identifies sponsors, athlete endorsements and resources. Additionally, tabs are used to organize the information into various sections, such as making complaints, legal information and resources, although there is no consistency in the organization of content across initiatives. In the majority of cases, accessing information on the various forms of athlete maltreatment was difficult and was categorized under headings ranging from "issues" to "fairness", "inclusion" and "discrimination", as examples. As can be seen in Table 1, all of the initiatives addressed the prevention of athlete abuse, but only five included content related to procedures for dealing with complaints of athlete abuse.

Table 1. Goals and means to achieve goals across initiatives.

Goals	Means to Achieve Goals	Number of Initiatives
Prevention	Awareness-Raising	7/7
	Provision of Educational Resources	7/7
	Provision of Structured Educational Modules or Workshops	4/7
	Establishment of Partnerships	6/7
	Incorporation of Research	6/7
Intervention	Identification of Procedures for Issuing a Complaint	7/7
	Duty to Report	7/7
	Identification of Procedures for Responding to a Complaint Against You	1/7
	Sample Policies and Procedures	7/7
	Recommendations for Athlete Advocate	4/7

All of the initiatives focused on prevention through the provision of educational resources and formal education programs, although they varied with respect to the format and delivery of educational content. Broadly, learning opportunities were available through short videos, worksheets, workshops or in-depth online programs; three of the seven initiatives provided all of these avenues for accessing content, while the remaining four initiatives offered at least one of the above options. Three of the seven initiatives charged a fee for some of their educational resources. One initiative charged a fee for accessing all of their educational materials.

Some, but not all, of the initiatives addressed intervention processes related to dealing with cases of athlete maltreatment. Of those that included measures of intervention, a wide variety of information and resources were observed with respect to complaint procedures, ranging from simply providing telephone numbers for abuse helplines, to the inclusion of detailed sample documents and procedures for filing a complaint and the importance of having an athlete advocate or athlete welfare officer to receive complaints.

The initiatives also differed organizationally with respect to their affiliations with non-sport child protection organizations. Three of the seven initiatives were situated within or affiliated with child protection initiatives that extend beyond the realm of sport. Five of the seven initiatives were linked with established non-governmental organizations outside of sport that were involved in humanitarian efforts (e.g., Red Cross), human rights associations and child services (e.g., ChildLine). One of the initiatives did not advertise any formal affiliations with other organizations.

4.3. Identification of Maltreatment

Each initiative was reviewed to assess the extent to which it identified, defined and provided examples of each form of relational maltreatment: sexual abuse, physical abuse, emotional abuse and neglect. Further, the inclusion of contextual influences on vulnerability was assessed. These results are illustrated in Table 2.

The following section will examine each form of maltreatment in relation to website content from the athlete protection initiatives.

4.3.1. Sexual Abuse

All seven initiatives identified, defined and provided examples of sexual abuse as a form of maltreatment. In terms of definitions, all initiatives perceived age as an important factor in sexually abusive behaviors, and as a result, sexual abuse was often identified as a sexual act or threat between an adult or adolescent and a child. The examples of sexual abuse identified included: being touched in inappropriate areas (e.g., genitals, buttocks) or coerced to touch others in this manner, forced to engage in oral sex or intercourse, indecent exposure, intrusive questions or being coerced to view sexually explicit videos or photographs.

4.3.2. Physical Abuse

As seen in Table 2, all but one of the initiatives identified physical abuse in their content, although definitions varied widely. Most of the initiatives referred to physical abuse as the use or threats of physical force on a child by a person in a position of trust or authority, but some referred to physical abuse as a response to misbehavior. The importance of an age difference between victim and abuser (e.g., physical harm caused by parent, caregiver or older child) was identified by many of the initiatives.

Table 2. Identification of maltreatment.

Variables of Interest			Number of Initiatives
Identification of Relational Maltreatment	Identification of Each Form of Relational Maltreatment	Sexual Abuse	7/7
		Physical Abuse	6/7
		Emotional Abuse	6/7
		Neglect	6/7
	Definition Provided for Each Form of Relational Maltreatment	Sexual Abuse	7/7
		Physical Abuse	6/7
		Emotional Abuse	6/7
		Neglect	4/7
	Examples Provided for Each Form of Relational Maltreatment	Sexual Abuse	7/7
		Physical Abuse	6/7
		Emotional Abuse	6/7
		Neglect	4/7
	Indicators of Signs and Symptoms	General recognition for signs/symptoms of maltreatment	5/7
Identification of Contextual Vulnerabilities	Identification of Factors of Vulnerability such as: power relations, opportunities for coach to be alone with athlete, "win-at-all-costs" ideology	Sexual Abuse	6/7
		Physical Abuse	4/7
		Emotional Abuse	2/7
		Neglect	0/7

Examples of physical abuse also varied across initiatives. Some initiatives discussed physical abuse broadly, using examples, such as slapping, punching, hitting or excessive exercise. Conversely, some initiatives provided more specific examples of physical abuse, including touching inappropriate parts of the body, physical acts that do not serve an instructional or congratulatory purpose, physical acts as a result of losing a game and acts that can be perceived by the victim as embarrassing or detrimental to his or her safety.

4.3.3. Emotional Abuse

Emotional abuse was identified, defined and described using examples by six of the seven initiatives. For this aspect of maltreatment, there appeared to be consistency amongst the athlete protection initiatives about the defining features of these behaviors. Most initiatives recognized the psychological nature of this maltreatment, suggested that emotionally abusive behaviors are often persistent over time and tend to result in poor emotional development or self-esteem issues. Examples of emotionally abusive behaviors frequently involved verbal acts, such as name-calling, swearing, ridicule, communicating a sense of worthlessness and threatening athletes. The initiatives typically identified two examples of non-verbal forms of emotional abuse, including ignoring an athlete or isolating the athlete from an activity.

4.3.4. Neglect

Neglect was the form of relational maltreatment that was addressed by the fewest number of initiatives. Although all but one initiative included a reference to neglect, only four initiatives defined and provided examples of neglect. Of these, neglect was characterized by a failure to provide basic necessities to children or adolescents over an extended period of time. Examples of neglect from the initiatives included using equipment that is unsafe, leaving young athletes unattended in sport environments that require supervision, forcing athletes to play through injury and engaging in practice or games in excessive weather conditions.

4.4. Identification of Contextual Vulnerabilities

As observed in Table 2, the identification of contextual factors that enhance the vulnerability of young athletes to experiences of maltreatment were lacking in many initiatives, except in the case of sexual abuse. In fact, three of the seven initiatives identified characteristics related to sport that may make an athlete vulnerable to sexual abuse, including: travel and overnight trips as a team, access to the locker room and a coach or trainer's frequent access to youth. Some of these initiatives also identified risk factors of individuals that may enhance their vulnerability to sexual abuse, including low self-esteem, unwavering allegiance to the coach and small physical size.

There were references to positions of authority or trust, particularly in reference to sexual and physical abuse, as increasing the vulnerability of athletes to experiences of maltreatment. Generally, references to the use or misuse of power, which is fundamental to all experiences of maltreatment, were lacking. Likewise, there was a relative absence of content related to the effects of a performance outcome or "win-at-all-costs" focus on child athletes' vulnerabilities to maltreatment.

4.5. Evaluations of the Initiatives

The final research question addressed by this study was the extent to which the initiatives had been evaluated empirically; in other words, do data exist to show that the initiatives are meeting their goals? Although the goals varied across the various initiatives, all of them sought to increase awareness and educate members of their communities regarding child maltreatment and protection. A review of the website content indicated that none of the initiatives had been evaluated in terms of the stated outcomes of enhancing awareness and knowledge, nor were there references to other publications sites that contained evaluative data.

5. Discussion

The findings indicate that theory and research were not the primary drivers of the development of most of the athlete protection initiatives. Instead, the majority of these initiatives emerged in response to high-profile media instances of athlete abuse and, more specifically, cases pertaining to the sexual abuse of athletes by their coaches. Such cases ignited fear and condemnation, as well as a passion for doing something about the problem of sexual abuse in sport. This passion, however, was not matched with empiricism. In fact, research on relational maltreatment in sport was fairly non-existent until these cases emerged. Although concerns about competitive sport for children had been raised long before this time, empirical research had not focused specifically on the maltreatment of athletes by their coaches. It appears, therefore, that these publicized cases of sexual abuse were stimulants for research on athlete maltreatment, as well as the development of athlete protection measures. It should be noted, however, that a wealth of information on maltreatment existed in the child development and social work literature at the time of these publicized cases that was not drawn upon in the development of the initiatives in sport, thus highlighting the prevailing ideology in sport of maintaining self-regulation and autonomy from the broader society.

Although cases of sexual abuse accounted for the origins of most of the initiatives, the content of all of the websites extended to include physical and emotional abuse in addition to sexual abuse (exclusive of the initiative that intentionally addresses sexual abuse only). However, the findings indicated that neglect was largely overlooked by most of the initiatives. Additionally, even when it was included, it was addressed in a very broad manner rather than distinguishing between the various forms of neglect (e.g., physical, educational, social). Such a narrow scope means that inadequate attention is devoted to the special needs of children, the developmental importance of relationships outside of the sport environment and the prioritizing of educational needs over sport training, as some examples. Given previously documented concerns about the over-emphasis on performance outcomes at the expense of the holistic development of children in sport [8], recommendations are made to expand upon content on neglect within these initiatives.

David [22] wrote almost 10 years ago that the child protection in sport measures established in Canada, the U.S. and Australia focused heavily on sexual abuse and tended to neglect other forms of maltreatment. It is encouraging to see that the initiatives have expanded the focus to include physical and emotional abuse, but clearly, more work needs to be done in regards to neglect. The absence of attention on neglect as a form of relational maltreatment in sport within these initiatives is also seen in the research; to-date, there is a paucity of empirical work that addresses the neglect of athlete's needs within the coach-athlete relationship. Even in the general child abuse literature, calls have been made for increased attention to neglect, particularly emotional neglect [32].

While it is encouraging to see that the initiatives identified, defined and provided examples of all of sexual, physical and emotional abuse, accuracy and specificity could be enhanced by drawing upon relevant research. For example, some initiatives used examples of sexual abuse interchangeably with physical abuse. Further, both physical and sexual abuse were seldom categorized into contact and non-contact forms, and emotional abuse was not differentiated into verbal and non-verbal forms. Failure to make such distinctions can narrow the scope of behaviors under consideration, potentially excluding some important abusive behaviors and, thus, leaving athletes vulnerable.

Of particular significance is the lack of attention to the notion of power, which is central to understanding critical relationships and maltreatment [4,22,33]. It may in fact be unreasonable to assume that researchers and practitioners can identify an exhaustive list of potentially abusive behaviors; however, it could be argued that if coaches understand the bases of the power they have over children and are cognizant of the ways in which this power can be used and misused, child protection would be enhanced.

Similarly, other aspects of the sport context that make it an environment ripe for the abuse of children were neglected in the content of the initiatives' websites. In spite of a plethora of literature on contextual influences on children's vulnerability to abuse in sport, such as the win-at-all-costs approach, these were largely overlooked in the content. Enhancing the focus on contextual influences would have the effect of shifting attention for prevention and intervention from the individual to the cultural level. Taken together, the findings indicate that the content of the various initiatives is loosely associated with scholarly work in the area.

In some countries, such as the United Kingdom and Australia, attempts have been made to address the problems inherent with the self-regulated nature of sport by bringing athlete protection into the wider legal and social welfare system. The Child Protection in Sport Unit, for example, is under the auspices of the broader NSPCC (National Society for the Prevention of Cruelty to Children), which has statutory powers that enable it to take action to safeguard children at risk of abuse. The remaining athlete protection initiatives however, are organizationally and functionally separate from general child protection services and, therefore remain insular and less well-equipped to deal with complaints effectively [34]. In Canada, for example, the general child protection agency, the Children's Aid Society, does not typically address child abuse in sport complaints, because it assumes sport has its own independent resolution mechanisms. This, however, ignores the fact that most cases in sport are dealt with by volunteers with limited confidence, abilities and experiences in addressing such concerns. The prevailing ideology within the sport context that it should be autonomous and self-policing has been highly criticized for these reasons. Further, future research should examine sport-specific websites for inclusion of child protection information, as these are the sources parents and athletes would most likely refer to for assistance.

Child protection measures in sport have also been criticized for lacking an integrated approach [4,22]. The initiatives in Canada and the U.S. are examples of a fragmented model with more than one athlete protection initiative, each with their own mission and goals, but separate from broader child protection agencies. On the other hand, progress has been made in the U.K. and Australia with an integrated national strategy and incorporation of sport-related child protection measures with broader child protection agencies.

All of the initiatives aim to reduce harm to children in sport by changing attitudes and behaviors of various stakeholders through awareness-raising and education. However, to-date, none of the initiatives has been evaluated empirically. As such, there is an absence of evidence to indicate whether or not these initiatives in sport have had an impact on the proximal outcomes of altering attitudes and behaviors of those in the community or on the more distal outcome of reducing harm to children. To move the field forward, systematic evaluation is necessary. Those responsible for the initiatives should be concerned about whether the initiatives do what they purport to do. This is especially the case for those initiatives that have compulsory educational modules and are funded by governmental agencies, although accountability should be of primary concern for all. Ideally, accountability would be assured through monitoring and evaluation by neutral, third-party bodies.

Future recommendations for the evaluation of child protection initiatives may include the integration of social and behavioral change theories. As all of the initiatives are intended to influence the attitudes and behaviors of stakeholders within their respective communities, such change theories may form an important theoretical foundation for future program evaluation. One such theory, the transtheoretical model [35], has been used widely to guide and assess behavior change and could be used to enhance the knowledge base and behavior change process with respect to coaches' conduct and use of power with young athletes. According to this model, effective behavior change occurs when individuals progress from a stage of knowledge acquisition and awareness of the desired behavior, to a stage in which one expresses intent to adopt the new behavior and prepares for the behavior change, to an action stage in which individuals commit to the new behavior in a sustained manner. Future research could assess the extent to which the child protection initiatives in sport affect behavioral change through data collection at each stage of the process.

In addition to theories of behavioral change that address impact at the individual level, social change processes focused on shifting the culture of a community should be implemented. Although all of the initiatives claim to be involved in advocacy endeavors to affect cultural shifts in the ways people understand and address child maltreatment in sport, the findings from this study indicate that the advocacy efforts lack theoretical and empirical grounding. Future work should address ways in which to strengthen the links between research, education and advocacy.

Finally, the initiatives addressed in this study focus almost exclusively on the protection of children from harm rather than the promotion of children's holistic health and wellbeing. As such, one could suggest that the sport context remains removed from the broader society, which has more recently focused on the prioritization of methods to optimize children's overall health and development. Further, with a focus on protection rather than growth, children are potentially viewed as objects in need of protection rather than as individuals with rights to participation and self-determination.

This study, while shedding light on the extent to which theory and research are incorporated into the development and evaluation of child protection in sport measures, is limited to data gathered through websites. It may be that supplementary information on the variables of interest in this study is available through other means of access aside from the website, such as educational workshops or modules or related documents and reports associated with the initiatives. Further, it must be acknowledged that some subjectivity was involved in analyzing the website data. As one of many examples, some website content included general statements related to the inclusion of research and partnerships, but did not specify what these were, nor were links provided for further information. In such cases, we subjectively determined that these criteria were not met, as this information was not available on the website. Similarly, there were many instances in which the content provided was so broad or general that it lacked the specificity required for inclusion in our assessment. The study was also limited to athlete protection initiatives in the English language; future research should advance the international perspective.

In sum, the development and implementation of these athlete protection initiatives are certainly important, but they represent a starting point only. If we are to move beyond the emotionally-charged responses to child maltreatment in sport, we need theoretically-grounded approaches and empirical research data upon which to base child protection measures. Conceptual clarity, as well as content that are congruent with the scholarly literature would facilitate discourse both among and between researchers and practitioners. Further, without monitoring and evaluation, it is unknown whether these initiatives are doing what they purport to do. Consistent with this view, Brackenridge ([4],

p. 203) writes that many in sport have "failed to attend to implementation or to the monitoring and evaluation processes by which accountability can be assured." To assure the sport community of transparency and accountability, evaluation should be conducted through an independent, neutral body. Only when these conditions are met can we gain a better sense of whether or not children in sport are being safeguarded. Perhaps, at that point, we can shift the focus from protection from harm to the advancement of children's holistic health and development through the sport experience.

6. Conclusions

As the focus on child maltreatment extends beyond intra-familial settings, there is growing awareness of occurrences of maltreatment within the sport context. In response to high profile cases of sexual abuse of athletes across several countries in the 1990s, a number of child protection in sport measures were developed and implemented internationally. This study examined seven child protection in sport initiatives with a focus on the extent to which they originated from research, had content that was consistent with scholarly work, and were evaluated empirically.

A web-based analysis indicated that these initiatives were not empirically or theoretically derived for the most part. The findings indicated that while most of the initiatives addressed sexual, emotional and physical abuse, neglect was largely overlooked, and of the information conveyed via the websites, much was inconsistent with scholarly work in the area. Of particular significance was the lack of attention to the notion of power and other contextual influences, which are central to understanding critical relationships and maltreatment. And finally, at the time of this study, none of the initiatives had been evaluated empirically.

Recommendations are made to more closely align research with these initiatives both with respect to their design and their evaluation. The content of these initiatives would benefit from an enhanced focus on the contextual influences on maltreatment; such a focus would shift attention for prevention and intervention from the individual to the cultural level. Additionally, finally, a shift in focus from protecting children from harm to the promotion of their holistic health and development would bring the initiatives used in the sport context closer in line with approaches used in other child-dominated domains.

Author Contributions

Gretchen Kerr, a Full Professor and Vice-Dean of the Faculty of Kinesiology and Physical Education at the University of Toronto, conceptualized the study and conducted the majority of the writing. Ashley Stirling, a Lecturer at the Faculty of Kinesiology and Physical Education at the University of Toronto, conceptualized the study and contributed to the analysis and writing. Ellen MacPherson, a Ph.D. student at the Faculty of Kinesiology and Physical Education at the University of Toronto, collected the data and assisted with the analysis and writing.

Conflicts of Interest

The authors declare no conflict of interest.

References

1. Stuart N. Hart. "From property to person status: Historical perspectives in children's rights." *American Psychologist* 46 (1991): 53–59.
2. Leonard Wankel, and Bonnie Berger. "The psychological and social benefits of sport and physical activity." *Journal of Leisure Research* 22 (1990): 167–82.
3. Ian Janssen, and Allana LeBlanc. "Systematic review of the health benefits of physical activity and fitness in school aged children and youth." *International Journal of Behavioral Nutrition and Physical Activity* 7 (2010): 1–16.
4. Celia Brackenridge. *Spoilsport. Understanding and Preventing Sexual Exploitation in Sport.* London: Routledge, 2001.
5. Statistics Canada. Ottawa: Government of Canada. Available online: http://www.statcan.gc.ca/pub/81-595-m/2008060/s6-eng.htm (accessed on 15 May 2014).
6. Youth Sport Statistics. Available online: http://www.statisticbrain.com/youth-sports-statistics/ 2013 (accessed on 18 May 2014).
7. Jen Fraser, and Alexandra Ziff. *Children's and Young People's Participation in Organized Sport. Omnibus Survey.* Research Report DCSF-RR135. London: Department for Children, Schools and Families, 2009.
8. Jay Coakley, and Peter Donnelly. *Sports in Society: Issues and Controversies*, 2nd ed. Toronto: McGraw-Hill Ryerson, 2009.
9. CBC News. "Former minor hockey coach charged with sexual assault: Allegations from 1987 to 1991 involving boy at bantam level in Ottawa." Available online: http://www.cbc.ca/news/canada/ottawa/former-minor-hockey-coach-charged-with-sexual-assault-1.1702950 (accessed on 18 May 2014).
10. Steven Downes. "OSM investigation: Sexual abuse by coaches." *The Observer*, Retrieved 4 January 2014.
11. Jan Tofetgaard Neilson. "The forbidden zone: Intimacy, sexual relations and misconduct in the relationship between coaches and athletes." *International Review for the Sociology of Sport* 36 (2001): 165–82.
12. Trisha Leahy, Grace Pretty, and Gershon Tenenbaum. "Prevalence of sexual abuse in organized sport in Australia." *Journal of Sexual Aggression* 8 (2002): 16–36.
13. Kari Fasting, Celia Brackenridge, and Jorunn Sungot-Borgen. "Prevalence of sexual harassment among Norwegian female elite athletes in relation to sport type." *International Review for the Sociology of Sport* 39 (2004): 373–86.
14. Sandra Kirby, Lorraine Greaves, and Olena Hankivsky. *The Dome of Silence: Sexual Harassment and Abuse in Sport.* Hailfax: Fernwood Publishing Ltd., 2000.
15. Misia Gervis, and Nicola Dunn. "The emotional abuse of elite child athletes by their coaches." *Child Abuse Review* 13(2004): 215–23.
16. Ashley Stirling, and Gretchen Kerr. "Defining and categorizing emotional abuse in sport." *European Journal of Sport Science* 8 (2008): 173–81.

17. Erik Brady. "Heat-related illness still deadly problem for athletes." Available online: http://usatoday30.usatoday.com/sports/2011–08–15-heat-stroke-still-causing-death-in-athletes_n.htm (accessed on 1 June 2014).
18. Scott Weich, Jacoby Patterson, Richard Shaw, and Sarah Stewart-Brown. "Family relationships in childhood and common psychiatric disorders in later life: Systematic review of prospective studies." *British Journal of Psychiatry* 194 (2009): 392–98.
19. Hannie Comijs, Eric van Exel, Roos van der Mast, Anna Paauw, Richard Oude Voshaar, and Max Shek. "Childhood abuse in late-life depression." *Journal of Affective Disorders* 147 (2013): 241–6.
20. Ashley Stirling, and Gretchen Kerr. "Abused athletes' perceptions of the coach-athlete relationship." *Sport in Society* 12 (2009): 227–39.
21. Gretchen Kerr, and Ashley Stirling. "Parents' reflections on their child's experiences of emotionally abusive coaching practices." *Journal of Applied Sport Psychology* 24 (2012): 191–206.
22. Nicola Maffulli. *Human Rights in Youth Sport*. London: Routledge, 2005.
23. Terry Orlick, and Carl Botterill. *Every Kid Can Win*. Chicago: Nelson Hall, 1975.
24. Peter Donnelly, Gretchen Kerr, Amanda Heron, and Danielle DiCarlo. "Protecting youth in sport: An examination of the status of harassment policies in Canadian Sport Organizations." *International Journal of Sport Policy and Politics*, in press.
25. Sally J. McMillan. "The microscope and the moving target: The challenge of applying content analysis to the World Wide Web." *Journalism and Mass Communication Quarterly* 77 (2000): 80–98.
26. Ashley E. Stirling. "Definition and constituents of maltreatment in sport: Establishing a conceptual framework for research practitioners." *British Journal of Sports Medicine* 43 (2009): 1091–99.
27. Claire V. Crooks, and David A. Wolfe. "Child abuse and neglect." In *Assessment of Childhood Disorders*, 4th ed. Edited by Eric J. Mash and Russell A. Barkley. New York: Guilford Press, 2007.
28. Cindy L. Miller-Perrin, and Robin D. Perrin. *Child Maltreatment*. London: Sage, 2007.
29. Gail Ryan, and Sandy Lane. *Juvenile Sexual Offending: Causes, Consequences, and Correction*. San Francisco: Jossey-Bass, 1997, 3–9.
30. Bruce Perry, David Mann, Ann Palker-Corell, Christine Ludy-Dobson, and Stephanie Schik. "Child physical abuse." In *Encyclopedia of Crime and Punishment*. Edited by David Levinson. Thousand Oaks: Sage, 2002, 197–202.
31. Danya Glaser. "Emotional abuse and neglect (psychological maltreatment): A conceptual framework." *Child Abuse and Neglect* 26 (2002): 697–714.
32. Nigel Parton. *Child Protection and Family Support: Tensions, Contradictions, and Possibilities*. London: Routledge, 1997.
33. Paul Tomlinson, and Dorothy Strachan. *Power and Ethics in Coaching*. Ottawa: Coaching Association of Canada, 1996.

34. Steve Boocock. "The Child Protection in Sport Unit." *The Journal of Sexual Aggression* 8 (2002): 99–106.
35. James O. Prochaska, and Wayne F. Velicer. "The transtheoretical model of health behavior change." *American Journal of Health Promotion* 12 (1997): 38–48.

Comparing Pedophile Activity in Different P2P Systems

Raphaël Fournier, Thibault Cholez, Matthieu Latapy, Isabelle Chrisment, Clémence Magnien, Olivier Festor and Ivan Daniloff

Abstract: Peer-to-peer (P2P) systems are widely used to exchange content over the Internet. Knowledge of pedophile activity in such networks remains limited, despite having important social consequences. Moreover, though there are different P2P systems in use, previous academic works on this topic focused on one system at a time and their results are not directly comparable. We design a methodology for comparing *KAD* and *eDonkey*, two P2P systems among the most prominent ones and with different anonymity levels. We monitor two *eDonkey* servers and the *KAD* network during several days and record hundreds of thousands of keyword-based queries. We detect pedophile-related queries with a previously validated tool and we propose, for the first time, a large-scale comparison of pedophile activity in two different P2P systems. We conclude that there are significantly fewer pedophile queries in *KAD* than in *eDonkey* (approximately 0.09% vs. 0.25%).

Reprinted from *Soc. Sci.*. Cite as: Fournier, R.; Cholez, T.; Latapy, M.; Chrisment, I.; Magnien, C.; Festor, O.; Daniloff, I. Comparing Pedophile Activity in Different P2P Systems. *Soc. Sci.* **2014**, *3*, 14131–14179.

1. Introduction

Pedophile activity is a crucial social issue and is often claimed to be prevalent in peer-to-peer (P2P) file-sharing systems [1,2]. However, current knowledge of pedophile activity in these networks remains limited.

Recently, research works have been conducted to improve this situation by quantifying pedophile activity in *Gnutella* and *eDonkey*, two of the main P2P systems currently deployed [3,4]. They conclude, respectively, that 1.6% and 0.25% of queries are of pedophile nature, but these numbers are not directly comparable as the authors use very different definitions and methods. Such comparisons are of high interest though, since differences in features of P2P systems, such as the level of anonymity they provide, may influence their appeal for pedophile users.

In this paper, we perform a comparison for the first time. We focus on the *KAD* and *eDonkey* P2P systems, which are the names given to the two underlying P2P networks used by the popular eMule file-sharing application. They are both widely used, accounting together for almost 10% of the global Internet traffic in Europe in 2012 [5], but they differ significantly in their architecture: while *eDonkey* relies on a few servers, *KAD* is fully distributed. This lack of centralization may lead users to assume that *KAD* provides a much higher level of anonymity than *eDonkey*. Comparing the two systems sheds light on the influence of a distributed architecture on pedophile behavior and increases general knowledge on pedophile activity in P2P systems.

The term pedophilia is popularly used to denote adult sexual engagement with children, both prepubescent and pubescent. The definition of pedophilia we use in this article thus encompasses both the medical definition of pedophilia (sexual interest in prepubescent children) and hebephilia (sexual interest in pubescent children not sexually mature).

We discuss related work in Section 2, to give an overview of the state-of-the-art on online pedophile activity detection and analysis. Section 3 presents a short introduction to P2P systems, before our description of our datasets and how we collected them (Section 4). We then present the details of our comparison of the amount of pedophile queries in *KAD* and *eDonkey* in Section 5. Section 6 focuses on an important feature of pedophile activity: ages entered in queries. Finally, in Section 7, we introduce a methodology to estimate the fraction of pedophile queries in *KAD* from the one in *eDonkey*.

2. Related Work

Collecting P2P traces is an active topic for years, but it is mostly aimed at analyzing peer behavior to help with future P2P protocol design. In 2006, authors of [6] and [7] explored the social and technical issues related to online child pornography and opened the way to the research in the field. The first detailed quantitative study focusing on a P2P system was proposed in [3], using an active methodology (sending specific queries and analyzing the answers provided by the search engine). Since then, several approaches have been proposed to gage the extent of the phenomenon. Among them, [8] presented filename categorization tool, while [9,10] proposed to label suspicious chat conversations. [11] especially analyzed aged-related queries.

A first large-scale study of P2P search-engine queries was presented in [12]. Their study focused on "onset", the first deliberate viewing of child pornography. They gathered the Top 300 queries submitted to the popular *Isohunt* tracker (part of the BitTorrent network) and published on the website Isohunt.com. Their study lasts for 3 months, a scale similar to ours, but they resort to manual classification of the queries. Their dataset is particular, as it only gives a relative popularity order for some queries, and may not provide any indication on the extent of child pornography in the network. Plus, with only 300 queries collected daily, they get very few pedophile queries (only 3), which leads to results with a limited statistical significance. However, their discussion is truly interesting, including comments on whether "regular pedophile users" are likely to submit several times the same query (to "build a collection"), while first-time users may not (they do not progress to downloading material once they have discovered the meaning of intriguing pedophile sequences such as *pthc*). This bias may lead query-based studies like ours to slightly overestimating the demand for child pornography, and would impact estimations on the number of pedophile users, but additional filtering based on the IP-address or the client ID could limit this issue.

In [4], the authors developed and assessed a dedicated tool for search engine query classification, and collected large-scale datasets on *eDonkey* (up to 28 weeks of uninterrupted experiment). We use here their tool and one of their datasets. Part of their work was later reused by another team to study another P2P network, BitTorrent [13]. The European Commission has set up a "Safer Internet" program [1], which funded some large research projects such as MAPAP [14] and iCOP [15].

In parallel, authors of [16,17] provided an extensive study (one-year long) on child pornography on Gnutella and eMule, partnering with law enforcement to develop software platforms and collect data on child pornography trafficking. They made a precious contribution to understand the "supply": how many users are involved in the distribution of files, what are their importance in the network, *etc*. In [16], they evaluated different strategies to best fight pedophile activity given the limited resources of law enforcement and proposed an efficient metric to target the most prominent peers.

While having a smaller scale, our study is the first to provide a methodology to gain new knowledge from the proper comparison of data collected from two P2P networks which architecture and monitoring capacity are totally different. Moreover, if the general user behavior in the *KAD* network was detailed in [18], our article is the first to study whether its decentralized architecture is prone to favor criminal activity.

3. P2P Systems

P2P systems are computer networks in which every user may share content with others members. They have become popular because they gather large amount of digital contents (books, movies, music) which can be obtained for free. Copyrighted material is available (however not authorized) and pornography is widespread. Accessing a P2P network is generally easy: a user only needs to download and install on his computer a single application, which will handle the connection process to the network. Then, he can search for files with some keywords, and gets a list of corresponding available files. The application sends messages to the network to find providers of the selected files, and then users interconnect directly to exchange them.

P2P networks are easy to access for both providers and consumers. Contents are obtained free of charge, and rather anonymously (no personal details are required). These features make such networks appealing for illegal activities such as pedophile material trafficking.

P2P networks account for approximately a fifth of the global bandwidth use on the Internet. Bittorrent is the most prominent P2P network nowadays, preceding *eDonkey* and *KAD* (the usage of which decline in Europe). For instance, an important *eDonkey* server received on average 8.8 million queries per week between 2009 and 2012 [4].

4. Experimental Setup and Datasets

In order to compare pedophile activity in two different P2P systems, we first need appropriate datasets, the collection of which is a challenge in itself. In *KAD* and *eDonkey*, different kinds of measurements are possible, depending on the details of the network's architecture.

In *eDonkey*, servers index files and providers for these files, and users submit keyword-based queries to servers to seek files of interest to them [19]. By monitoring such a server, one may collect all those queries [20]. Here, we record all queries received by two of the largest *eDonkey* servers during a three-month period in 2010. The servers are located in different countries (France and Ukraine) and have different filtering policies: the French server indexes only non-copyrighted material, while the Ukrainian server openly indexes all submitted files. Monitoring two such different servers will allow us to compare them in order to know if server policy impacts our results.

To collect *KAD* data, we use the HAMACK monitoring architecture [21], which makes it possible to record the queries related to a given keyword by inserting distributed probes close to the keyword ID onto the *KAD* distributed hash table. We supervise 72 keywords, which we choose to span well the variety of search requests entered in the system, with a focus on pedophile activity: a set of 19 *paedophile* keywords (*babyj, babyshivid, childlover, childporn, hussyfan, kidzilla, kingpass, mafiasex, pedo, pedofilia, pedofilo, pedoland, pedophile, pthc, ptsc, qqaazz, raygold, yamad, youngvideomodels*), which are known to be directly and unambiguously related to pedophile activity in P2P networks; a set of 23 *mixed* keywords (*1yo, 2yo, 3yo, 4yo, 5yo, 6yo, 7yo, 8yo, 9yo, 10yo, 11yo, 12yo, 13yo, 14yo, 15yo, 16yo, boy, girl, mom, preteen, rape, sex, webcam*) frequently used in pedophile queries but also in other contexts (for instance, *Nyo* stands for *N years old* and is used by both pedophile users and parents seeking games for children of this age); and a set of 30 *not paedophile* keywords (*avi, black, christina, christmas, day, doing, dvdrip, early, flowers, grosse, hot, house, housewives, live, love, madonna, man, new, nokia, pokemon, rar, remix, rock, saison, smallville, soundtrack, virtual, vista, windows, world*) used as a test group and *a priori* rarely used in pedophile queries. The sets of keywords were established using the work on pedophile query detection presented in [4]. Notice that our set of keywords contains mainly common English words (*love, early, flowers*), but some are in other languages (*saison, pedofilia*), and some are also brand names (*pokemon, nokia*).

Because of the differences in architectures of the two networks and of the measurement methodologies, we obtained very different datasets, which are not directly comparable: in *eDonkey*, we observe all queries from a subset of users whereas in *KAD* we only observe queries related to a given keyword, but from all users. In addition, based on various versions of *KAD* clients, the measurement tool only records the queries containing a monitored keyword placed in first position or being the longest in the query. As a consequence, with a short keyword such as *avi*, a name extension for video files, we almost only record queries in which it is the unique keyword, because otherwise it most likely is neither the longest nor the first word in any query. In order to obtain comparable datasets, we therefore limit our study to a subset of our datasets: the queries composed of exactly one word among the 72 keywords we monitor.

As a result of this construction process, we obtain three datasets, which we call *eDonkeyFR*, *eDonkeyUA* and *KAD*. They contain 241,152, 166,154 and 250,000 queries respectively, all consisting of a unique keyword from our list of 72 monitored keywords, which ensures that they are comparable. The server corresponding to the *eDonkeyFR* dataset is located in France, while the one corresponding to *eDonkeyUA* is in Ukraine. Their large sizes make us confident in the reliability of our statistical results presented hereafter.

5. Amount of Pedophile Queries in *eDonkey* versus *KAD*

The most straightforward way to compare the pedophile activity in different systems certainly is to compare the fraction of pedophile queries in each system. Figure 1 presents the fraction of queries for each category of keywords. This plot clearly shows that there are very distinct search behaviors in the two networks, since values obtained for the *paedophile* and *not paedophile* categories significantly differ between *KAD* and the two *eDonkey* datasets. More surprisingly, the fraction of pedophile queries is significantly lower in *KAD* than in *eDonkey* which is in sharp contradiction with previous intuition, as *KAD* is assumed to provide a higher level of anonymity. The plot also shows that values obtained for the two *eDonkey* servers are similar, which indicates that very different filtering policies have no significant influence on the amount of pedophile queries.

In order to gain a more detailed insight on this phenomenon, we study the frequencies of each keyword separately in the three datasets. As we want to explore possible correlations between the pedophile nature of a keyword and its frequency, we need a way to quantify the pedophile nature of a keyword. To do so, we use the 28-week dataset and the pedophile query detection tool from [4], which divides a dataset between *paedophile* and *not paedophile* queries (with a precision above 98% and a recall above 75%). We denote by Q the whole dataset of queries, and by $Q(k)$ the set of queries containing a given keyword k. For each keyword k, we obtain $Q(k) = N(k) + P(k)$, where $N(k)$ and $P(k)$ are the subset of queries containing keyword k and tagged as *not paedophile* or *paedophile*, respectively. We then define the *paedophile coefficient* $\pi(k)$ of keyword k as: $\pi(k) = \frac{|P(k)|}{|Q(k)|}$. If all the queries with keyword k are pedophile queries, $\pi(k) = 1$, and if none of them are, $\pi(k) = 0$. All keywords in the *not paedophile* category have a *paedophile coefficient* below 0.006. For keywords in the *mixed* category, the *paedophile coefficient* is above 0.01 and below 0.4. All *paedophile* keywords have a *paedophile coefficient* above 0.885. Finally, we plot in Figure 2 the ratios $\frac{f_{eDonkeyFR}(k)}{f_{kad}(k)}$ and $\frac{f_{eDonkeyUA}(k)}{f_{kad}(k)}$, where $f_s(k)$ denotes the frequency of queries composed of keyword k in the dataset s, for each of our 72 keywords. We rank keywords on the horizontal axis in increasing order of *paedophile coefficient*. The horizontal line represents *y = 1*, which enables a visual comparison of the values: if the point is below the line, then the keyword is more frequent in *KAD*, otherwise it is more frequent in the *eDonkey* dataset.

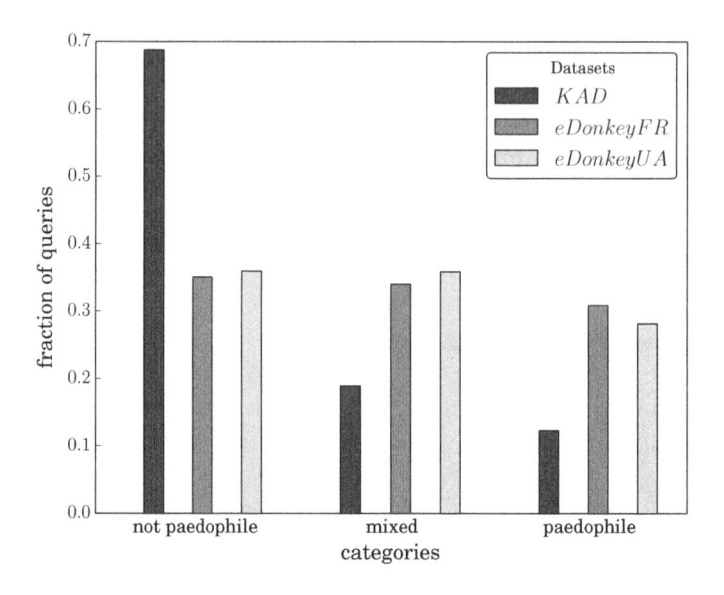

Figure 1. Fraction of queries of each kind in our three datasets.

Figure 2. Ratio of keyword frequencies in *eDonkey* vs. *KAD*. Keywords are ranked in increasing order of *paedophile coefficient*. Points above the $y = 1$ horizontal line indicates keywords more frequent in the corresponding *eDonkey* dataset; below the line keywords are more frequent in *KAD*.

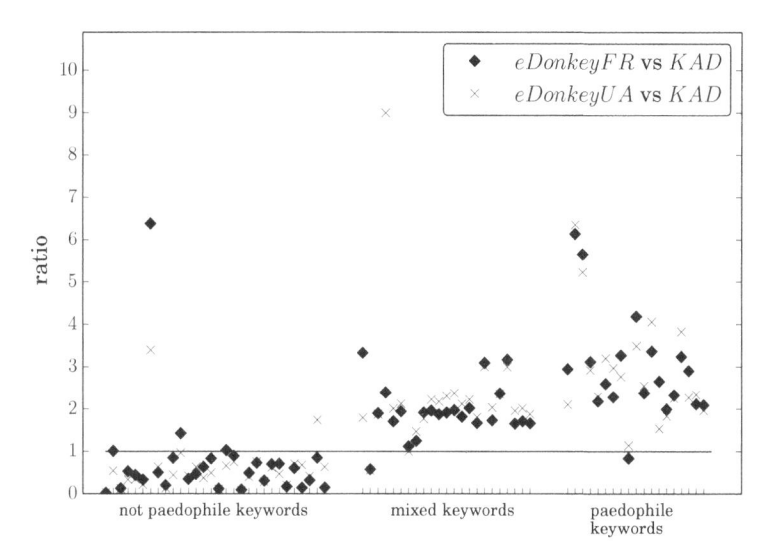

This plot gives a clear evidence for a correlation between the pedophile nature of a keyword and its higher presence in *eDonkey* than in *KAD*. In addition, the frequencies in both *eDonkey* datasets are very similar for the vast majority of keywords.

We therefore conclude that anonymity is not the prevailing factor when pedophile users choose a network, since neither the decentralized architecture of *KAD* nor the different filtering policies increase the frequency of pedophile queries. Instead, the frequency of pedophile queries is even higher in *eDonkey* than in *KAD*. Finding an explanation for this unexpected phenomenon is still an open question. The higher technical skills required to use *KAD* may be part of the explanation. Users may also search content on *eDonkey* while protecting their privacy with other tools, such as Virtual Private Networks or TOR [22]. The fact that in *KAD* search requests are sent over UDP and cannot benefit from TOR anonymization could explain the difference in the network usage.

6. Ages Indicators in Queries

A way to gain more insight on observed pedophile activity is to study the distribution of age indicators in queries [11]. Notice that age indicators are sometimes used in other contexts than pedophile activity, especially when parents seek content suitable for children of a certain age. However, one can observe on Figure 2 that ages indicators have similar behavior to those obtained for the *pedophile* group, and are therefore closely related to the topic.

We plot the distribution of age indicators on Figure 3: for each integer n lower than 17, we plot the number of queries of the form *nyo* in each dataset (*yo* stands for *years old*). The three plots have similar shape, with mostly increasing values from 1 to 10, a little drop at 11, a peak at 12 and a fall from 13 to 16. These values for *KAD* are below the values for the *eDonkey* servers, which is due to the fact that this dataset is a bit smaller than others and that pedophile queries are rarer in it. The key point here is that the distributions are very similar in all three datasets. This indicates that, although the *amount* of pedophile activity varies between systems, its nature is similar, at least regarding ages.

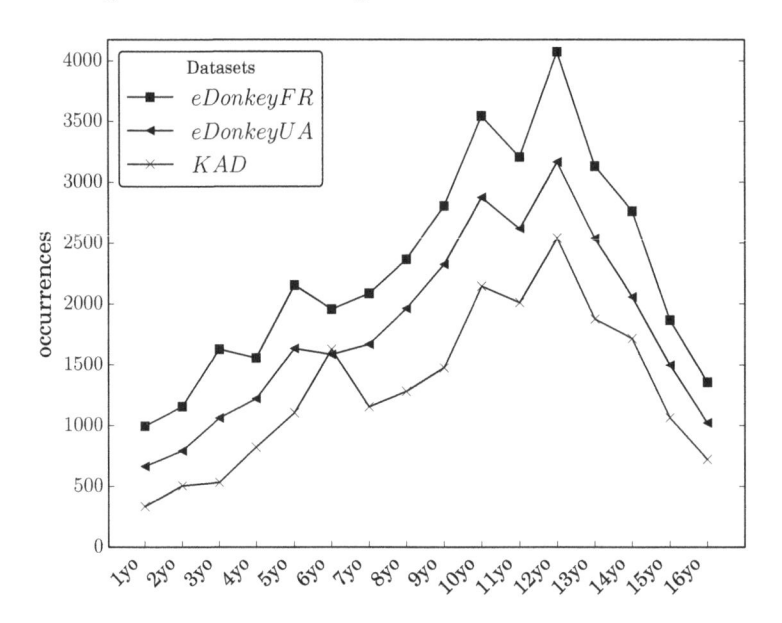

Figure 3. Distribution of age indicators in our three datasets.

7. Quantifying Pedophile Activity in *KAD*

In [4], the authors establish a method to quantify the fraction of pedophile queries in *eDonkey*. It relies on a tool able to accurately tag queries as pedophile or not, and on an estimate of the error rate of this tool. Such an approach cannot directly be applied to *KAD* though, as only a small (and biased) fraction of all queries may be observed in this system. We however show in this section how to derive the fraction of pedophile queries in *KAD* from the one in *eDonkey*.

In a given system, *eDonkey* or *KAD* here, we consider different sets of queries and we denote by Q the set of all queries, P the subset of pedophile queries in Q, $\overline{Q}$ the subset of queries composed of one word among the 72 monitored keywords, $\overline{P}$ the subset of pedophile queries with one word, *i.e.*, consisting of one of the 19 monitored pedophile keywords (and so: $\overline{P} = \overline{Q} \cap P$). Figure 4 illustrates our notations.

In both our *eDonkey* measurements, $|P|$ and $|Q|$ may be directly estimated, as shown in [4], and one can then obtain the fraction $\frac{|P|}{|Q|}$ of pedophile queries in the dataset. We give the results for our two measurements in Table 1. On the contrary, in *KAD*, one may only estimate $|\overline{P}|$ and $|\overline{Q}|$.

Figure 4. The different sets of queries defined for each dataset.

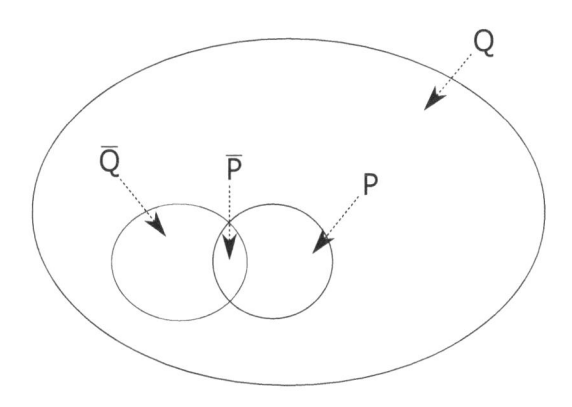

Table 1. Results for our three datasets.

Dataset	$\frac{|P|}{|Q|}$	$|\overline{P}|$	$|\overline{Q}|$	α	β
edonkeyFR	$2.554 \cdot 10^{-3}$	74,557	241,152	$1.431 \cdot 10^{-3}$	0.2502
edonkeyUA	$2.668 \cdot 10^{-3}$	46,763	166,154	$1.538 \cdot 10^{-3}$	0.2251
KAD	n/a	30,821	250,000	n/a	n/a

However, we define $\alpha = \frac{|\overline{Q}|-|\overline{P}|}{|Q|-|P|}$ and $\beta = \frac{|P|}{|\overline{P}|}$, which capture the probability for a non pedophile query, respectively pedophile, to make a query of one word among one of our monitored keywords. Given the definition of α and β, there is no *a priori* reason to assume that they have significantly different values between *eDonkey* and *KAD*. From the definitions of α and β, we have:

$$\alpha = \frac{|\overline{Q}| - |\overline{P}|}{|Q| - |P|} \implies |Q| = \frac{\alpha|P| + |\overline{Q}| - |\overline{P}|}{\alpha}$$

$$\beta = \frac{|P|}{|\overline{P}|} \implies |P| = \frac{|\overline{P}|}{\beta}$$

Then, the following expression holds:

$$\frac{|P|}{|Q|} = \frac{|\overline{P}|}{\beta} \times \frac{\alpha}{\alpha|P| + |\overline{Q}| - |\overline{P}|}$$
$$= \frac{\alpha|\overline{P}|}{\beta|\overline{Q}| + (\alpha - \beta)|\overline{P}|} \quad (1)$$

We now use expression (1) to infer the fraction of paedophile queries that were submitted in the *KAD* P2P network during our experiment. Using the values from Table 1 and the average values of α and β between our *eDonkey* datasets, we obtain:

$$\frac{|P|}{|Q|} \approx 0.087\% \pm 0.008$$

This value is of similar magnitude to the one of *eDonkey* (approx. 0.25%) but close to three times lower.

This estimation of $\frac{|P|}{|Q|}$ relies on the value of α. One may wonder whether the choice of keywords from which we built $\overline{Q} \setminus \overline{P}$ has a significant impact on the estimated value of $\frac{|P|}{|Q|}$ in *KAD*. We check this as follows: we randomly select 1,000 subsets of 26 keywords out of the 53 keywords which compose the queries in $\overline{Q} \setminus \overline{P}$. We then compute, for each subset, the number of queries consisting of exactly one of those keywords and the resulting value of alpha. For *eDonkeyFR*, we obtain an average value of $\overline{\alpha} = 0.000889$ (minimum: 0.000256, maximum: 0.00153, and 90% of the values in [0.000463;0.00133]). For *eDonkeyUA*, we obtain an average value of $\overline{\alpha} = 0.00105$ (minimum: 0.000352, maximum: 0.00172, and 90% of the values in [0.00062;0.00148]). This means that we would obtain very similar results with 26 keywords only and so we may be confident in our estimate obtained with 53 keywords.

8. Conclusions

We performed a comparative study of two large-scale peer-to-peer networks, *KAD* and *eDonkey*, with regards to the queries related to child pornography. We designed a methodology to collect and process datasets allowing to compare them in a relevant manner. We obtained the counter-intuitive result that pedophile keywords are significantly more present in *eDonkey* than in *KAD*, despite the higher anonymity level it provides. On the contrary, our study of age indicators in queries showed that the nature of pedophile queries is similar in these systems. We finally established the first estimate of the fraction of pedophile queries in *KAD*. We obtained a value close to 0.09%, which is of the same magnitude but significantly lower than in *eDonkey* (0.25%).

Our approach here is similar to the one used in [4]: we focus on search queries, which help to grasp the demand for pedophile material. It differs from [16,17] which focused on the files. In P2P networks such as *eDonkey* and *KAD*, a single file may have several names, most of which describe its content. However, filenames are prone to pollution and often exhibit keywords unrelated to the real content of the file, for instance a pedophile file may have a non-pedophile name [23,24]. Thus, estimations relying on specific filenames are likely to underestimate the true extent of child pornography distribution, while estimations relying on file-based honeypots are likely to overestimate the demand due to false-positive download requests. Query-based estimations using search requests do not suffer from such a bias, but, as mentioned earlier, may be impacted by repetitive queries from regular pedophile users. Nevertheless, both the considered P2P networks (*KAD* and *eDonkey*) should be equally affected, thus making their comparison valid to this regard.

Our contributions open various directions for future work. In particular, our methodology may be applied to compare other systems, and our datasets may be used to perform either deeper analyses on pedophile activity or on general search engine behaviors.

Acknowledgments

This work is supported in part by the MAPAP SIP-2006-PP-221003 and ANR MAPE projects.

Author Contributions

RF participated in the study design, carried out analyses and interpreted the data, before writing the first manuscript in consultation with the co-authors. TC, IC and OF participated in the study design, data collection and experiment analysis. ML and CM participated in the study design and data analysis. ID was of significant help to collect data.

Conflicts of Interest

The authors declare no conflict of interest.

References

1. European Commission. "Safer Internet Programme: Empowering and Protecting Children Online." 2010. Available online: http://ec.europa.eu/information_society/activities/sip/index_en.htm (accessed on 4 June 2014).
2. Declan McCullagh. "RIAA: Child porn rife on P2P networks." *CNet*, 9 September 2003. Available online: http://news.cnet.com/RIAA-Child-porn-rife-on-P2P-networks/2100-1028_3-5073817.html (accessed on 4 June 2014).
3. Daniel Hughes, James Walkerdine, Geoff Coulson, and Stephen Gibson. "Peer-to-Peer: Is Deviant Behavior the Norm on P2P File-Sharing Networks?" *IEEE Distributed Systems Online* 7 (2006): 1–11.
4. Matthieu Latapy, Clémence Magnien, and Raphaël Fournier. "Quantifying paedophile activity in a large P2P system." *Information Processing & Management* 49 (2013): 248–63.
5. Sandvine Network. "Global Internet Phenomena Report: Spring 2011." 2012. Available online: http://fr.scribd.com/doc/94722096/Sandvine-Global-Internet-Phenomena-Report-1H-2012 (accessed on 4 June 2014).
6. Munish Chopra, Miguel Vargas Martin, Luis Rueda, and Patrick C. K. Hung. "Toward New Paradigms to Combating Internet Child Pornography." Paper Presented at Canadian Conference on Electrical and Computer Engineering (CCECE), Ottawa, ON, Canada. IEEE, 7–10 May 2006, pp. 1012–15.
7. Asaf Shupo, Miguel Vargas Martin, Luis Rueda, Anasuya Bulkan, Yongming Chen, and Patrick C.K. Hung. "Toward efficient detection of child pornography in the network infrastructure." *IADIS International Journal on Computer Science and Information Systems* 1 (2006): 15–31.
8. Alexander Panchenko, Richard Beaufort, Hubert Naets, and Cedrick Fairon. "Towards Detection of Child Sexual Abuse Media: Categorization of the Associated Filenames." In *Advances in Information Retrieval*. Edited by Pavel Serdyukov, Pavel Braslavski, Sergei O. Kuznetsov, Jaap Kamps, Stefan Rüger, Eugene Agichtein, Ilya Segalovich and Emine Yilmaz. Lecture Notes in Computer Science. Springer: Berlin Heidelberg, Germany, 2013, vol. 7814, pp. 776–79.

9. April Kontostathis, Andy Garron, Kelly Reynolds, Will West, and Lynne Edwards. "Identifying Predators Using ChatCoder 2.0." Paper Presented at CLEF Conference 2012 Evaluation Labs and Workshop, Rome, Italy, 17–20 September, 2012. Edited by Pamela Forner, Jussi Karlgren and Christa Womser-Hacker.
10. Nick Pendar. "Toward Spotting the Pedophile Telling Victim from Predator in Text Chats." Paper Presented at International Conference on Semantic Computing, Irvine, CA, USA, 17–19 September 2007, pp. 235–41.
11. Chad M.S. Steel. "Child pornography in peer-to-peer networks." *Child Abuse & Neglect* 33 (2009): 560–68.
12. Jeremy Prichard, Paul A Watters, and Caroline Spiranovic. "Internet subcultures and pathways to the use of child pornography." *Computer Law & Security Review* 27 (2011): 585–600.
13. Moshe Rutgaizer, Yuval Shavitt, Omer Vertman, and Noa Zilberman. "Detecting Pedophile Activity in BitTorrent Networks." In *Passive and Active Measurement (PAM)*. Edited by Nina Taft and Fabio Ricciato. Lecture Notes in Computer Science. Springer: Berlin Heidelberg, Germany, 2012, vol. 7192, pp. 106–15.
14. MAPAP project. 2010. Available online: http://antipaedo.lip6.fr (accessed on 4 June 2014).
15. iCOP. 2014. Available online: http://scc-sentinel.lancs.ac.uk/icop/ (accessed on 4 June 2014).
16. Janis Wolak, Marc Liberatore, and Brian Neil Levine. "Measuring a year of child pornography trafficking by US computers on a peer-to-peer network." *Child Abuse & Neglect* 38 (2013): 347–56.
17. Ryan Hurley, Swagatika Prusty, Hamed Soroush, Robert J. Walls, Jeannie Albrecht, Emmanuel Cecchet, Brian Neil Levine, Marc Liberatore, Brian Lynn, and Janis Wolak. "Measurement and analysis of child pornography trafficking on P2P networks." Paper Presented at International World Wide Web Conference (WWW), Rio de Janeiro, Brazil, 13–17 May 2013. Edited by Daniel Schwabe, Virgilio A. F. Almeida, Hartmut Glaser, Ricardo A. Baeza-Yates and Sue B. Moon. pp. 631–42.
18. Thomas Locher, David Mysicka, Stefan Schmid, and Roger Wattenhofer. "A Peer Activity Study in eDonkey and Kad." Paper Presented at International Workshop on Dynamic Networks: Algorithms and Security (DYNAS), Wroclaw, Poland, 5 September 2009.
19. Oliver Heckmann, Axel Bock, Andreas Mauthe, and Ralf Steinmetz. "The eDonkey File-Sharing Network." Paper presented at Jahrestagung der Gesellschaft für Informatik, Ulm, Germany, 20–24 September 2004. Edited by Peter Dadam and Manfred Reichert. Lecture Notes in Informatics; vol. 51, pp. 224–28.
20. Frédéric Aidouni, Matthieu Latapy, and Clémence Magnien. "Ten weeks in the life of an eDonkey server." Paper Presented at International Workshop on Hot Topics in P2P Systems, in conjunction with 23rd IEEE International Symposium on Parallel and Distributed Processing, IPDPS 2009, Rome, Italy, 23–29 May 2009.
21. Thibault Cholez, Isabelle Chrisment, and Olivier Festor. "Monitoring and Controlling Content Access in KAD." Paper presented at International Conference on Communications - ICC 2010 IEEE, Cape Town, South Africa, 23–27 May 2010.

22. The Tor Project, Inc. TOR project, 2012. Available online: https://www.torproject.org/ (accessed on 4 June 2014).
23. Guillaume Montassier, Thibault Cholez, Guillaume Doyen, Rida Khatoun, Isabelle Chrisment, and Olivier Festor. "Content Pollution Quantification in Large P2P networks: A Measurement Study on KAD." Paper presented at 11th IEEE International Conference on Peer-to-Peer Computing (IEEE P2P'11); IEEE Communications Society, Kyoto, Japan, 31 August–2 September 2011; pp. 30–33. Projects: ANR MAPE and GIS 3SGS ACDAP2P.
24. Maggie Brennan, and Sean Hammond. "Complete critical literature review." *iCOP: Identifying and Catching Originators in P2P Networks.* Technical report, 2011. Available online: http://scc-sentinel.lancs.ac.uk/icop/sites/scc-sentinel.lancs.ac.uk.icop/files/D4.1LiteratureReview.pdf (accessed on 4 June 2014).

"Under His Spell": Victims' Perspectives of Being Groomed Online

Helen C. Whittle, Catherine E. Hamilton-Giachritsis and Anthony R. Beech

Abstract: The aim of this paper is to highlight key themes within the process of online grooming from the victim's perspective. Eight adolescents who experienced online grooming were interviewed and data were analysed using Thematic Analysis. It was found that participants, who had been both sexually abused online and/or offline, were subjected to a range of grooming experiences. Consistent grooming themes within this sample included: manipulation; deception; regular/intense contact; secrecy; sexualisation; kindness and flattery; erratic temperament and nastiness; and simultaneous grooming of those close to the victim. These themes are similar to those identified by the literature surrounding grooming offline. Analysis demonstrated that once a participant was 'enmeshed' in the relationship with the offender, they were more likely to endure negative feelings associated with the grooming, than if the victim was not 'enmeshed'. This paper supports the notion that grooming is a varied and non-linear process. Recommendations are made for practitioners, parents and carers, as well as suggestions for primary preventative education.

Reprinted from *Soc. Sci.* Cite as: Whittle, H.C.; Hamilton-Giachritsis, C.E.; Beech, A.R. "Under His Spell": Victims' Perspectives of Being Groomed Online. *Soc. Sci.* **2014**, *3*, 404–426.

1. Introduction

Social media and portable technology has contributed to young people becoming accessible to sexual abusers on a scale never known before [1–4]. While child sexual abuse has long existed and still exists offline [5], the Internet has altered the way in which abuse can be carried out. The concept of grooming was first addressed by UK legislation within Section 15 of the Sexual Offences Act (2003) and this legislative advancement enabled the prosecution of individuals who take preparatory steps towards abusing a child [6]. Following a review, Craven, Brown and Gilchrist ([7], p. 297) proposed that grooming is: "A process by which a person prepares a child, significant adults and the environment for the abuse of this child. Specific goals include gaining access to the child, gaining the child's compliance and maintaining the child's secrecy to avoid disclosure. This process serves to strengthen the offender's abusive pattern, as it may be used as a means of justifying or denying their actions."

The prevalence of online grooming is difficult to gauge particularly given the low reporting rates of sexual abuse [8]. Therefore the true figure will be far greater than prevalence statistics indicate, but 64% of 2391 reports made to the Child Exploitation and Online Protection Centre (CEOP) in the UK by members of the public, in 2009 and 2010 were related to grooming [9]. In prevalence studies, Ospina, Harstall and Dennet's [10] meta-analysis found most studies report between 13% [11] and 19% [12] of young people aged 10–17 years had received sexual solicitations online. However, in a recent study of adolescent behaviour online, Whittle, Hamilton-Giachritsis, Bishopp and Beech [13] found 33% of 354 thirteen and fourteen year olds reported having been approached sexually online. However, in most of these studies, the age of the person soliciting was unknown. In contrast, Swedish based research found that 25% of 14–15 year olds had received online sexual solicitations from an adult within the last year [14].

Manipulation techniques utilized during the grooming process can vary considerably [1] and are likely to incorporate both physical and psychological grooming to sexualize the child [7,15]. The process often involves one or several of the following tactics: flattery, blackmail, threats, sexualized games, deception or bribery [4,16–18].

O'Connell [18] was one of the first researchers to identify the process of online grooming, noting the following sequential process: friendship forming, relationship forming, risk assessment (whereby the offender attempts to assess the likelihood of detection), exclusivity (through intensified conversation, a sense of mutual respect is established, with an emphasis on trust and secrecy), and sexual and fantasy enactment. More recently, research has suggested that grooming is more likely to be a cyclical process and offenders do not progress through the stages sequentially [19,20]. In particular, Williams *et al.* [20] outlined various themes and sub-themes, notably surrounding rapport building, sexual content and assessment of the situation.

However, most research in this area stems from the perspective of the offender (e.g., [19,21,22]), and relies on the honesty of reporting of the perpetrators. However, as part of the Risk-taking Online Behaviour Empowerment through Research and Training (ROBERT) project, Quayle, Jonsson and Lööf [23] conducted research with 27 young victims of online grooming. The research identified five thematic categories within the grooming process: (1) the feeling that something is missing from one's life; (2) the importance of being someone who is connected online; (3) getting caught in a web and making choices; (4) others' involvement; and (5) closing the box and picking up the pieces (whereby victims attempted to make sense of what has happened and move on [23]. Research from the victim's perspective remains scarce, and these themes are yet to be tested and verified by further qualitative research.

Therefore, acquiring knowledge from victims themselves is imperative to better understand the processes involved in online grooming. Thus the purpose of this research was to provide an insight into the experience of the groomed victim, contributing to the limited research base currently available. Specifically, the aim of this research was to explore how the process of grooming takes place online.

2. Method

2.1. Ethics

Ethical considerations were paramount to this research and the study was approved by the University of Birmingham Ethics Committee (Reference ERN_11-0083) and the CEOP Research Panel, ensuring all possible steps were taken to protect the participants. Participants were only interviewed on completion of consent forms from the professional associated with the case, their parent/primary carer and the participant. The professionals were asked to put forward only victims who they believed would have no detrimental effects from involvement. All data was anonymized in that all personal details (including their name, names of others, place names and any other identifying features) were changed before analysis commenced. All references to the interview use the pseudonym and fictional information. Therefore, the only information given about participants is their age and gender. All pre-anonymized transcripts and voice recordings were destroyed.

2.2. SAMPLE

Eight young people were interviewed as part of this research; (see Table 1 for participant details).

Table 1. Information about Participants.

Gender	Six Females and two Males
Ethnicity	White British
Geographical Spread	Across England
Mean Age at Time of Interview	15.88 years
Range of Ages at Time of Interview	13–18 years
Standard Deviation of Ages at Time of Interview	2.17
Mean Age at Onset of Grooming	12.88 years
Range of Ages at Onset of Grooming	12–14 years
Standard Deviation of Ages Onset of Grooming	0.84
Range in Grooming Length	10 days–1 ½ years
Contact or Non-Contact Abuse	3 contact abuse 5 non-contact abuse

Notes: Onset of grooming refers to the first point of contact with the offender; grooming length refers to the time from the first point of contact to the last point of contact with the offender.

All the young people in this study experienced online grooming to the point of sexual abuse, whether online or offline. The length of time between the offense and the interview varied between participants, from one to six years (M = 3.00, SD = 1.77). There was a considerable range in the abusive experiences of the participants and the offences committed by the abusers. All of the females ($n = 6$) in this study considered their abusers to be a "boyfriend" at some point during the contact. Both males in this study were groomed by the same offender; the boys knew their male abuser in the offline, but were unaware their online female "friend" was this individual. The abuser targeted the boys specifically because of their offline friendship. Both males were under the impression they were talking to a female and sent "her" several semi-naked photos of themselves. Neither of the males considered the abuser to be a girlfriend.

Three of the young people met with their abusers offline and experienced contact sexual abuse: one participant travelled out of her home town with the abuser, another met the abuser twice during a year and the third participant had sex with her abuser several times a week for three months. Of the young people who did not meet their abusers offline, abusive experiences again varied considerably. One victim's abuser was 17 years old and thus the case could be interpreted as "sexting" (peers sharing sexually explicit photos via technology); however, the characteristics of this case were similar to the findings from others. This case and one other did not result in a conviction. The age of the offenders spanned from 17 up to approximately 50, all were male and white British. Most of the offenders had no previous convictions. The majority of the victims (including two of those who met their offender offline) were incited to send a range of naked photos to the offenders, and some received similar photos in return. One victim was regularly incited to create images and videos during the course of a year, some of which were of an extreme nature (for example, the use of objects in sexual acts).

2.3. Procedure

The sample of victims was identified via professional contacts at CEOP, including police officers and social services. An email was sent to approximately 2500 professional contacts who had attended the CEOP Academy training courses during the last five years. Furthermore, professionals who had previously worked with CEOP or who were known to have cases of online grooming were approached individually via phone and email. The professionals were given an information sheet with the following inclusion criteria: (1) the young person is between 12 and 18 years old at the time of interview; (2) the young person had been a victim of online grooming in the past; (3) the case relating to the grooming has now been closed; (4) the victim would like to participate in the research; (5) the professional associated with the case agrees that participation will have no detrimental effects for the young person; (6) the parent or guardian of the young person consents for the interview to take place. The following exclusion criteria were also outlined: (a) the young person is known to have mental health difficulties; (b) the young person has severe learning difficulties. These tight inclusion criteria led to a select sample, but ensured that all cases could contribute to the research aims.

The professionals were asked to put forward young people known through their work, who had been victimized through online grooming. The young person was required to fit the inclusion criteria and be deemed psychologically ready by the professional to participate in the research. Due to poor response rates from professionals and tight inclusion criteria, the young people who were identified as potential participants were limited. Depending on the recommendation, the professional would then either approach the victim and their family or give details to the main researcher to approach the family. The parent/primary carer and the victim were each given an information sheet to help them consider the research. If the victim and their family were happy for the young person to participate, a consent form was given to the professional, the parent and the victim to sign. The first author then corresponded with the victim and their parent to arrange a mutually convenient time and place for the interview.

The victims were involved in a semi-structured interview that took between 45 and 120 min, depending on the pace of the individual. The young people were given as much information as possible about the research, prior to their involvement. This was provided via the information sheet, the consent form and explained in person immediately prior to interview. Interviews took place in a neutral setting of the victim's choice; this was either a victim suite at police property or an appropriate room in a Children's Services or charity property. It was stipulated that the researcher would not attend the home of the young person, as it was not deemed a neutral space. The young person was given the option of having their parent or Guardian attend the research interview. All participants declined parental presence. To enhance rapport and informality, only one interviewer was present at and led all interviews (with the exception of the first interview, where a second interviewer was present to assess the quality of the interview structure).

To enable the interviewer to give full attention to the young person, no notes were taken; instead the interview was recorded using a Dictaphone. This was outlined on the information sheet and explained to the young person prior to interview. Before the interview commenced, it was explained that the participant was in control of the interview and could stop or take breaks at any time. Emphasis was placed on the interviewee feeling able to ask for clarification if necessary and informing the interviewer if they would prefer not to answer a question. It was explained that the interview was confidential, with the limits that confidentiality could not be guaranteed if reference was made to a crime that the police are unaware of, which would have to be reported. Information was given regarding withdrawal from the research and that participants could withdraw at any time before a specified date. The interview commenced only after the consent forms had been discussed and any questions had been answered. All interviews followed the same semi-structured format. All interviews began with a free narrative for the participant to summarize what happened. Following this, events were generally discussed chronologically with some questions used to gain information about key themes/issues. During the debriefing, the participant was given a debriefing sheet with further information about the research, a reminder about the process of withdrawing (including the contact details of the interviewer) and details of a range of agencies that could provide additional support if required.

2.4. Data Analysis

As soon as possible after each interview, the first author did an exact transcription of the Dictaphone recording. Transcribing the interviews enabled the first author to become familiar with the data. Once the interview was transcribed, all personal information mentioned during interview (including individual names, place names, *etc.*) were anonymized. These alterations were recorded in a document and stored on an encrypted computer at CEOP (a secure Government building). Anonymous transcripts were then imported into NVivo9 qualitative analysis software. Qualitative analytic approaches vary significantly [24] and are either entrenched within a theoretical perspective, or independent of theory. Thematic Analysis is often considered the foundational technique for qualitative work and is independent from specific theoretical perspectives [25]. Hence, Thematic Analysis seeks to identify, analyse and report themes within a set of data and has the flexibility to explore rich and detailed data without theoretical constraint [25]. For these reasons, Thematic Analysis was chosen as an appropriate methodology for this research.

A bottom-up or data driven technique was utilized for this study, whereby no pre-existing theory was overlaid and consequentially themes were identified purely based on the content of the data. The first author coded each interview in turn by generating initial nodes within NVivo9. Initial coding was considered complete when each line of the data set had been allocated to one or more nodes. Following this, each interview was recorded again to ensure that any nodes created by subsequent interviews were connected to data across all interviews where necessary. At this stage, sections of the text were analysed by the second author to provide inter-rater reliability. The codes identified by the second author were very similar to those identified by the first author and dissimilar codes were resolved through discussion.

Having established a set of single nodes (approximately 800) covering all interviews, themes were searched for across the nodes. Nodes that were very similar or shared meaning were amalgamated into one node (for example, "family money problems" and "claimed benefits" were combined to become 'low income family') and nodes that were related to each other were combined to create themes using tree nodes (for example, "given presents" and "offered money" were joined under the tree of "bribery"). Using data from all interviews, tree nodes gradually expanded to connect over-arching, inter-related themes (e.g., offender manipulation techniques). Throughout this process, the first author worked with the second author to discuss emerging themes and analytic progress. Thus, having established a comprehensive set of tree nodes through discussion with the second author, the first author then reviewed, defined and renamed themes until confident that the tree nodes and branches accurately reflected the data.

3. Results

Early analysis of the interviews produced three superordinate themes based on timeframes; pre-offense, during the offense and post-offense. The results of this paper primarily focus on themes identified relating to "during offense" analysis. There were a range of sub-themes within the "during offense" superordinate theme, including: (1) the grooming behaviour; (2) victim feelings at the time; (3) protective factors; (4) risk factors; (5) perpetrator characteristics; and (6) relationship status. This range is demonstrative of the variety of victim experiences of grooming. The grooming varied dramatically in duration and over half of the abusers were grooming other victims at the same time. The sub-themes that generated the most information regarding the process of grooming were "grooming behaviour" and "victim feelings at the time". A sub-sub-theme within "grooming behaviour" was "offender manipulation techniques"; this identified a range of grooming techniques with various effects on victims (see Table 2). Please note that all ages given in this paper are the age of the victim during the grooming, not their age at interview.

Table 2. Subthemes of offender manipulation techniques and effect on victim.

Technique	Effects Reported by the Victims
Conversations (Including normal, mutual interests, victim focused and confiding)	Built familiarity, trust and basis for relationship.
Deception (Including lies about interests, lies about identity and webcam trickery)	Attracted to abuser, fitted ideals, false sense of security.

Table 2. *Cont.*

Technique	Effects Reported by the Victims
Regular/intense contact (Including increasing methods of contact, talking through the night)	Enmeshed in relationship, addiction to contact, abuser infiltrated into victim's life, relieves boredom, distancing from family.
Secrecy (Including techniques to keep it secret, encouraging victim secrecy, allowing victim to decide secrecy)	Special and exclusive relationship, distancing from friends and family, lying.
Sexualisation (Including sexual chat, sexual photos and videos, sexual compliments, sexual contact and overemphasis on sexual side of relationship)	Feeling out of control, boosting confidence, wanting sexual experience, excitement, pressurised, enjoys reciprocity, believes will keep abuser interested, hold over victim, love.
Kindness and Flattery (Including generosity, good listener, genuine, fun, helping with homework, supportive, traditional and sexual compliments, promises about the future, personality and physical compliments)	Feeling good, builds trust and basis for a relationship, confiding in abuser, wanting to talk more, receiving gifts, love, feeling special, feeling beautiful, confidence boost, hopeful about future, enmeshed in relationship.
Erratic Temperament & Nastiness (Including blackmail, threats, bribery, possessiveness, anger, encouraging jealousy, fights, being contradictory)	Fear, helplessness, lack of control, irritation, annoyance, worrying about losing abuser, confusion, dependence, desire to please offender, hold over victim.
Grooming others (Including friends and family)	Familiarity, part of victim's wider life, builds trust.

3.1. Conversations

Common to all but one victim was that the abusers initiated contact; in the remaining case, conversation started due to a mutual online friend. In two instances, the first contact from the abusers was sexual; this could be considered atypical to "normal" peer interactions online. One victim reacted negatively to this but agreed to "forgive" the offender because he seemed interesting, the other continued speaking to the abuser sexually and non-sexually, before meeting him later that day.

> "One day I just logged on and I got a friend request like so I accepted it. And that's like how it all started." [Jonathan, 13]

> "Well he offered me first £200 to sleep with him...(laughs). So he offered me [that] first and I was like I'm not a prozy [prostitute] and everything and so then he went, I'll give you £400 and I went, I told ya I'm not like that, I don't go around getting money off people for sex." [Jenna, 12].

All participants described having normal conversations with their abusers (in a similar way to how they talked to their friends), about general things such as discussing mutual interests, music, their day at school, and others known to them. However, this normal conversation was often in the context of intense levels of contact (see below) and thus may be distinct from regular online friendship formation patterns.

> "Just like normal really; normal conversation." [Jonathan, 13].

Six victims articulated how they confided in the offenders about problems within their life, particularly family problems, and found emotional support in the relationship. These conversations resulted in the abusers feeling familiar to the victims and built a level of trust. For 63% (n = 5) of the victims in this study, friendship became the basis of a romantic relationship with the abuser. This emotional connecting is likely to have been influenced by the vulnerabilities that the victims were experiencing in their lives and increased their reliance on the offenders. On several occasions, the victims described feeling emotionally attached to their offender relatively quickly; potentially quicker than would be expected with online relationships more generally. Half of the participants mentioned that the conversation generally focused on them (although they did not necessarily notice this at the time). This dimension of the relationship may distinguish theses dynamics from age appropriate online friendships, as non-offending friendships are likely be more balanced and reciprocal.

> "I told him everything, he knew just about everything that was going on. Whenever my Mum and me had had a row, the first person I'd tell, I'd start speaking to was him."[Charlotte, 12].

> "If I had a bad day at school, I'd come in and I'd speak to him about it. Erm, or if someone said this about my sister, I'd speak to him about that. So I trusted him a hell of a lot with a lot of my life basically." [Shelley, 13].

3.2. Deception

Over half of the abusers lied to the victims about their identities; most commonly the abusers implied they were younger than their true age. In half the cases, victims were sent a photo of an attractive teenager of the opposite sex and led to believe this was the identity of the person they were speaking to. One offender used a picture of his teenage son to groom the victim. The lies told by the abusers were generally believed by the victims at the time yet, with hindsight, all but one victim thought that the abuser had frequently lied to them. Of the victims that were deceived, no substantial suspicions were apparent and all were shocked when they found out the truth.

> "He'd find things out about me first and then say yeah I like that too and I like this. So it was like, it was almost like he was using my responses to shape who he was, so he could pretend to be this person that I liked in order to get what he wanted from me." [Chloe, 12].

> "He made an account that wasn't him; he pretended to be someone else." [Lucas, 13].

On a few occasions the victims would have benefitted from questioning and critically evaluating some of the information given by the offenders, as some aspects of who the offenders were purporting to be were inconsistent with realistic peer relationships online. It is likely that victim vulnerabilities prevented this process.

> "He told me he was a model, so all his photos on Tagged are of him modelling. So I found out obviously when it all came about, that the photos were actually a model from London." [Shelley, 13].

> "How he could work two jobs and have loads of stuff at 18? ...The little things that would've if I'd had listened to, would have, might have given some of it away." [Joanne, 14].

Of the three victims who met their abusers, two found he was roughly as expected and one was shocked by how much older the offender was. The fact that this victim stayed despite this shock, indicates the extent to which she had been groomed by this point. In three cases, the abusers told the victims they did not have a working webcam, to avoid sending any videos back. The offender using his son's identity had pre-recorded video footage on webcam and streamed this so it would play to the victim, as if it were himself.

> "I was a bit shocked 'cos apparently he was meant to be really young and then when I see that he wasn't, I just like stood there and froze." [Joanne, 14].

> "I'd say well why won't you go on webcam and he'd always be like oh it's broken and then this one time, he, I don't I honestly don't know how he did this, but there was a video of a person, like the person I thought I was talking to." [Chloe, 12].

3.3. Regular or Intense Contact

The majority of the victims were in regular and intense contact with their abusers; the prevalence and extent to which this theme was discussed leads this to be noted as a substantial element of the grooming process. The number of methods of contact with the abusers gradually increased in the majority of cases, usually involving instant messaging, texting, webcam use and phone calls. Most victims described talking to their abusers frequently, and often through the night, which appeared to increase the young persons' dependency on the offender and enmeshed the abusers more centrally within the victims' day to day life. The word "addiction" was used by two victims when describing their need to contact the abusers; this included the victim from the "sexting" case. The intensity of the contact between victims and offenders is likely to be a distinguishing feature of grooming in comparison to other age appropriate online relationships. Several victims felt that the intense contact was indicative of a loving relationship and regularly spoke of love with the abusers.

> "I couldn't like hardly ever have anytime to myself." [Jenna, 12].

> "It had got to about, probably about for about 4 h a day and that's not including texting." [Mona, 14].

"By the end we were texting all the, like texting through the day, talking online in the evening and then like a phone call at night, so it was quite frequently." [Chloe, 12].

"I was constantly on the phone. I could be in bed and I could be on the phone all night and I'd actually fall asleep on the phone….And like wake up in the morning and the phone would be still on. So it was like an addiction." [Joanne, 14].

"I was kind of addicted to talking to him…he'd text me and I'd be online within minutes and then we'd chat, when I had to log off my Facebook, I'd then begin texting him. And that'd probably be about 9 o'clock and I'd text him until 2 o'clock in the morning." [Charlotte, 13].

Of the two victims (the boys) who were not communicating with the abuser intensively, relief from boredom appeared to be a contributory factor dictating when they would engage in chat with the offender ("Just someone to talk to really." [Jonathan, 13]). The lack of regular and intense contact is likely to contribute to why the boys did not become enmeshed in their relationship with the offender.

3.4. Secrecy

In all but one instance, the victims' parents did not know anything about the abusers. In the vast majority of cases, one or more of the victims' friends knew they were talking to a "boyfriend" or a "girl" online, but details of the relationships were shared to varying extents. A few victims were warned about the relationship by their friends who became uneasy about the extent of contact the victim was having with a stranger. One friend eventually reported the abuser to the victim's parent because she was aware that the abuser was older and was worried by this.

"I could have told my Dad, but I can't trust him because I think oh he's gonna go mad at me, it's all my fault." [Jenna, 12].

"The only thing I was worried about was him telling my Dad that I'd said things and sent things to him. But then if I continued doing what he'd ask me, then he wouldn't tell my Dad so there was nothing to worry about." [Chloe, 12].

"I told…my Dad's girlfriends' son, he's same age as me... I spoke to him one night, but that was it, I didn't say anything to anyone else." [Jonathan, 13].

In some cases the abusers explicitly told the victim not to tell anyone about their relationship, but in the majority of circumstances, the victims described not wanting to tell anyone (particularly their parents) about the offenders. Again, secrecy surrounding contact with the abuser is a unique feature of grooming and is likely to differ from typical peer friendships online, particularly in the cases where the offender insisted that the relationship remain a secret. This could be considered a warning sign for young people. On a couple of occasions one of the reasons for the secrecy was that the victims felt the "relationship" would be perceived by others as wrong, usually due to the sexual elements of the contact and the fact the offender was a stranger. Thus, a variety of techniques were used by the victims to keep the relationships secret, including: (1) lying about where they were; (2) deleting messages; (3) saving conversations under a different name; and (4) terminating the conversation if interrupted by a parent. Secrecy seemed to make the relationship feel more exclusive, special and exciting to the victim. This lack of sharing information also had the effect of distancing the victim from their family and in some instances, their friends.

> "I wanted to keep to myself cos it was cos it was like that nice, you know, the stuff that he was saying, I didn't like wanna tell everybody. So….deep down, it was like my own little ya know, person that likes me." [Joanne, 14].
> "I usually deleted them (messages) once they were sent." [Chloe, 12].

> "She (Mum) thinks she's taken my phone but she's taken my decoy phone. I had a little, rubbish little phone that I used when I was around her." [Charlotte, 12].

The fact that some of the secrecy tactics employed by the victims were quite extreme highlights the importance of the relationship to the victim and thus how enmeshed they had become.

3.5. Sexualisation

All victims experienced sexualisation to the point of sexual abuse online and in some cases offline sexual abuse. This theme was extremely prevalent in the data and should be considered a dominant component of the grooming process. Sexualisation involved one or several of the following: sexual chat, sexual compliments, creating and receiving sexual photos, creating and receiving sexual videos over webcam, and sex with abuser during a meeting. Sexualisation was apparent in all cases, but the process varied considerably. Most victims talked sexually with their abusers and, in the majority of cases, the offenders initiated this.

Half of the victims felt uneasy and pressured by this aspect of the relationship; despite this, these victims and a couple of others also found the sexual elements exciting, at least initially. The majority of victims described sexualisation as a slow force that emerged and intensified over a long period of time (several months in some cases); however one victim engaged in sexual chat with the abuser immediately (and met him later that day), and another after a few days. A couple of victims were originally excited by the sexual side but became scared as it intensified, whilst others who were initially reluctant began to initiate the sexual elements more often over time. For many female victims, sexuality eventually dominated the relationship and it was described often as the principal time when they felt out of control. In contrast, while sexualisation was a component for the male victims, it did not dominate. However, both males talked less openly in interview about the sexual elements of the grooming and this finding may be a reflection of this.

> "It was just started off normal chat for quite a while I think and then a bit more provocative." [Lucas, 13].

> "It went from him saying… you're pretty, to beautiful, to sexy, to f'ing lush, erm, I'd have you in my bed tonight and it went, just kind of through getting more and more…I would have stopped it because I would've realised that we've been, we'd known each other two weeks and we're already doing that. What would we have been like in a month? We'll be already having sex and stuff." [Charlotte, 12].

The quote above relates to the "sexting" case and the victim explained that she continued sharing sexual images with the abuser because she enjoyed it, however the speed at which the relationship and content of the images was progressing made her uneasy.

All but one victim created sexual photos and/or videos for the abusers and all said these received positive responses, which made them feel good. Photos and videos often increased in volume and became more extreme over time. In half of the cases the abusers also sent photos and/or videos to the victim in return, these received mixed responses from the victims. In most cases the abusers instigated the idea of sharing photos and videos, but there were mixed responses regarding pressures to do so. Several abusers told victims that other young people commonly send sexual photos thus, several female victims described feelings of obligation, concerned that they may lose the abusers' interest and/or love if they withdrew participation, others felt they owed the abusers for their emotional support, but others, (including the boys), said they were not pressured. However, most victims of both genders described feelings of excitement at some point.

> "I was under his spell so I'd do anything he wanted. Just come home from school, speak to him, do this, do that (sexual activity via webcam), go to bed…He was showing me so much attention in the beginning and talk to me near enough every day about everything and help me with my homework and stuff I thought in return, I'd do what he wants. So he'd request it and I'd do it." [Shelley, 13].

> "There wasn't really any pressure until after I sent one or two like after, like the first one, that was like that was just fun, you know that was just exciting and I had my underwear on so it wasn't like massively bad or anything, I thought oh well it's only like being in a bikini; that was my justification in my head you know….Other stuff happened as well like when he asked me to do things on webcam and you know I did because it was fun and you weren't supposed to do it, which made it even more fun."[Chloe, 12].

> "I was excited 'cos it was something different, something new. Um he like he apparently a load of people do it so, it was like that's what he said. So it was like an exciting feeling." [Joanne, 14].

> "But I was on Facebook at the time so I weren't really watching it (a video of the offender masturbating), cos it kind of freaked me out in some ways, it was just kind of argh!...For a 12 year old girl I was quite scared!" [Charlotte, 12].

Two victims had been keen to meet up, but were discouraged by the abusers (who had lied about their identity), although one of these victims was planning the meeting with the offender at the point of police involvement. In some cases the abusers were encouraging the victims to meet.

> "Oh I was excited; I thought it would be really fun you know. I got to meet my boyfriend, awesome." [Chloe, 12].

Three female victims met their abusers offline and had been eager to do so. All had sexual intercourse on the first meeting. But while two of these young people often spoke quite positively about sexual intercourse with the abusers, the third victim generally talked more negatively it and fought back when the offender attempted to have sexual intercourse on a second occasion. The first two both had previous sexual experience; the third had no previous sexual experience. Despite, the general reflections noted above, victims sometimes made contradictory statements about the sexually abusive part of the relationship; on occasion describing feelings of excitement and enjoyment and other times describing concerns, discomfort and fear.

> "The second time I just wasn't bothered honestly it's the only way of putting it!" [Mona, 14].
>
> "In, some ways it wasn't just all him doing it, it was me too…The police and everything class it as rape and groomed. I don't class it as that because like, I, I loved him."[Jenna, 12].

> "He was more like shouting and stuff saying like, you should do it and, and stuff like that really, just erm, but I was like standing my ground, I was like I don't, don't want to. Not, I cou, I couldn't do it again. Erm, and I think what was running through my head as I, I was like, it doesn't matter whether he was to hurt me or anything, I just couldn't put myself through that again." [Joanne, 14].

Despite the fact that some online peer relationships may well involve sexual elements, the sexualisation of victim-offender interactions within this sample (often instigated and controlled by the abuser) built over time and in several cases began to dominate the relationship. This is likely to be more exclusive to grooming and therefore could be considered a warning sign.

3.6. Kindness and Flattery

All victims described the abusers with positive adjectives for the majority of the contact, such as lovely, nice and kind; however this was to a lesser extent for the boys. This may also have contributed to why they were less enmeshed in the relationship. Victims often felt the abusers were fun, good at listening to their problems, interesting and supportive and, in one case, regularly helped with homework. Such interactions made them feel good and loved. This was a considerable theme across the interviews. However, given the clear overlap with typical adolescent relationship development it is difficult to draw distinctions between the two behaviours. Two victims who met their abusers, described the abusers paying for food and taxi fares and one of these victims also received money and gifts from the abuser for her birthday, which she explained made her feel special. This kindness, on several occasions, contributed to the victims becoming enmeshed or hooked on contact with the offenders.

> "Genuine, as he seemed like the nice person everyone wants ya to go out and be with, he just seemed really nice to me." [Mona, 14].

> "Oh no he was lovely, he was just [like]. another teenager who liked the stuff that I liked and was fun to talk to or whatever." [Chloe, 12].

> "He was really like kind and caring and uh he's a really nice person to talk to um, like you'd like him if you met him." [Joanne, 14].

All victims felt familiar with and trusted the abusers, furthermore they all felt unconcerned at the time of the grooming, often describing it as feeling normal. This lack of concern may directly relate to the young people's vulnerabilities and is likely to have decreased the accuracy of a critical assessment of the risks involved in such an online friendship.

"I trusted him with my whole life and everything like that." [Jenna, 12].

"I never suspected anything." [Jonathan, 13].

All but one victim expressed feeling a confidence boost from talking to the abusers, and in all female cases; this flattery was consistent and frequent with most describing feeling special, beautiful, enjoying the attention and becoming 'enmeshed' in the relationship. The girls described considerably more flattery than the male victims. Compliments were predominantly (but not exclusively) based on the victims looks, incorporating both traditional and sexual stances. Sexualized compliments, once established, generally became the most consistently used form of flattery. Half of the victims reported that the abusers were promising them a better future and regularly discussed staying together.

"He'd just like tell me I was pretty and beautiful and he'd tell me that he loved me you know; yeah that sort of thing just that I was sort of a good person and that he liked me."[Chloe, 12].

"It was mainly like everything a girl would like to hear, like you're beautiful, um you deserve good things and I can do all that for you and stuff like that" [Joanne, 14].

All the female victims in this study felt that the abusers were their boyfriend and half of all participants reported they believed they were in love with the abusers.

"He made me love him well he...yeah he made me love him." [Jenna, 12].

"He was kind, made you feel special, made you fall in love with him." [Charlotte, 12].

"He'd say he loved me and I'd say oh yeah I love you too because I was 12 and didn't know what that was so like yeah I love you too and yeah we'd just be like that." [Chloe, 12].

In contrast, the two male victims described having a mediocre interest in the girl that the abuser purported to be: "Just nice to talk to, if you're bored someone to talk to, just catch up and stuff. Nothing really serious going on, but still friends." [Lucas, 13]. This is likely to have helped them stay more distant from their abuser, potentially restricting the types of manipulation the offender felt able to engage in (e.g., intense contact) and/or the extent of their abusive experiences.

3.7. Erratic Temperament and Nastiness

Some victims referred to occasions when the abusers had been possessive, jealous, controlling, or blowing hot and cold with them. On occasion this resulted in arguments and victims feeling irritated and annoyed, but more commonly, this resulted in the victim feeling confused and out of control. Some victims mentioned disliking the abusers as a result and the only victim who experienced the abuser becoming nasty in person described feeling scared by him. While typical peer relationships may involve arguments, the one-sided nature of the nastiness and erratic temperament experienced by some of the victims indicates a possible distinction for this type of abuse. Most victims who witnessed an erratic or nasty side to the abusers were anxious to please the offenders in attempts to regain their kindness and maintain the relationship. Such offender behaviour appears to highlight the hold they had over the victims and victims who experienced this type of temperament described already feeling enmeshed in the relationship with the abusers. This form of manipulation equated to one of the few times any of victims described feeling concerned by the relationship.

> "If I was in an exam or something, erm if I'd turn my phone off and he'd tried ringing, he was like, oh you're ignoring me even though he knew I was in school. So and then I had to get like, like, loads of messages saying like, "oi bitch, answer your phone" and stuff like that." [Joanne, 14].

> "There was quite a few times when I said something he didn't like and he's just like oh go away I wish you were dead, all that type of stuff… he occasionally tried to make me feel really bad about myself like oh you're so ugly, you're so fat, I'm surprised more people don't hate you….It was a bit of a rollercoaster, because there were times when I thought I loved him and then others when I hated him and didn't want to speak to him ever again and it went on like that for about a year." [Mona, 14].

> "It made me feel like he, like I'm not wanted anymore…and it made me like harder fast, because like losing somebody that you think you love it's dead hard." [Jenna, 12].

The victim who travelled out of her home-town with her abuser described him getting progressively nastier while they were away, despite having been kind and loving before they met. This was the victim that spoke negatively about sexual intercourse with the abuser and fought back against the abuser on a second occasion.

> "He just started going really mad and getting really angry um cos we was on the park on our own and he was just like had like really evil eyes, I just remember his eyes, erm like he grabbed hold of my wrists and then was like well you're not going, you're staying with me." [Joanne, 14].

Two victims were blackmailed with threats of showing parents if they did not send more sexual photos, and this emphasized their lack of control to these victims. Blackmail might be considered atypical of normal peer interactions online and thus could be a warning sign for grooming. However, young people need to be provided with information about where to seek help if they have reached the point where they are being blackmailed.

> "Because you know you'd done it once or twice they just expect it all the time and then if you try and say like oh I don't want to talk about that or whatever, he'd like threaten or black(mail), like I'll send your Dad all the chat logs if you don't." [Chloe, 12].

3.8. Grooming Others

On several occasions, victims' friends were also in contact with the abusers, either when with the victim or as a means of the offender getting in contact with the victim if they were not responding. At points, the victims were warned to be careful by a friend, but more typically, the friend found the relationship exciting, as they too had been groomed. In the one case where the parents did know their daughter was talking to the abuser, they too were regularly speaking on the phone with him and were manipulated by him. This contact with family and friends led the victim to feel increasing familiarity with the abuser and misplaced trust. The two male victims knew their abuser offline, and the families knew and liked this man offline. In the case of Jonathan, his mother trusted the offender to the extent that he regularly babysat for Jonathan and his brother, including an overnight stay on one occasion.

> "They knew that we were talking to each other and like he was sending me messages saying like I love you and stuff like that. And my mum knew about that 'cause my mum had, my mum would speak to him as well, like when he's speaking to my mum, he'd say like um I really, really like your daughter, I think she's lovely, I can't wait to come and meet you all and like um, just stuff that a normal lad would say when they're seeing your daughter….So it was like nothing out the ordinary to my mum or dad." [Joanne, 14].

> "I knew he was a [person in authoritative role] and I knew him as like well kind of a friend I suppose, cos I know he looked after me a few times when my Mum was working." [Jonathan, 13].

All of these grooming techniques and subsequent effects on the victims (see Figure 1) increased the chances of the victims becoming enmeshed in the relationship. All female victims in this study implied they were "hooked" on their offenders, for some this even transferred to after the arrest when they still believed it had been a relationship. Such victim beliefs gave the abusers increased control over the relationship and the young person. In contrast, the male victims were subject to fewer grooming techniques or often to a lesser extent, thus neither felt enmeshed; in particular one of the males appeared relatively uninterested in the relationship.

> "We were like puppets, once we were under his control, anything he said would make me, would make me do it." [Shelley, 13].

> "Once they've got you in that certain position they want ya, they can do anything with you because you didn't know that you loved them and you'd do anything for them." [Jenna, 12].

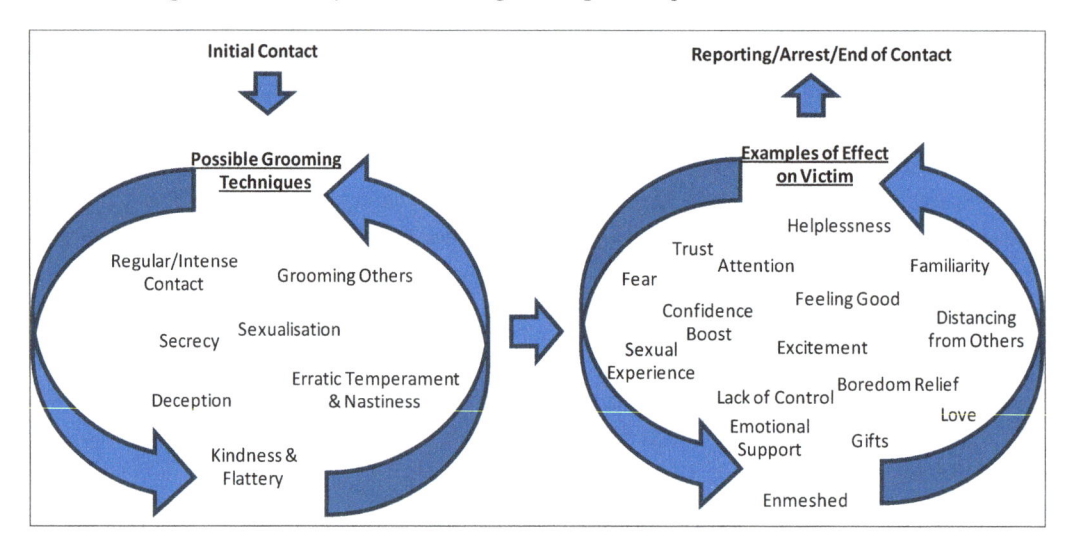

Figure 1. Summary of non-linear grooming techniques and effect on victim.

4. Discussion

The results of this study illustrate the range of experiences of victims of online grooming and highlight that grooming within this sample was not a linear or homogeneous process; offenders did not move through the phases of grooming in any particular order. Instead, it may be cyclical by nature and groomers may adopt, relapse and re-adopt various manipulation strategies as necessary. Despite the heterogeneity of victim experiences, the themes above highlight commonalities in the way that the adolescent victims in this study were groomed and these techniques often had similar effects on the victims. Given the age group of victims within this sample and the potential for offenders to tailor their grooming style to fit what they know of the victims; the results are discussed in the context of grooming adolescents (rather than children).

This study cannot make inferences about the prevalence of online grooming, but while recent US research suggests that online sexual solicitations are in fact decreasing [26] and most forms of harassment online actually come from peers [27], the current study highlights that online grooming by adults remains an issue requiring greater understanding. Existing literature recognizes grooming others can be a phase within the grooming process [7,20,28], and this is apparent through many of the victims' experiences within this study. This study suggests that any phase within grooming (e.g., sexualisation) can occur extremely quickly and is likely to vary. This finding is consistent with existing literature which recognizes variation in grooming periods [29]. Furthermore, the fact less than half of the victims in this study met with their offenders offline, is supportive of the notion that not all offenders are contact driven [1].

The most commonly utilized online grooming strategies experienced by the victims in this sample were manipulation through conversation, deception, regular/intense contact, secrecy, sexualisation, kindness and flattery, erratic temperament and nastiness, and grooming others. These grooming techniques are similar to those identified by previous research from both an offender perspective [17,18] and a victim perspective [16], although the use of deception was more prevalent within this study than previous [30]. Interestingly, this grooming process and techniques within it are similar to those identified as being used by offenders' offline [7,15]. This study therefore provides support for the notion that grooming behaviour remains constant, irrespective of the environment and that child sexual offenders utilize technology both to facilitate access to victims and facilitate the abuse.

However, one key element of the current research is that different manipulation techniques are utilized by different offenders (sometimes differing by victim) and that, although regularly sharing similar themes, the process of grooming is a unique experience to each victim. Notably, however, the experiences described by the victims in this study appear to be consistent with (but also go beyond) the themes of rapport building and sexual content, as outlined by Williams and colleagues [20]. Furthermore, the findings correlate with the theme of "caught in a web", as identified by Quayle *et al.* [23], which includes: seeming like a normal relationship, telling lies, being groomed, losing control and betrayal. The current research found that victims experienced these phases in different ways and at different points within the grooming process.

The grooming techniques endorsed by the abusers in this study generated a range of immediate positive and negative effects on the adolescent victims. The victims commonly felt immediate positive effects of the grooming such as trust, love, attention, support, excitement and confidence boosting; these tended to enmesh the victim and establish the abusers hold over them. In some cases, the grooming techniques gradually evoked more overtly negative effects on the victim such as fear, confusion, lack of control, and distancing from family. The victims who were already enmeshed with the abusers endured this and continued contact, despite experiencing more overtly nasty grooming strategies. These victims were focusing on maintaining the relationship and seeking to regain the positive effects of it. Notably, the two males in this study did not report any nastiness or erratic temperament by the abuser. It is likely that the abuser was aware the boys were not yet enmeshed in the relationship and therefore such grooming techniques would not have been tolerated at this stage. Using grooming techniques which evoked overtly negative effects on victims who were not enmeshed in the relationship could result in the loss of the relationship entirely. This finding contributes to knowledge of grooming as it indicates there is likely to be a 'tipping point' at which the offender knows the victim is enmeshed.

4.1. Implications of This Research

The heterogeneous nature of grooming as reported by this study is a challenge for preventative strategy; however this study generates important implications for prevention. Sexualisation was a key theme within this study, evoking a range of complicated and often contradictory feelings for the victims. The internet gives young people new ways to explore their sexuality and adolescents are known to behave sexually online [31]; thus the findings from this study must be viewed within the context of sexual behaviour between peers. For some young people, however, even relationships with adults who clearly state their sexual intentions can be perceived as a romantic relationship. Some of the young people in this sample believed they were in a relationship with the offender, therefore education messages which distinguish age appropriate relationships from inappropriate sexual relationships could contribute to prevention.

Consistent educational awareness-raising is required to highlight the uncertainty about with whom you are speaking online, as well as the permanent nature and digital footprint of everything posted online (whether via text, apps, photos or images). This will help young people to make more informed decisions about how they interact online and consider the potential consequences more fully. Empowering young people to risk-assess relationships and recognize potentially abusive elements, will enable them to seek help at an earlier stage.

However, it cannot be overlooked that many of the grooming techniques identified and subsequent effects on the victims are typical of adolescent friendship/relationship development. Parallels between grooming behaviour and typical adolescent relationship forming online are problematic for preventative education, as warning signs of grooming may be discreet or in some cases, virtually non-existent. Despite this, some of the themes identified by the analysis in this study are likely to be indicative of the subtle signs of grooming. In particular, intense contact, nastiness and erratic temperament, encouraged secrecy, disproportionate focus on the young person's life during conversation and sexual elements (especially when instigated, persisted and controlled by another) should be considered warning signs, most notably when a combination of these factors are experienced. Educating young people about these indicators will contribute to protection. Furthermore, extending sex education to incorporate sexuality online and the inherent risks could further equip young people with the knowledge to assist them in protecting themselves.

A small number of victims discussed that, with hindsight, some of the offenders' lies did not make sense; therefore teaching young people to objectively evaluate online friendships and relationships, regardless of emotional attachment may help them to identify risks which would be otherwise overlooked. If the victims had had a better understanding of the intricacies of online grooming techniques, how quickly it can progress and the consequences, there is a greater possibility they would have been suspicious and better equipped to resist the abusers. Young people learning directly from the experiences of young victims could assist them in understanding these subtleties and being able to recognize the warning signs among their peers. On the occasions when the victims in this sample did feel worried about the relationship (e.g., when Chloe was being blackmailed to send more photos), they were not equipped with the knowledge of how to stop the cycle. Educating young people about how to report concerns about online relationships, at any stage, is imperative.

Within this sample, other than a few concerns regarding specific issues, most victims felt largely unconcerned by their relationship with the offenders, and on occasion this lack of concern extended beyond the point of sexual abuse. Despite current research suggesting that disclosure rates are increasing [27], all cases of grooming in this study only ended due to someone reporting on behalf of the victims or the offender getting caught as part of a wider police investigation. This lack of victim suspicion is likely to be associated with the parallels between the offenders' grooming techniques and typical adolescent peer relationships, but also demonstrates the extent to which victims had been groomed. Similarly, two out of eight victims experiencing blackmail is a relatively small proportion, which further indicates the offenders' confidence and ability to incite sexual acts without the need for blackmail. The emotional hold some offenders had over their victims mirrors aspects of interpersonal violence within relationships. Therefore, it is imperative that young people are educated to also look out for signs of grooming among their peers, who may be too enmeshed within the process to identify the warning signs.

Aftercare of victims of sexual abuse can be enhanced by better understanding the effects of sexualisation on the victims; in particular the confusion victims may feel. All the victims in this study felt an element of attraction to their offenders or who the offenders were purporting to be, and all the girls considered the offenders to be boyfriends at some stage. The emotional connection and sexual relationship (online or offline) that the victims may have with the offenders needs to be recognized and sensitively addressed by professionals who provide after-care and support.

For parents and carers, there are also important lessons to be learnt. The speed with which grooming can occur needs to be emphasized and that, for all of the young people in this sample, the grooming progressed to experiencing sexual abuse online, sometimes also offline. The additional difficulty for protection is that parents may believe their child is safe upstairs in their own home and, in many cases, may remain naïve to the potential dangers in the online world. This has become more complicated by the rise in smartphones and other technologies allowing young people easy and on-going access to the internet outside of the home (including in friends' homes) and when they are to some degree beyond parental control. Despite being a difficult issue, potential risk could also be identified by encouraging young people to communicate with their parents and carers (or other trusted adults in their lives) about their online activities. If adults can facilitate these open discussions (without insinuating blame), then it is more likely a young person will discuss online relationships, thus giving adults the opportunity assist with risk assessment and intervene if necessary. As was the case for one victim in this study, parents are also at risk of being groomed by offenders and thus awareness raising and education for parents and carers is also imperative.

For child protection professionals, teachers, parents and adolescents themselves, there is a need to balance the huge advantages to be gained through the medium of the internet with the need to keep young people safe and this can only be achieved, in part, through greater awareness of the process of online grooming and abuse.

In light of the fact that this research found that offenders were required to use different strategies with different victims to keep them engaged, additional analysis has considered why some young people are more vulnerable to online victimization. In particular, analysis has considered whether vulnerabilities are the same as or different to those for offline victimization and whether these different vulnerabilities are related to the impact of the grooming and abuse on victims (see Whittle, Hamilton-Giachritsis, & Beech [32]).

4.2. Limitations of This Research

There are several limitations of this study that must be considered when interpreting results. Only one interview session was scheduled with each victim and while all possible attempts to achieve and maintain rapport were made, it is possible that the victims may have held back information on the basis of not knowing the interviewer. This is likely to be particularly relevant with the two male participants, who generally provided less information. It is possible that the male victims felt less comfortable discussing the offense generally or that it was specifically due to having a female interviewer. As a result of this, the finding that they were less enmeshed in the relationship is tentative; as it is possible they did not wish to share the extent of their feelings in interview.

Another limitation is that the length of time between the offense and the interview varied between participants, thus victims are likely to have been in different stages of recovery. Consequentially, the memories and reflections of each participant are likely to vary in quality. In addition, the participants within this sample were selected by professionals who felt their involvement would have, "no detrimental effects for the young person." Therefore, this sample is unlikely to be representative of all victims of online grooming and sexual abuse, given that those who were displaying current psychological difficulties would not have been included. Similarly, the victims were aged between 13 and 18 at the time of interview and at different developmental stages. This is likely to impact on the way in which they recall and interpret their experiences.

Finally, perhaps the main limitation of this study is the relatively small sample size. Due to the qualitative nature of the research, the sample size of eight victims is small and therefore applicability of findings to wider populations is tentative. The authors sought additional participants but encountered difficulties in recruiting further. The diversity in the experiences of the victims may be a reflection of their individual differences (e.g., gender, perception of the relationship, age of the offender, *etc.*); consequentially research which explores victims who are more similar to one another may offer a more robust contribution for that specific group. Further studies could also incorporate a larger sample of victims and compare the themes with those identified in this research. Additionally, studies comparing victim experiences to a wider sample of non-abused counterparts would help explore the links between grooming behaviours and typical adolescent relationship development online.

5. Conclusions

This research supports the notion that online grooming of adolescents is varied and cyclical, involving the abuser adopting and re-adopting a variety of manipulation techniques throughout the process. These techniques may include manipulation through conversation, deception, sexualisation, regular/intense contact, kindness and flattery, erratic temperament/nastiness, grooming others and secrecy which are notably similar to offline offender grooming strategies. Effects these tactics are likely to have on the victims include feelings of familiarity, love trust, confidence boosting, emotional support, excitement, but also, lack of control, confusion, reliance on the offender and distancing from family. Victims who considered themselves enmeshed in the relationship were more likely to tolerate immediately negative effects of the grooming, in the hope of maintaining the relationship and regaining the positive effects. Further research is required, from the perspective of the victims, to gain a deeper knowledge of grooming, what the impact is on the young person and how professionals can better respond to and prevent this form of abuse in the future.

Acknowledgments

The first author of this paper is funded by The University of Birmingham and The Child Exploitation and Online Protection Centre (CEOP) as part of a collaborative studentship. CEOP have approved submission of this paper. Thank you to Elly Farmer and Tom Simmons for reading early drafts of this paper. Thank you also to Joe Sullivan for contributions during the analysis.

Author Contributions

Helen Whittle wrote, conducted and transcribed the research interviews as part of her Ph.D. thesis. Helen was the principal analyst and generated the first draft and subsequent revisions of this paper. Catherine Hamilton-Giachritsis is first supervisor of the Ph.D. Catherine assisted in writing the semi-structured interviews and at various stages during analysis, including providing inter-rater reliability. Catherine also significantly contributed to the writing and re-drafting of this paper. Anthony Beech is second supervisor of the Ph.D. Tony provided feedback during the analysis of the interviews and contributed to re-drafting and editing of this paper.

Conflicts of Interest

The authors declare no conflict of interest.

References

1. Peter Briggs, Walter T. Simon, and Stacy Simonsen. "An exploratory study of internet-initiated sexual offenses and the chat room sex offender: Has the Internet enabled a new typology of sex offender?" *Sexual Abuse: A Journal of Research and Treatment* 23 (2011): 72–91. doi:10.117/1079063210384275.
2. Stefan C. Dombrowski, John W. LeMasney, C. Emmanuel Ahia, and Shannon A. Dickson. "Protecting children from online sexual predators: Technical, psychoeducational, and legal considerations." *Professional Psychology: Research and Practice* 35 (2004): 65–73. doi:10.1037/0735.
3. Jennie G. Noll, Chad E. Shenk, Jaclyn E. Barnes, and Katherine J. Haralson. "Association of maltreatment with high-risk internet behaviors and offline encounters." *Pediatrics* 131 (2013): 510–17. doi:10.1542/peds.2012-1281.
4. Helen Whittle, Catherine Hamilton-Giachritsis, Anthony Beech, and Guy Collings. "A review of online grooming: characteristics and concerns." *Aggression and Violent Behavior* 18 (2013): 62–70. doi:10.106/j.avb.2012.09.003.
5. Yvonne Jewkes, and Maggie Wykes. "Reconstructing the sexual abuse of children: 'Cyber-paeds', panic and power." *Sexualities* 15 (2012): 934–52. doi:10.1177/1363460712459324.
6. Anne-Marie McAlinden. "Setting 'em up': Personal, familial and institutional grooming in the sexual abuse of children." *Social and Legal Studies* 15 (2006): 339–62. doi:10.1177/0964663906066613.
7. Samantha Craven, Sarah Brown, and Elizabeth Gilchrist. "Sexual grooming of children: Review of literature and theoretical considerations." *Journal of Sexual Aggression* 12 (2006): 287–99. doi:10.1080/13552600601069414.

8. Savi Report. "Sexual Abuse and Violence in Ireland, a national study of Irish experiences, beliefs and attitudes concerning sexual violence." Available online: http://www.drcc.ie/wp-content/uploads/2011/03/SAVI_Revisited.pdf (accessed on 30 May 2012).
9. Child Exploitation and Online Protection Centre. "Annual Review 2009–2010." Available online: http://ceop.police.uk/Documents/CEOP_AnnualReview_09-10.pdf (accessed on 20 March 2013).
10. Maria Ospina, Christa Hartstall, and Liz Dennet. "Sexual exploitation of children and youth over the internet: A rapid review of the scientific literature." Available online: http://www.ihe.ca/documents/Online%20Sexual%20Exploitation.pdf (accessed on 2 May 2012).
11. Janis Wolak, Kimberly J. Mitchell, and David Finkelhor. "Online victimisation of youth: Five years later." Available online: http://www.missingkids.com/en_US/publications/NC167.pdf (accessed on 4 May 2012).
12. David Finkelhor, Kimberly J. Mitchell, and Janis Wolak. "Online victimization: A report on the nation's youth." Available online: http://www.missingkids.com/en_US/publications/NC62.pdf (accessed on 5 May 2011).
13. Helen C. Whittle, Catherine E. Hamilton-Giachritsis, Daz Bishopp, and Anthony R. Beech. "Young people's behavior online: The impact of their lives offline." submitted to *Psychological Science*, 2014.
14. Brå (The Swedish National Council for Crime Prevention). "Vuxnas Sexuella Kontakter med Barn via Internet [Adults' Sexual Contact with Children Online]." Available online: http://www.google.co.uk/url?sa=t&rct=j&q=&esrc=s&source=web&cd=1&cad=rja&uact=8&ved=0CCAQFjAA&url=http%3A%2F%2Fwww.eucpn.org%2Fdownload%2F%3Ffile%3Dbra_online_sexual_solicitation_children.pdf%26type%3D8&ei=i9nkU8GTOYfG7Aa-64C4Bw&usg=AFQjCNH_xamrNxaevHukMgD_PQECOXLsoQ (accessed on 4 May 2012).
15. Lucy Berliner, and Jon R. Conte. "The process of victimization: The victims' perspective." *Child Abuse and Neglect* 14 (1990): 29–40. doi:10.1016/0145-2134(90)90078-8.
16. Faye Mishna, Alan McLuckie, and Michael Saini. "Real-world dangers in an online reality: A qualitative study examining online relationships and cyber abuse." Available online: http://icbtt.arizona.edu/sites/default/files/Mishna,_McLuckie,_&_Saini_Social_Work_Research_KHP_Cyber_Abuse_0.pdf (accessed on 4 May 2012).
17. Kimberly J. Mitchell, David Finkelhor, and Janis Wolak. "The Internet and family and acquaintance sexual abuse." *Child Maltreatment* 10 (2005): 49–60. doi:10.1177/1077559504271917.
18. Rachel O'Connell. "A typology of cyber sexploitation and online grooming practices." Available online: http://www.uclan.ac.uk/host/cru/docs/cru010.pdf (accessed on 24 May 2011).
19. Stephen Webster, Julia Davidson, Antonia Bifulco, Petter Gottschalk, Vincenzo Caretti, Thierry Pham, Julie Grove-Hills, Caroline Turley, Charlotte Tompkins, Stefano Ciulla, and *et al.* "European Online Grooming Project Final Report." Available online: http://www.european-online-grooming-project.com/ (accessed on 21 April 2012).

20. Rebecca Williams, Ian A. Elliott, and Anthony R. Beech. "Identifying sexual grooming themes used by internet sex offenders." *Deviant Behavior* 34 (2013): 135–52. doi:10.1080/01639625.2012.707550.
21. L. Webb, Jackie Craissati, and S. Keen. "Characteristics of internet child pornography offenders: A comparison with child molesters." *Sexual Abuse: A Journal of Research and Treatment* 19 (2007): 449–65. doi:10.1007/s11194-007-9063-2.
22. Janis Wolak, David Finkelhor, Kimberly J. Mitchell, and Michele L. Ybarra. "Online 'predators' and their victims: Myths, realities and implications for prevention and treatment." *American Psychologist* 63 (2008): 111–28. doi:10.1037/0003-066X.63.2.11.
23. Ethel Quayle, Linda Jonsson, and Lars-Gunnar Lööf. "Online behavior related to child sexual abuse: Interviews with affected young people." Available online: http://www.childcentre.info/robert/public/Interviews_with_affected_young_people.pdf (accessed on 1 February 2014).
24. Immy Holloway, and Les Todres. "The status of method: Flexibility, consistency and coherence." *Qualitative Research* 3 (2003): 345–57. doi:10.1177/14687941030330004.
25. Virginia Braun, and Victoria Clarke. "Using thematic analysis in psychology." *Qualitative Research in Psychology* 3 (2006): 77–101. doi:10.1191/1478088706qp063oa.
26. Lisa M. Jones, Kimberly J. Mitchell, and David Finkelhor. "Trends in youth internet victimization: Findings from three youth internet safety surveys 2000–2010." *Journal of Adolescent Health* 50 (2012): 179–86. doi:10.1016/j.jadohealth.2011.09.015
27. Lisa M. Jones, Kimberly J. Mitchell, and David Finkelhor. "Online harassment in context: Trends from three internet safety surveys (2000, 2005, 2010)." *Psychology of Violence* 3 (2013): 53–69. doi:10.1037/a0030309.
28. Joe Sullivan. "Professionals who sexually abuse the children with whom they work." Ph.D. Dissertation, University of Birmingham, 2009.
29. Samantha Craven, Sarah Brown, and Elizabeth Gilchrist. "Current responses to sexual grooming: Implication for prevention." *Howard Journal of Criminal Justice* 46 (2007): 60–71. doi:10.1111/j.1468-2311.2007.00454.x.
30. Janis Wolak, David Finkelhor, and Kimberly Mitchell. "Internet-initiated sex crimes against minors: Implications for prevention based on findings from a national study." *Journal of Adolescent Health* 35 (2004): e11–20. doi:10.1016/j.jadohealth.2004.05.006.
31. Kimberly J. Mitchell, David Finkelhor, and Janis Wolak. "Youth internet users at risk for the most serious online sexual solicitations." *American Journal of Preventative Medicine* 32 (2007): 532–37. doi:10.1016/j.amepre.2007.02.001.
32. Helen C. Whittle, Catherine E. Hamilton-Giachritsis, and Anthony R. Beech. Victims' voices: The impact of online grooming and sexual abuse. *Universal Journal of Psychology* 1 (2013): 59–71.

The Australian Royal Commission into Institutional Responses to Child Sexual Abuse: Dreaming of Child Safe Organisations?

William Budiselik, Frances Crawford and Donna Chung

Abstract: On 12 November 2012 the then Australian Prime Minister Julia Gillard announced she was recommending to the Governor General the establishment of a Royal Commission into Institutional Responses to Child Sexual Abuse. Following inquiries in Australia and elsewhere much is already known about institutional and inter-institutional child protection failures and what is required to address them. That Australia's national government has pursued another abuse inquiry with terms of reference limited to institution-based (excluding the family) sexual abuse is of interest given the lack of political will to enact previous findings and recommendations. This article examines the background to the Government's announcement, the Commission's terms of reference and some of its settings, and literature on the nature of royal commissions across time and place. After the lack of success in implementing the recommendations of previous inquiries into how to better protect Australia's children, the question is: how will this Royal Commission contribute to Australian child protection and safety? Will the overwhelming public support generated by "truth speaking to power" in calling for this inquiry translate into action?

Reprinted from *Soc. Sci.* Cite as: Budiselik, W.; Crawford, F.; Chung, D. The Australian Royal Commission into Institutional Responses to Child Sexual Abuse: Dreaming of Child Safe Organisations? *Soc. Sci.* **2014**, *3*, 565–583.

1. Introduction

The sexual abuse of children is widely regarded as one of the most morally unacceptable forms of (mainly male) adult human behaviour. The public "outings" of abusers over the past 20 or so years of those once regarded as pillars of the community—clergymen, police and judicial officers, entertainers, teachers, sporting coaches, youth workers and the like—took the public by surprise for two reasons: it contradicted community expectations about who it thought sexually abused children and the extent of the abuse. Due to victims and their supporters speaking out, increased research and professional interventions, and greater numbers of investigative journalists' media reports, the prevalence and nature of sexual abuse of children is now better understood but still shocking to the community [1]. In this article we critically examine the most recent response to child sexual abuse that is taking place involving Australian institutions. Acknowledging the importance of "truth speaking to power" in the activities leading to the government's decision to hold this royal commission, our examination is underpinned by a concern about the importance of implementing recommendations to bring about change along with redress for the past. The evidence is that knowledge generated through previous inquiries has failed to be translated into practice, often through a lack of political and populist commitment to the resourcing protecting children requires. In an era of user pays who are the users of protected children?

2. The Australian Royal Commission into Institutional Responses to Child Sexual Abuse

On 19 November 2012, a week after the Australian Prime Minister's announced intention to establish a Royal Commission into Institutional Responses to Child Sexual Abuse (the Commission), the Commission's secretariat released a consultation paper seeking input from interested individuals and organisations concerning "the arrangements for the establishment of the Royal Commission, including the scope ... the form ... the number and qualifications of Royal Commissioner/s and the reporting timetable" [2]. The response deadline of 26 November 2012 betrayed the pressure on those designing the Commission and preparing its budget. The Commission's terms of reference were presented on 15 January 2013 and Justice Peter McClellan from the New South Wales Supreme Court of Appeal was appointed the Commission's Chair.

The Commission's terms of reference require the royal commissioners to inquire into and report on: what institutions and governments should do to better protect children against child sexual abuse and related matters in *institutional contexts* in the future;

a what institutions and governments should do to achieve best practice in encouraging the reporting of, and responding to reports or information about, allegations, incidents or risks of child sexual abuse and related matters in *institutional contexts*;

b what should be done to eliminate or reduce impediments that currently exist for responding appropriately to child sexual abuse and related matters in *institutional contexts*, including addressing failures in, and impediments to, reporting, investigating and responding to allegations and incidents of abuse;

c what institutions and governments should do to address, or alleviate the impact of, past and future child sexual abuse and related matters in *institutional contexts*, including, in particular, in ensuring justice for victims through the provision of redress by institutions, processes for referral for investigation and prosecution and support services (emphases added) [3].

In our opinion, the time pressure on those designing the Commission was driven more by ephemeral political forces and less associated with the Australian Government's desire to establish a considered response to past abuse and to prevent it in the future. An appropriation of $434,000,000 (US$403,000,000) was granted for the Commission's operation. Other costs associated with agency effort (government and non-government) and securing professional advice and legal representation are not known, in part because non-government entities, such as the Catholic Church, are not obligated to advise its members or the public of such expenditure.

This considerable expenditure of money and human resources raises the question of whether these could have been better used to further a broad Australian child protection and abuse response agenda and services, rather than the re-examination of issues associated with past institution-based child sexual abuse. It remains to be seen whether the Commission is an opportunity lost or whether it delivers reforms commensurate with Australia's investment in it.

3. What Led to the Establishment of the Commission?

Events leading to the Australian Government's decision to establish the Commission are numerous and complex. There was both community organising and media campaigning to raise public consciousness of the issue. These were driven by continuing grass roots outrage at the sexual abuse of children and the treatment of the abused who complained as adults. In this complexity two champions stand out: Hetty Johnston and Joanne McCarthy. Johnston established Bravehearts in 1997 in Queensland as a community-based initiative to "educate, empower and protect Australian kids from sexual assault" and "move this once taboo subject into the light" [4]. In 2005 and 2012 Johnston was an author of papers, with Carol Ronken, about the need for a royal commission, refuting all arguments that had circulated against the idea [5,6]. McCarthy was recognized in 2013 with the top Australian journalism award for stories that helped spark the Commission [7]. Amplifying this groundwork was one specific catalyst for the Government's announcement: Detective Chief Inspector Peter Fox's open letter in the *Newcastle Herald* on 8 November 2012 to New South Wales' Premier Barry O'Farrell calling for a royal commission into the Catholic Church's cover-up of sexual abuse. Part of Fox's letter read:

> I have seen the worst society can dredge up, particularly the evil of paedophilia within the Catholic Church… Many police are frustrated by this sinister behaviour… The whole system needs to be exposed; the clergy covering up these crimes must to be brought to justice and the network protecting paedophile priests dismantled. There should be no place for evil or its guardians to hide… Many priests don't want a royal commission nor does the hierarchy of the church, but God knows we need one [8].

It seems Fox's status as a serving New South Wales' police officer warranted a response from the New South Wales Premier: "One cannot hear allegations from someone with the stature of Detective Chief Inspector Peter Fox and do nothing". ([9], pp. 16, 684) On 9 November 2012 the then Premier O'Farrell announced his intention to establish the "Special Commission of Inquiry into matters relating to the Police investigation of certain child sexual abuse allegations in the Catholic Diocese of Maitland Newcastle" (the Special Commission). The Special Commission established on 21 November 2012 and headed by Margaret Cunneen SC had two terms of reference: to establish whether in relation to child sexual abuse the Catholic Church hindered or obstructed, failed to report or discouraged witnesses and the circumstances in which Fox was asked to cease investigating church-based sexual abuse in the Newcastle–Maitland region of New South Wales [10].

When Tony Jones, the Australian Broadcasting Commission's *Lateline* host, tested Fox about various claims, including that "the church covers up, silences victims, hinders police investigations, alerts offenders, destroys evidence and moves priests to protect the good name of the church", Fox replied:

> Oh, not only do I have evidence, it's irrefutable… The greatest frustration is that there is so much power and organisation *behind the scenes* (emphasis added) that police don't have the powers to be able to go in and seize documents and have them disclose things to us [11].

Fox's letter to Premier O'Farrell is straightforward: The target the Catholic Church, not only child sex offenders in the Catholic Church who are abusing children, but the "organisation" that operates "behind the scenes" to protect them.

While Fox's letter was addressed to a state premier, and despite the national government's decision not to accede to earlier calls for a royal commission from victims and victims' advocacy groups [6], this call for a royal commission was taken up nationally. In the days following the release of his letter, a Fairfax Nielsen poll suggested that 95% of Australians supported a royal commission (cited in [12], p. 8).

On 26 November 2012 at the conclusion of the consultation period Australia's then Attorney General, Nicola Roxon, advised:

> The commission needs to focus on systemic issues of child sexual abuse to make sure that recommendations can be implemented in a timely manner. It is very clear that the community wants the commission and all governments across Australia to do everything we can to make sure what happened in the past is never allowed to happen again ([13], pp. 13, 146).

Relevantly, the consultation paper had noted:

> While it is important that the Royal Commission form its own opinions and recommendations, there is a large body of work already on hand from recent inquiries. The Terms of Reference for the Commission can request that this work be taken into account, both to ensure that the relevant findings, recommendations and responses are considered as well as to ensure that survivors who have already shared their stories in these inquiries do not need to do so again if they do not want to [2].

The Commission's terms of reference accommodated this concern by including in its Letters Patent a direction for the Commission to take (or not take) action or consider.

> the need to establish appropriate arrangements in relation to current and previous inquiries, in Australia and elsewhere, for evidence and information to be shared with you in ways consistent with relevant obligations so that the work of those inquiries, including, with any necessary consents, the testimony of witnesses, can be taken into account by you in a way that avoids unnecessary duplication, improves efficiency and avoids unnecessary trauma to witnesses [3].

4. The Sexual Abuse of Children and Moral Panic

A number of authors and media analysts have argued that moral panics about childhood sexual abuse in their most recent iteration during the past 20 or so years have been largely due to media reporting [14,15]. In contrast, professionals in this area of work suggest that it is not so much a moral panic but that the abuse is now spoken about and better understood even if still taboo. The moral panic which is induced around the sexual violation of children's bodies evokes a strong reaction by the public to which politicians need to be seen to be doing something—either stopping its occurrence in the future and/or supporting the seeking of justice for those abused and the punishment of its perpetrators. Responses have been largely in the areas of legal and policy changes including changes to processes for giving evidence and stricter gatekeeping of people working with children. Whilst these changes have been welcomed, there remains a community stigma associated with being a victim of such abuse or of being associated with or identified as a perpetrator of child sexual abuse [14]. Governments operate to stop and redress childhood sexual abuse within a highly sensitive political environment of hyper moral judgment about those committing the crimes and their representatives, alongside an equally worried public concerned with having legal systems so robust that nobody is ever accused of such abuse "unfairly" due to the highly stigmatized identity it represents. The nature of these criminal acts is such that they often occur without witnesses or other evidence and victims are intimidated into silence; therefore the capacity of legal system to deal with such crimes is particularly challenged. It is within this socio-political context that the current Australian inquiry is taking place.

5. On the Nature of Royal Commissions

The Australian Government's decision to initiate a royal commission symbolically signals the seriousness of the problem of children being sexually abused within institutions. Royal commissions are traditional in British Commonwealth countries as a well-endowed institution at arms-length from government, authorised to draft a plan to address for the long-term a publically problematic issue [16]. Australia has conducted 132 royal commissions since federation with more held at state level [17]. The literature from the United Kingdom (UK), Canada and New Zealand as well as Australia suggests royal commissions can serve many purposes and these are not always under the control of those commissioning them. Thomas and Field ([18], p. 14) analysed the 1991 UK Royal Commission on Criminal Justice. The authors describe this Royal Commission as an institution for crisis management in that "the terms of reference may be so written as to mute the debate by changing the focus of attention". They argue the UK government was able to prioritise the recommendations to suit their ideological agenda, ignoring the generating concern and ensuring "the parade of pluralist reasoned debate (was) replaced by the parade of ideological populism" ([18], p. 160).

In contrast, Inwood [16] argues that a royal commission can be a vehicle for a transformative moment in a nation. The focus of the Royal Commission analysed by Inwood was concerned with deciding the agenda for the Canadian political economy. This Royal Commission operated as a site for the rigorous and regulated interplay of ideas, institutions and interests. Research was open and transparent and included the active canvassing of submissions from the public. Inwood ([16], pp. 10–11) identifies three factors in the possibility of transformative moments arising out of royal commissions. The first lies in "political viability, economic viability and political and bureaucratic leadership". In the end decision makers need to be swayed to a course of action. The second revolves around the concept of credibility and leverage to action. "Who says something is sometimes more important than how many say it". The final factor shared by transformative royal commissions is that ensuing "policies must mobilise support from coalitions of actors upon whose support, electoral and financial, elected politicians depend".

A process of collective learning through argument and persuasion is the description that Owens and Rayner [19] arrive at in analysing the UK continuing Royal Commission on Environmental

Pollution. Started in the 1960s it operates as a knowledge broker in leveraging emerging research on environmental matters and removing difficult decisions for the state from the public arena. Such brokerage is always about the negotiation and performance of power in situ and in regard to the environment the credibility of scientific knowledge was an instrument to be wielded for change. The authors conclude:

> "Knowledge always matters but has most effect when it is skilfully framed to resonate in the climate of the day, originates from or is mediated by a trusted source, and is deployed in a timely manner or persistently over time, until conditions converge into a situation ripe for change" ([19], p. 18).

In contrast, an analysis of the 2001 New Zealand Royal Commission into the Genetic Modification of Crops concludes that the language of science in an era of neoliberalism and marketisation can be used to silence active participation in democracy by citizens concerned as to the limits of scientific certainty ([20], p. 585). Goven [20] queries this Royal Commission's suggestion that citizens interested in science should not express doubts unless they have evidence from appropriately funded and conducted research projects. The author argues that the Commission accepts "an idealised science innocent of power relations (and) the current role of commercial interests in research and development in the biosciences. In this way (idealised) science acts as a vector through which economic liberalism (or neoliberalism) trumps democracy".

All of these analyses have potential relevance for the current Commission. Also relevant is a much earlier piece of work. Biskup [21] in his classic look at "The Royal Commission that never was" unveils some further dynamics as to the workings of royal commissions. The topic under consideration to be referred to a royal commission in 1938 was the relationship between the State of Western Australia and church missions. This focus emerged from considerable public and media concern in response to evidence of abuse on missions including the sexual abuse of children. In bringing the abuse to light a Minister in Western Australia's government stated at the time:

> the natives [Aboriginal Australians] are first and foremost a charge upon the State, whoever may subsequently be delegated more directly to handle them, and our duty is to ensure that the job is efficiently undertaken by those best qualified to do so ([21], pp. 89–90).

This language captures a significant difference to current discourse in a marketised, privatised and commodified society where services are outsourced and a provider is responsible for meeting specified pre-determined quality standards. In 1938, alongside the discourse of state responsibility there was also a taken-for-granted acceptance of the vulnerability of Aboriginal people including their children. While the public expressed great concern at the stories of abuse in church-run missions, power was negotiated behind the scenes between the government and its departments, churches and pastoralist power holders. Despite many meetings and much media talk of calling a royal commission it never evolved. An editorial in *The West Australian* newspaper of 17 February 1939 commented after a large public conference on the issue: "It is good to see a number of people getting excited about the matter. The doubt is whether they got excited about the conditions of the (vulnerable) or about their own personal feelings" (cited in [21], p. 108).

This historical event can be viewed from this distance as necessarily steeped in colonialism, racism, religion and political ideology. At the time however there were concerned citizens able to name child sexual abuse and other forms of abuse. They proved not able to organise to move to action against those with investment in the status quo.

More recently an Inquiry (not a royal commission) for the Northern Territory Government documented extensive crimes of child sexual abuse in that jurisdiction [22]. This time there was a swift and organised response at the national level. Then Prime Minister John Howard used his federal powers to intervene in the governance of the Territory. As Fawcett and Hanlon [23] describe, the emotion of outrage at child sexual abuse was used to justify widespread intervention, much of which had neither direct link to established knowledge in child protection nor impact on the incidence of these crimes. Certainly the timing and nature of this intervention met few of the factors necessary for a transformative moment in addressing this problem. The lack of open collaboration in planning a response meant an ongoing lack of coordinated child protection in the Northern Territory.

Prasser identifies a changing pattern in the use and nature of Australian royal commissions since the 1970s [24]. This change has particularly been in the balance between inquisitorial forms investigating publically unacceptable incidents and issues, and advisory forms investigating major policy areas like health. There has been an increasing use of royal commissions to address what are perceived to be political and ideological issues but overall "Commonwealth Coalition governments have a lower rate of appointing royal commissions in relation to their length of time in office" ([24], p. 29). Certainly John Howard, a former Coalition Prime Minister, was clear in his rejection of a royal commission into child abuse in 2003 when he stated: "I would rather spend the $60 million to $100 million involved in a royal commission on further intervention (in child care) than I would on lining the pockets of lawyers" (cited in [24], p. 43). It is arguable that Howard acted on these beliefs when he commissioned the Northern Territory National Emergency Response in 2007 [23].

Independence is a valued characteristic of royal commissions but there is no certainty that the knowledge on an issue so generated will guide the actions of government. As Prasser notes, governments establish royal commissions for "politically expedient reasons such as to show concern about an issue, give an illusion of action, show responsiveness to a problem, co-opt critics, reduce opposition, delay decision-making and reassert control of the policy agenda" ([24], p. 34).

Royal commissions, as a means of identifying the extent, dynamics and effects of a problem, typically offer robust insights and recommendations, which are necessarily comprehensive, in order to address complex problems. The difficulty or often disappointment lies post-commission when recommendations are not acted on, not implemented as envisaged or a small number of recommendations are acted on which do not comprehensively remedy the problem into the future. The present Commission will report to an administration different from the one which appointed it. That there is a possible "disconnect" between the administration in power and the Commission is a further confounding factor in attempting to discern the Commission's likely efficacy. It makes for uncertainty both in terms of achieving redress for those bearing witness as to their abuse and for the major implementation of any changes designed to make children safer from child sexual abuse in the future.

6. Current and Previous Inquiries

It is beyond the scope of this article to comprehensively present the large number of relevant previous and current inquiries, and their recommendations germane to the current Commission. Consideration of all relevant inquiries is difficult because not all are reported publicly, and a national register of relevant inquiries into matters related to child protection and child abuse does not exist. Indeed, it is likely some are held as confidential documents in various organisations.

The Australian Institute of Family Studies provided to the Commission a list of 23 inquiries conducted in the last decade in Ireland, the United Kingdom, Canada and New Zealand excluding reviews and reports into individual deaths or government annual reports into child deaths [25]. The Australian Institute of Health and Welfare's (AIHW) 2011/2012 report into child protection provides a list of 16 Australian state and territory child protection inquiries conducted in the "past few years" ([26], p. 136).

Since the AIHW report provided its list of inquiries from the "past few years", Victoria's "Betrayal of Trust: Inquiry into the handling of child abuse by religious and other non-government organizations" (Victorian Betrayal of Trust Inquiry) [27] has been completed and the New South Wales Special Commission [5] reported on 31 May 2014. In Western Australia in September 2012 a relevant inquiry report entitled "St Andrew's Hostel Katanning: How the system and society failed our children" [28] was provided to the Western Australian Parliament by a former president of the Western Australian Children's Court, Peter Blaxell.

In addition to these inquiries there are inquiries conducted by organisations themselves, for example, Olsson and Chung's "Report of the board of inquiry: Into the handling of claims of sexual abuse and misconduct within the Anglican diocese of Adelaide" [29] established by the Synod of the Diocese of Adelaide in 2003, and Parkinson, Oates and Jayakody's "Study of reported child sexual abuse in the Anglican Church" [30]. Commissioned by the Church's Professional Standards Commission, this latter study aimed to examine abuse reports in the Australian Anglican church. The authors reported that while all 23 diocese were invited to participate in the research, three declined ([30], p. 13).

Last, given the focus of the current Commission is on past sexual abuse, earlier inquiries conducted at the time are relevant, as are Government and organisational responses to recommendations.

7. Recommendations of Earlier Inquiries

In 2009, a Senate Committee (the Committee) report entitled "Lost Innocents and Forgotten Australians Revisited" [31] examined the responses of Australia's governments (federal, state and territory) to two earlier federal government inquiries, one about child migrants [32] and the second about children who had experienced institutional or out-of-home care [33]. The Committee's conclusion on revisiting the impact of these inquiries was "the responses to the recommendations of earlier inquiries by the Commonwealth and State governments, the churches and agencies has been variable…in other areas progress is slow or no action has been taken" ([31], p. 6).

In reviewing these earlier inquiries the Committee reconsidered the Forgotten Australians inquiry recommendation that the government consider initiating a "narrowly conceived" royal commission of "short duration" into state, charitable and church-run institutions and out-of-home care if within a period charitable and church-run institutions had failed to open their files and premises and provide full cooperation to authorities to investigate the nature and extent of *criminal assault, sexual assault* and report on *past criminal practice* and *persons suspected of having committed crimes against children in care* (emphases added) ([31], p. 65). Australia's federal and state governments did not favour this recommendation at that time ([31], p. 69).

In short, past inquiries have commonly found that there have been various forms of assault and abuse committed against children by those in positions of power over others. These forms of abuse involved organised groups of perpetrators in some organisations and in other areas there were instances of individuals using their position to assault and silence victims without the systematic involvement of others. Some key common issues stand out: those victims disclosing to authorities during or closely following the abuse were often not believed and their characters were often maligned leaving them in a worse position and the perpetrator without scrutiny. The reputation of the organisations and individuals involved often drove the apparent lack of response and disparagement of whistleblowers. Consequently, where allegations were made, organisational representatives did not consistently—or in some cases ever—refer the allegations to the police for investigation. Therefore many recommendations of past inquiries focused on the organisational cultures, values and lack of transparency that enabled these abusive situations to continue. Another aspect noted is the adversarial role of lawyers and their recommendations for organizational risk avoidance that served to dissuade organisational representatives speaking out about abusive or suspected abusive individuals and the organisation. Recommendations generally include changes to organisational practices to become more accountable and transparent within the organisation and in working with the relevant authorities when abuse is disclosed and to prevent future abuse.

In 2009 the Committee canvassed arguments for and against a royal commission and concluded against establishing one:

> The Committee's conclusion was ultimately based on an assessment of the likely success of a Royal Commission in achieving successful exposure and prosecution of perpetrators of criminal acts. The Committee senses that there may be unrealistic expectations held by many as to the outcome of a Royal Commission. Despite the wider powers of royal commissions, the Committee considers that any such inquiry would face the same barriers to success as outlined above in relation to judicial inquiries, and accordingly would be unlikely to produce outcomes that would justify the significant expenditure of both time and finances ([31], p. 225).

The Committee then sensed there might be unrealistic expectations about the outcomes of such a royal commission. The current Commissioners are struggling to respond to the large number of people wishing to come forward and individually meet with them. By April 2014, Justice McClellan advised the community "the Commissioners have held 1426 private sessions… received 1328 written accounts from survivors or their family and friends…1065 people in the queue awaiting a session… receive about 40 requests for a private session each week". He estimated by the end of

2015 there may be 2000 people who will have requested a private session which could not be accommodated [34].

The Committee's consideration may have also been influenced by the reduction of the number of children in traditional forms of institutional/residential care: a social issue on a trajectory to fade with time.

> The number of children in institutional/residential care has decreased markedly from approximately 27,000 in 1954 to less than 2000 currently. Most states and territories have phased out large institutions, with the majority of residential care now provided in small facilities caring for three to eight children. ([31], p. 62).

Today, in Australia, children in out-of-home care and other forms of care (e.g., day care) are cared for in ways not resembling the institutions that existed through to the last quarter of the twentieth century: "The majority of children (93%) in out-of-home care at 30 June 2012 were in home-based care—44% in foster care, 47% in relative/kinship care and 2% in other types of home-based care" ([25], p. 38). This raises the critical question of whether the resources could have been better used trying to implement past recommendations that have been consistently identified and partially implemented. The lack of thorough implementation can be attributed to a few factors including the obvious issue of financial cost, trying to engage and coordinate multiple jurisdictions and authorities, and a less tangible cultural aspect that child sexual abuse is still thought of by some as a rare occurrence not requiring this level of attention and investment.

8. Systemic Failures and the Protection of Church Located Abusers

The systemic problems in addressing church located child abuse have long been raised and reported in Australia. In the 1990s the New South Wales' Royal Commission into the New South Wales Police Service (the Wood Royal Commission) [35] in part addressed the issue of child sexual abuse and Australian churches. Commissioner Justice James Wood identified the problem as the substantial incidence of sexual abuse involving those associated with churches. He wrote that the failure to properly investigate allegations or pursue allegations through the courts was "suggestive of either protection or failure on the part of the official agencies involved to exercise their powers impartially" ([35], p. 991). Fox's assertion in November 2012, that "power and organisation behind the (Church) scenes" blocks effective action, is consistent with Wood's earlier assessment.

9. Working with Children Checks

In light of the Wood Royal Commission, Australia's (state and territory) community services ministers agreed to implement safety screening of persons employed in a paid or voluntary capacity in services for children. Characteristic of Australian federalism, each state and territory has, since Wood's report, developed different legislation, procedures and requirements to screen its working with children workforce ([36], p. 350).

Australia's peak intergovernmental forum, the Council of Australian Governments (COAG), promotes reforms of national significance and those requiring inter-jurisdictional coordination. In April 2009 COAG released its "National Framework for Protecting Australia's Children

2009–2020" (the national framework) [37]. The national framework announced that all Australian governments had endorsed a long-term approach to child protection. The national framework report emphasised a shift towards a "public health" model of child protection ([37], p. 6). Stated aims of the national framework included developing a "nationally consistent approach to working with children checks and child safe organisations across jurisdictions" ([37], p. 14).

In 2011, an update was provided by the state and territory officers responsible for achieving "a nationally consistent approach" to working with children checks:

> Harmonisation of state and territory legislation would require substantial investment of resources to bring the data and related information management mechanisms into line. *Current fiscal constraints make additional financial commitments untenable as part of an agile response* (emphasis added). There is insufficient evidence to inform a best practice screening model [38].

Australian states and territories do not have a common child workforce checking process. State and territory child protection authorities do not have mechanisms in place to systematically exchange information about persons believed responsible for child abuse. That Australia does not have a national approach to screening its working with children workforce seems in part to be the result of "fiscal constraints". At the present time there is no indication of any future commitment to such national efforts.

10. The Australian Catholic Church, Cardinal Pell and the Ellis Defence

In response to demands for inquiries and commissions into the Catholic Church, its most senior Australian representative, Cardinal George Pell, positioned the Catholic Church in the following way:

> If there was need for another general inquiry it should be wide ranging, covering not only the Catholic Church but all religions and charities, and not only non-government organisations but government organisations also. I cannot see the need for a state-wide Royal Commission at this time but if there was one the Catholic Church authorities would cooperate fully [39].

Pell's testimony to the Commission has been widely reported in the Australian press. Part of Pell's testimony and that which is most widely reported related to a 2007 case, *Trustees of the Roman Catholic Church v Ellis & Anor* (2007) NSWCA 117 (the Ellis case) and the Church's use of the so called "Ellis defence", which the authors understand to mean the Catholic Church is not liable for the criminal activity of its clergy. This is largely a legalistic argument by the Catholic Church not to take responsibility for abuse by its clergy. It was viewed publicly as yet another example of an abuse victim seeking justice and being denied it by the Church.

Victoria's Betrayal of Trust inquiry report dealt with the issues raised in the Ellis case in the following terms:

> The Committee recommends that the Victorian Government consider requiring organisations it funds or provides with tax exemptions and other entitlements to be

incorporated and adequately insured. It also suggests that the Victorian Government work with the Australian Government to require religious and other non-government organisations that engage with children to adopt incorporated legal structures. ([27], p. xxxix).

11. Child Safe Institutions: A Worthy Aspiration for ever Vigilant Organisations

The current Commission's activities are broadly delimited by the meanings of the word *institution* and the phrase *institutional context*. In the child welfare literature "institutional abuse", a phrase used since the early 1980s, is much broader than sexual abuse and those behaviours related to it. For example, Gil defines institutional child abuse as when a system is "detrimental to a child's health, safety, or emotional and physical well-being or in any way exploits or violates a child's basic rights" [40].

"Institution" and "institutional context" are defined in the Commission's Letters Patent [3]:

(institution) means any public or private body, agency, association, club, institution, organisation or other entity or group of entities of any kind (whether incorporated or unincorporated), and however described, and:

i. includes, for example, an entity or group of entities (including an entity or group of entities that no longer exists) that provides, or has at any time provided, activities, facilities, programs or services of any kind that provide the means through which adults have contact with children, including through their families; and
ii. does not include the family.

institutional context: child sexual abuse happens in an *institutional context* if, for example:

a. it happens on premises of an institution, where activities of an institution take place, or in connection with the activities of an institution; or
b. it is engaged in by an official of an institution in circumstances (including circumstances involving settings not directly controlled by the institution) where you consider that the institution has, or its activities have, created, facilitated, increased, or in any way contributed to, (whether by act or omission) the risk of child sexual abuse or the circumstances or conditions giving rise to that risk; or
c. it happens in any other circumstances where you consider that an institution is, or should be treated as being, responsible for adults having contact with children.

The Commission's issue paper "Child Safe Institutions" uses interchangeably the phrase "child safe institutions" and "child safe organizations", while emphasising it is concerned about child sexual abuse in an institutional context.

In this paper, the first question posed by the Commission assumes the possibility of creating a "child safe organisation":

Of particular interest to the Royal Commission is:

The essential elements of establishing a "child safe organization" that protects children from sexual abuse in an institutional context. In particular, are there core strategies that should be present and others that are less critical?

The question is premised on a (comforting) belief that a child safe organisation is achievable rather than aspirational. To reinforce the Commission's presumption and to assist those making submissions, a number of resources are provided that set out various child safe frameworks and checklists. Unfortunately, this certainty of child safe organisations cannot be guaranteed to be attained and maintained. Organisations can be more or less safe and unsafe. Organisations that are safer have mechanisms to demonstrate how they are not "unsafe" and provide avenues to facilitate the reporting and addressing of anything that is unsafe. At its most cynical, working towards a child safe organisation can be a risk management strategy to protect the organisation and its workers by denying children the opportunity for development associated with manageable risk.

That a child safe organisation is an aspiration that is not achievable might seem to some a trite distinction. Arguably, it is an important distinction to those shaping the Australian community's response to these issues. To offer solace to parents and others interested in child welfare by encouraging a belief that an organisation is capable of being made safe is to suggest certainty is possible. Rather, this territory requires their constant vigilance and their acceptance of limits to certainty as to what is happening to children. The private nature of much abuse perpetrated and the silencing tactics of abusers means there will not be "full information" available. Use of the term "best practice" in the Commission's terms of reference works to silence concerns about uncertainty by suggesting that knowledge to control the incidence of child sexual abuse in institutional care exists and is both identifiable and applicable. It promotes the perception that continuing risks to children are measurable and manageable through instruments such as insurance.

Consider the National Disability Service's response to the issues raised by the Commission in respect of services to children with disability:

> (In some cases) providers have unique access to people's home environments… Out-of-home care (including respite) is a high-risk category. Children in these services may have heightened vulnerability due to factors such as childhood trauma, estrangement from family and instability associated with multiple placements. They are also exposed to situational risk factors associated with extensive periods of unsupervised one-on-one contact with a staff member, or they may be living with other children with the potential to cause harm to them [41].

12. Breaking the Cycle: Well-Funded Inquiries Alongside Poorly Resourced Services

The federal government's assertion that systemic institutionally located abuse is able to be eliminated given sufficient funding is tantalising. In February 2013, the then Attorney-General Mark Dreyfus assured the Australian community that: "our government is going to do everything it can to make sure that what has happened to children in the past is never allowed to happen again…since its very inception we have made clear to the royal commission and we make it clear to the Australian community that this government is determined to ensure the royal commission is adequately resourced" [42]. The Commission's funding enables it to provide appropriately trained staff and support to victims coming forward. For example, Justice McLellan's description of the sensitive way in which people coming forward to the Commission are received describes a level of resourcing not available to services which have attempted to provide responses to past abuse victims: "We have been careful to employ appropriately trained people to answer the telephone when the initial contact is made and we have in place professional counsellors to assist people who come to a session. Recognising that many people will experience a decline in mood following their session we are careful to follow people up to ensure they have adequate support available" [34].

The promise that the Commission can wrestle with sexual abuse and create environments which are safe might be viewed in the context of a statement made in the Victorian Parliament in March 2014 (noting the Victorian Betrayal of Trust inquiry report [27] was delivered in November 2013 and the Commission commenced in January 2013):

> Victoria needs an open, properly resourced inquiry into the allegations that vulnerable children in the care of the state have been groomed and exploited for criminal sexual abuse. The Napthine government will fail its duty of care if it refuses to immediately launch an inquiry into such systemic failures. The inquiry should run in tandem with police investigations into specific offences. This model of coordinated investigations into child sexual abuse was efficient and effective in revealing systemic failures by religious and other non-government organisations.
>
> The government should stop resisting such an inquiry following today's admission by the principal commissioner of the Commission for Children and Young People, Bernie Geary, that the system is "shabby". He also disclosed he was unsurprised by reports that up to 40 children as young as 12 were being exploited while in the care of the state. This is an indictment of the system which must be exposed and fixed as a matter of the utmost urgency ([43], p. 623)

The Youth Affairs Council of Victoria released a statement welcoming the announcement of an inquiry by the Victorian Commissioner for Children and Young People, which advised that the inquiry would look at the sexual exploitation and assaults of children in care by outsiders, and sexual violence committed by other children in care. The statement read: "it (the inquiry) also responds to concerns about vulnerable and traumatized young people being *housed in settings which are understaffed and underfunded* (emphasis added)" [44].

13. Conclusions

On 23 July 2014 the South Australian premier, Jay Weatherill, made a statement to that State's parliament advising it that if allegations under police investigation about child abuse of children in the state's residential care facilities by a *Families SA* employee were proven true, he would initiate a royal commission into them. The details of the allegations are apparently so appalling that the premier is not ruling out barring males from caring positions within the department. Ironically, in South Australia *Families SA* administers paragraph 8A(h)(i) of the *Child Protection Act 1993* (SA), which requires it "to monitor progress towards child safe environments in the government and non-government sectors and to report regularly to the Minister on that subject".

With respect to the Commission, Weatherill said: "I think it is also probably worth mentioning at this juncture that there is an existing royal commission into child sexual abuse which is currently on foot at the federal level. It is more likely than not that this matter could be the subject of interest by that royal commission, but it may well also be the case that there would be a separate need for South Australia to have its own inquiry, having regard to the needs of its own system." [45].

As discussed there are various reasons contributing to the implementation gap concerning the take-up of child protection recommendations by governments. Additionally, in Australia a structural impediment exists: its federal system of government. While there are national policy and decision making forums such as the Coalition of Australian Governments and various ministerial councils, representing national and state and territory interests, and these have considered issues and developed plans for children's safety, on a constitutional and operational level, state and territory governments are responsible for child protection. So, in the case of the Commission, we have a national government that will receive recommendations with state and territory governments not having an obligation (or in the absence of the national government's support, possibly the financial resources) to implement them. Therefore at this time there is no obvious "fit" between the national government's recommendations, and responsibility and funding for their implementation. Without such a fit, the main incentive for states and territories may be the moral imperative of their desire to improve the safety of children in out-of-home forms of care (and associated programs). Because of its terms of reference the Commission will not address how to better prevent child sexual abuse occurring within family, which is a major area of state and territory child protection responsibility. In this respect, the Commission's limited focus can send the message that governments are less concerned to stop family-based sexual abuse.

It seems inevitable, in keeping with a culture of forgetting about previous inquiries, that even before the Commission has concluded its hearings and prepared its recommendations, Australia's Governments will have commissioned further inquiries and more recommendations will be generated. How will the findings of the present Commission impact the future in keeping children safe from child abuse?

There is plenty of existing evidence as to what factors need to be addressed in providing for children's wellbeing and what impact child abuse has on individual development. At the same time there is also longstanding evidence that the resources required to adequately implement this knowledge are beyond what is considered politically feasible to governments of all political persuasions. Child sexual abuse and related acts are committed by those who rest assured that children's vulnerability will not be protected by vigilance. Will a focus on the language of legal redress cover all that is required in the everyday practices of making organisations safer for children?

It is a value-based principle that the sexual abuse of children is abhorrent and to be prevented. In an era of economic rationalism there could be a case made for the economic benefit of organisations investing in child protective practices so as not to have to pay redress to those abused and to prevent the impairment of trauma on future workers. In leveraging the political capital to bring about the Commission it would seem values rather than the market forces shaped the outcome of calling a royal commission. Hetty Johnston and Joanne McCarthy were among many Australians embodying the age-old principle of "truth speaking to power". The past history of royal commissions suggests that success in calling a royal commission does not guarantee any control over the outcome. To this end in the case of this Commission, is it possible to "mobilise support from coalitions of actors upon whose support, electoral and financial, elected politicians depend?" ([16], p. 9).

Julia Gillard, at her final press conference as Prime Minister, after being initially reluctant to call the Commission, took the opportunity to predict the outcome: "This royal commission is now working its way around the country. I believe it will have many years of work in front of it. But it will change the nation." (cited in [12], p. 8). Only the future will determine her prescience on this matter.

This article concludes by posing a question directed toward Australia's decision makers (be they citizens, politicians, professionals and/or policy makers): How can better outcomes be achieved from the effort put into inquiries? The Commissioner has been authorized to draft a plan to address for the long-term the publically problematic issue of sexual abuse of children in institutional contexts. Knowing what has happened to the recommendations of previous inquiries into child abuse, how can such a plan address the issue of implementation of recommendations from this inquiry?

Acknowledgments

Thanks to three anonymous reviewers for their valuable comments on an earlier draft.

Author Contributions

Budiselik initiated the writing process, produced early drafts and synthesized authors' contributions; Crawford reviewed and revised the article, contributed to its structure and reviewed the literature on royal commissions; Chung reviewed and revised the article, contributed to the theoretical approaches used, and its structure and argument.

Conflicts of Interest

The authors declare no conflict of interest.

References

1. John Pratt. "Child sexual abuse: Purity and danger in an age of anxiety." *Crime, Law and Social Change* 43 (2005): 263–87.
2. Secretariat, Royal Commission into Child Sexual Abuse. "Consultation Paper on the Establishment of the Royal Commission into Institutional Responses to Child Sexual Abuse". 2012. Available online: http://parlinfo.aph.gov.au/parlInfo/download/media/pressrel/2056920/upload_binary/2056920.pdf;fileType=application/pdf (accessed on 18 June 2014).
3. Australian Government ComLaw. "Letters Patent for the Royal Commission into Institutional Responses to Child Sexual Abuse." Available online: http://www.comlaw.gov.au/Details/C2013G00083 (accessed on 26 July 2014).

4. Bravehearts. "Bravehearts' Key Purpose Is to Educate, Empower and Protect Australian Kids from Sexual Assault." Available online: http://www.bravehearts.org.au/pages/about-us.php (accessed on 15 August 2014).
5. Hetty Johnston, and Carol Ronken. "Position Paper: The Need for a Royal Commission into the Sexual Assault of Children in Australia." 2005. Available online: http://www.bravehearts.org.au/files/pos_paper_royal_commission.pdf (accessed on 26 July 2014).
6. Hetty Johnston, and Carol Ronken. "Position Paper: The need for a royal commission of inquiry into the sexual assault of children in Australia." 2012. Available online: http://www.bravehearts.org.au/files/Royal%20Commission_2012.pdf (accessed on 15 August 2014).
7. Lucy Carroll. "Reluctant Reporter Wins Nation's Top Journalism Prize the Sydney Morning Herald." Available online: http://www.smh.com.au/national/reluctant-reporter-wins-nations-top-journalism-prize-20131129–2yh34.html (accessed on 15 August 2014).
8. Peter Fox. "Don't block your ears to abuse Mr Premier." *Newcastle Herald*, 8 November 2012. Available online: http://www.theherald.com.au/story/757111/opinion-dont-block-your-ears-to-abuse-mr-premier/?cs=308 (accessed on 26 July 2014).
9. Barry O'Farrell, and Garry Edwards. "Hunter Child Sexual Abuse Allegations." Available online: http://www.parliament.nsw.gov.au/prod/parlment/hansart.nsf/0/16610DA0B94C902FCA257AC500118262 (accessed on 26 July 2014).
10. State of New South Wales. "Special Commission of Inquiry into Matters Relating to the Police Investigation of Certain Child Sexual Abuse Allegations in the Catholic Diocese of Maitland-Newcastle." Available online: http://www.lawlink.nsw.gov.au/lawlink/Special_Projects/ll_splprojects.nsf/vwFiles/Updated_Terms_of_Reference__12_February_2014.pdf/$file/Updated_Terms_of_Reference_-_12_February_2014.pdf (accessed on 26 July 2014).
11. Tony Jones. "Lateline Studio Interview with Peter Fox." Available online: http://www.abc.net.au/news/2014–05–30/lateline-studio-interview-with-peter-fox/5490908 (accessed on 26 July 2014).
12. David Marr. *The Prince: Faith, Abuse and George Pell.* Australia: Black Inc. Publishing, 2013.
13. Nicola Roxon. "Royal Commission into Child Sexual Abuse." Available online: http://parlinfo.aph.gov.au/parlInfo/search/display/display.w3p;query=Id%3A%22chamber%2Fhansardr%2Fc94905e2–4370–462f-b408-d06e0d0a5c8e%2F0143%22 (accessed on 26 July 2014).
14. Philip Jenkins. *Moral Panic: Changing Concepts of the child Molester in Modern America.* New Haven: Yale University Press, 2008.
15. Kathryn J. Fox. "Incurable Sex Offenders, Lousy Judges & The Media: Moral Panic Sustenance in the Age of New Media." *American Journal of Criminal Justice* 38 (2013): 160–81.
16. Gregory J. Inwood. *Continentalizing Canada: The Politics and Legacy of the Macdonald Royal Commission.* Toronto: University of Toronto Press, 2005, vol. 21.
17. Parliament of Australia. "Royal Commissions and Commissions of Inquiry." Available online: http://www.aph.gov.au/About_Parliament/Parliamentary_Departments/Parliamentary_Library/Browse_by_Topic/law/royalcommissions (accessed on 26 July 2014).
18. Steward Field, and Philip A. Thomas. "Introduction: Justice and Efficiency? The Royal Commission on Criminal Justice." *Journal of Law and Society* 21 (1994): 1–19.

19. Susan Owens, and Tim Rayner. "When knowledge matters: The role and influence of the Royal Commission on Environmental Pollution." *Journal of Environmental Policy & Planning* 1 (1999): 7–24.
20. Joanna Goven. "Processes of Inclusion, Cultures of Calculation, Structures of Power Scientific Citizenship and the Royal Commission on Genetic Modification." *Science, Technology & Human Values* 31 (2006): 565–98.
21. Peter Biskup. "The royal commission that never was: A chapter in Government—Missions relations in Western Australia." *University Studies in History* 5 (1967): 89–113
22. Rex Wild, and Pat Anderson. "Ampe Akelyernemane Meke Mekarle 'Little Children are Sacred': Report of the Northern Territory Board of Inquiry into the Protection of Aboriginal Children from Sexual Abuse 2007." Department of the Chief Minister, 2007. Available online: http://www.inquirysaac.nt.gov.au/pdf/bipacsa_final_report.pdf (accessed on 26 July 2014).
23. Barbara Fawcett, and Maurice Hanlon. "Child sexual abuse and Aboriginal communities in Australia: A case study of non-inclusive government intervention." *European Journal of Social Work* 12 (2009): 87–100.
24. Scott Prasser. "Royal Commissions in Australia: When should governments appoint them?" *Australian Journal of Public Administration* 65 (2006):28–47.
25. Australian Institute of Family Studies. "Institutional child sexual abuse inquiries 2002–2013." Available online: http://www.aifs.gov.au/institute/pubs/carc/4.html (accessed on 26 July 2014).
26. Australian Institute of Health and Welfare. "Child protection in Australia 2011–2012." Available online: http://www.aihw.gov.au/WorkArea/DownloadAsset.aspx?id=60129542752 (accessed on 26 July 2014).
27. Family and Community Development Committee. "Inquiry into the Handling of Child Abuse by Religious and other Organisations." Available online: http://www.parliament.vic.gov.au/fcdc/article/1788 (accessed on 26 July 2014).
28. Peter Blaxell. "St Andrews Hostel Inquiry: How the system and society failed our children." Available online: http://www.publicsector.wa.gov.au/document/st-andrew%E2%80%99s-hostel-katanning-how-system-and-society-failed-our-children (accessed on 26 July 2014).
29. Leslie T. Olsson, and Donna Chung. "Report of the Board of Inquiry into the Handling of Claims of Sexual Abuse and Misconduct within the Anglican Diocese of Adelaide." Anglican Church of Australia, Diocese of Adelaide, 2004. Available online: http://www.adelaide.anglican.com.au/assets/Uploads/Reports-and-Publications/14–24504finalboireportfinal.pdf (accessed on 26 July 2014).
30. Patrick Parkinson, Kim Oates, and Amanda Jayakody. "Study of reported child sexual abuse in the Anglican Church." Available online: http://www.adelaide.anglican.com.au/assets/Uploads/Reports-and Publications/07-Study-of Reported-Child-Sexual-Abuse-in-the-Anglican-Church-2009.pdf (accessed on 26 July 2014).

31. Australian Senate Community Affairs Committee. "Lost Innocents and Forgotten Australians Revisited: Report on the Progress with the Implementation of the Recommendations of the Lost Innocents and Forgotten Australians Reports." Available online: http://www.aph.gov.au/~/media/wopapub/senate/committee/clac_ctte/completed_inquiries/2008_10/recs_lost_innocents_forgotten_aust_rpts/report/report_pdf.ashx (accessed on 26 July 2014).
32. Australian Senate Community Affairs Committee. "Lost Innocents: Righting the Record on Child Migration." Available online: http://www.aph.gov.au/~/media/wopapub/senate/committee/clac_ctte/completed_inquiries/1999_02/child_migrat/report/report_pdf.ashx (accessed on 26 July 2014).
33. Australian Senate Community Affairs Committee. "Forgotten Australians: A Report on Australians Who Experienced Institutional or Out-of-home Care as Children." Available online: http://www.aph.gov.au/~/media/wopapub/senate/committee/clac_ctte/completed_inquiries/2004_07/inst_care/report/report_pdf.ashx (accessed on 26 July 2014).
34. Peter McClellan. "2014 Families Australia Oration." Available online: http://www.childabuseroyalcommission.gov.au/media-centre/speeches/2014-families-australia-oration (accessed on 26 July 2014).
35. James Wood. "Royal Commission into the New South Wales Police Service—Final Report Volume IV: Paedophile Inquiry." 1997. Available online: http://www.pic.nsw.gov.au/files/reports/RCPS%20Report%20Volume%204.pdf (accessed on 26 July 2014).
36. William Budiselik, Frances Crawford, and Joan Squelch. "The Limits of Working with Children Cards in Protecting Children." *Australian Social Work* 62 (2009): 339–52.
37. Council of Australian Governments. "Protecting Children is Everyone's Business: National Framework for Protecting Australia's Children 2009–2020." Available online: http://www.dss.gov.au/sites/default/files/documents/child_protection_framework.pdf (accessed on 26 July 2014).
38. Australian Government Department of Social Services. "Position Paper: Toward a Nationally Consistent Approach to Working with Children Checks." Available online: http://www.dss.gov.au/our-responsibilities/families-and-children/publications-articles/a-nationally-consistent-approach-to-working-with-children-checks-2011 (accessed on 26 July 2014).
39. The Catholic Communities of St Mary Magdalene, Rose Bay St Therese, Dover Heights. "Statement from Cardinal George Pell." 4 and 5 August 2012. Available online: http://www.rosebaydoverheightscatholics.com.au/wp-content/uploads/2012/08/Bulletin-4th-5th-August-2012.pdf (accessed on 26 July 2014).
40. Eliana Gil. "Institutional Abuse of Children in Out-of-home Care." *Child and Youth Services* 4 (1982): 7–13.
41. National Disability Service. "Child Safe Institutions (submission to the Royal Commission into Institutional Responses to Child Sexual Abuse)." Available online: http://www.childabuseroyalcommission.gov.au/getattachment/d26219d7-cfdf-493b-b4f4-e567426c09b4/33-National-Disability-Services (accessed on 26 July 2014).

42. Mark Dreyfus. "Royal Commissions Amendment Bill 2013 Second Reading Speech." Available online: http://parlinfo.aph.gov.au/parlInfo/genpdf/chamber/hansardr/e1b9741b-6117–42e6-bb54 219d93714fe7/0013/hansard_frag.pdf;fileType=application%2Fpdf (accessed on 26 July 2014).
43. Frank McGuire. "Child Protection." Available online: http://tex.parliament.vic.gov.au/bin/texhtmlt?form=jVicHansard.one&house=ASSEMBLY%0A&pageno=623&date1=12&date2=March&date3=2014&speech=124&title=Child+protection%0A&db=hansard91&query= (accessed on 26 July 2014).
44. Youth Affairs Council of Victoria. "'Inquiry Into Sexual Abuse In State Care Shows The Value Of Having An Independent 'Watchdog'." Available online: http://www.yacvic.org.au/news/media-releases/477-media-release-inquiry-into-sexual-abuse-in-state-care-shows-the-value-of-having-an-independent-watchdog (accessed on 26 July 2014).
45. Jay Weatherill. "Child Protection." Available online: https://hansardpublic.parliament.sa.gov.au/Pages/HansardResult.aspx#/docid/HANSARD-11–16992 (accessed 28 July 2014).

Forty Years of Forensic Interviewing of Children Suspected of Sexual Abuse, 1974–2014: Historical Benchmarks

Kathleen Coulborn Faller

Abstract: This article describes the evolution of forensic interviewing as a method to determine whether or not a child has been sexually abused, focusing primarily on the United States. It notes that forensic interviewing practices are challenged to successfully identify children who have been sexually abused and successfully exclude children who have not been sexually abused. It describes models for child sexual abuse investigation, early writings and practices related to child interviews, and the development of forensic interview structures from scripted, to semi-structured, to flexible. The article discusses the controversies related appropriate questions and the use of media (e.g., anatomical dolls and drawings). It summarizes the characteristics of four important interview structures and describes their impact of the field of forensic interviewing. The article describes forensic interview training and the challenge of implementing training in forensic practice. The article concludes with a summary of progress and remaining controversies and with future challenges for the field of forensic interviewing.

Reprinted from *Soc. Sci.* Cite as: Faller, K.C. Forty Years of Forensic Interviewing of Children Suspected of Sexual Abuse, 1974–2014: Historical Benchmarks. *Soc. Sci.* **2015**, *4*, 34–65.

1. Introduction

The mid-1970s marked a renewed awareness of the extent and seriousness of child sexual abuse. In the United States, this awareness was related to concern about child maltreatment in general [1], to the pioneering research of David Finkelhor on the prevalence of child sexual abuse among college students in six New England colleges and universities [2], and to social justice movements, for example the women's movement and the civil rights movement [3]. This article will describe the unique and important response to child sexual abuse, the forensic interviewing of children as a method to determine if they have been sexually abused. The article will focus primarily on forensic interviewing in the U.S., but with reference to parallel developments and collaborations involving other developed countries.

Who are the forensic interviewers? In the U.S., the first forensic interviewers were professionals with mental health backgrounds [4], but they are not the professionals who are mandated investigators of child sexual abuse; child protection workers and law enforcement officers are. In addition, the Children's Advocacy Center movement in the U.S. led to a new group of professionals, specially trained forensic interviewers, whose role initially was to interview children alleged to have been sexually abused, but over time, they have come to be responsible for interviewing children alleged to have been maltreated in other ways [5].

In this article, I will first address the impact of professional and public perceptions about the credibility of sexual abuse allegations on forensic interviewing practices and its effect on forensic interviewing. Second, I will describe the policy initiative in the United States that led to the need to evaluate children's allegations of sexual abuse. Third, I will briefly describe models for evaluating child sexual abuse in the U.S. Fourth, I will discuss early writing that defined interviews of alleged sexual abuse victims. Fifth, I will describe the development of forensic interviewing structures. Sixth, I will discuss select influential interview structures. Seventh, current endeavors to train child forensic interviewers will be documented; included in this discussion will be challenges related to the implementation of training in actual interview practice. Finally, in the conclusions, progress to date and remaining controversies will be summarized. Then modest proposals for future practice and research will be covered.

2. Belief and Disbelief about Child Sexual Abuse: Impact on Forensic Interviewing

Professional and public belief and disbelief about allegations of child sexual abuse have varied over the course of history [6]. The source of the ebb and flow in belief is complex. In part, it derives from the inability of adults to accept that sexual abuse of children occurs and a counter reaction of rage when sexual victimization is believed [7]. In the domain of forensic interviewing these complex reactions have resulted in a tension between using interview practices that enable disclosure and interview practices that avoid false allegations [8].

In the mid-1970s, when sexual abuse was "rediscovered" [1], the initial professional response was to gather information about sexual abuse "by any means necessary". The means included interviewing the child multiple times, asking leading questions, and using other suggestive techniques [9].

In the mid-1980s, however, concerns about false allegations began to drive interview practices. Events that led to this "backlash" were are series of multi-victim cases [10,11]. In the United States, most of these cases involved day care centers. The cases received a great deal of media attention, initially focused on the enormity of harm to children [12] and later highlighting questionable interview practices and doubting children's disclosures [13]. There were comparable cases in England, for example one in Cleveland [14] and in Scotland, a case on the Orkney Islands [15].

Professional views about the veracity of the sexual and other abuse described in these multi-victim cases remains mixed [16]. Nevertheless, these high profile cases have played a major role in shaping forensic interview practice. They have driven interview strategies that avoid false positives (children determined to have been sexually abused, but who were not) as opposed to false negatives (children who were sexually abused, but were not identified in the investigative process) [8].

3. The Challenge of the Child Abuse Prevention and Treatment Act

In the United States, the passage of the Child Abuse Prevention and Treatment Act in 1974 (CAPTA) [17] had implications for child welfare policy and practice beyond what the U.S. Congress could have anticipated. Among other provisions in CAPTA that transformed the child welfare system was mandated reporting of child maltreatment. This provision in federal law both expanded the professions who were mandated to report and the types of maltreatment to be reported. Subsequent to the passage of CAPTA, virtually every state amended or promulgated a state law to comply with

CAPTA. States did this because there were federal discretionary funds tied to a state statute in compliance with CAPTA provisions [17].

Mandated reporting resulted in an exponential increase in reports of suspected child maltreatment to local child protection agencies. In 1978, the first year of data collection under CAPTA, fewer than 700,000 cases, or 10.1 per 1000 children, were reported [18]. In 2012, the most recent year for which there are aggregated data, there were 3.4 million cases reported involving approximately 6.3 million children, 46.1 per 1000 children [19].

Although initially sexual abuse was not among the required types of child maltreatment to be reported, it was added in 1981 [20]. This addition resulted in states amending their statutes to include sexual abuse as a reportable type of child maltreatment [21]. Unlike physical abuse, which is usually determined by the pattern of a child's injuries, and physical neglect, which is usually determined by a child's physical condition or living conditions, as a rule, child sexual abuse rarely leaves physical signs. Physical indicators are found in about 10% of girls and rarely in boys [22]. Sexual abuse is generally determined by the child's statements and sometimes by the child's behavior [23]. Child welfare professionals were therefore tasked with gathering information from children to determine whether they had been sexually abused.

4. Models for Investigation

In this this section, models that have evolved in the United States for investigating allegations of sexual abuse and their rationale will be discussed. This article focuses on the forensic interview, but the result of this interview are only one piece of information gathered during the investigation and should be regarded as a means to the end of understanding what sexual abuse, if any, the child has experienced. That said, although the forensic interview is once piece, it is the centerpiece of the investigation.

4.1. An Early Approach to Investigation of Sexual Abuse

In the early days post-CAPTA, child welfare professionals followed their own intuition in data gathering about possible child sexual abuse [24]. For example, the model for investigating physical abuse or neglect involved child protection investigators going to the home and "confronting" the parents with the allegations. Applying this model to sexual abuse cases, child welfare professionals were interviewing children in the presence of their parents, when the alleged abuser was in the family [25]. Soon, however, professionals came to understand that children were unlikely to disclose sexual abuse in the presence of the perpetrator.

4.2. School-Based Interviews by First Responders

Because in-home investigations were ineffective, communities and states developed policies for interviewing school-aged children in school and informing their caretakers after the child interview [26]. Interviewing children in their school setting remains an important approach for first responders, who may be child protection workers or law enforcement. Depending upon the resources in the community, an interview by the first responder may be followed by a joint investigation or a forensic interview at a Children's Advocacy Center, both described below.

This model, however, does not address investigation of cases of pre-school children who may have been sexually abused. This child population remains a serious challenge for both mandated investigators and forensic interviewers. Children ages four and older have been successfully interviewed [27], but younger children may also be victims of sexual abuse and lack the verbal and non-verbal skills to communicate their experiences in a forensic interview [28–30]. They remain a population in need of protection.

4.3. Joint Investigation by Child Protection and Law Enforcement

Child sexual abuse is not only harmful to the child, jeopardizing child safety and well-being; it is also a crime. Cases in which the offender is in the family and those that involve caretakers who are negligent and fail to protect children in their care from sexual abuse fall within the purview of child protective services. Cases where caretakers are not culpable are the responsibility of law enforcement. Sexual abuse prevalence studies indicate that about 70% of offenses are extra familial [31]. In the mid-1980s, virtually every state in the U.S. amended its child protection laws to foster collaboration between law enforcement and child protection investigators on sexual abuse cases, and often on other serious maltreatment cases [32,33]. Joint investigation models involving child protection, law enforcement, and the local prosecutor for intra-familial sexual abuse cases were developed. These models vary by locality. Child protection workers and law enforcement might jointly interview the child, often one or the other taking the lead [32]. The case might be divided so that the child protection worker interviews the child and law enforcement the alleged offender along with other witnesses. Information might be shared through exchange of notes, sharing of interview recordings, or conferring [32]. If there is a Children's Advocacy Center in the community, the model described in the next section usually will be followed.

4.4. The Development of the Children's Advocacy Center Model

Because investigation of child sexual abuse may involve a range of professionals—for example, child protection workers, medical professionals, law enforcement, and prosecutors, children were often interviewed multiple times in multiple contexts [34]. The process of having to repeatedly disclose what was, for many children, a shameful and frightening experience, to multiple adult strangers was felt to be traumatic.

As a response to the above troubling scenario, in 1985, Huntsville, Alabama, District Attorney Bud Cramer announced a new concept, a Children's Advocacy Center (CAC), a child friendly place, where alleged victims of sexual abuse would receive a single interview by a trained professional. The interview could be observed, either through a one-way mirror or on a remotely located TV monitor, by all the professionals who needed to hear the child's account [34]. Moreover, other services the child required were intended to be located at the Children's Advocacy Center, so the child experienced "one stop shopping." These services might include a medical exam, victim advocacy, and treatment. The National Children's Advocacy Center (NCAC) was thus founded in Huntsville,

Alabama, and continues to be located in Huntsville. NCAC plays a leadership role in knowledge development and dissemination related to forensic interview models and structures, through its annual International Symposium, its on-site and remote training endeavors, and its internet webinars. NCAC conducts about 600 child interviews per year [35] and houses an electronic library, Child Abuse Library Online (CALiO) on child maltreatment that serves the professional community [36].

Not only did the concept of a Children's Advocacy Center (CAC) resonate with professionals charged with investigating child sexual abuse, but CACs became widespread because, in 1990, District Attorney Bud Cramer became U.S. Congressman Bud Cramer. One of his first acts as a Congressman was to foster a bill to fund CACs [36]. To date, there are over 800 CACs in all 50 states and in 10 countries. Two-thirds of the communities in the United States now have access to a Children's Advocacy Center [37]. So far, this funding has been sustained.

The National Children's Alliance (NCA) administers the funding for CACs and has established a set criteria that Children's Advocacy Centers must meet to obtain funding. Today, for a CAC to be an accredited member of the National Children's Alliance and receive federal funding, organizations must have: (1) Child-Appropriate/Child-Friendly Facility; (2) Multidisciplinary Team (MDT), which includes representation from law enforcement, child protective services, prosecution, mental health, medical, victim advocacy, and the Children's Advocacy Center; (3) Organizational Capacity, both fiscal and programmatic to sustain the CAC; (4) Cultural Competency and Diversity, acknowledged and hopefully integrated into its investigative and interviewing endeavors; (5) Forensic Interviews; (6) Medical Evaluations; (7) Therapeutic Intervention; (8) Victim Support/Advocacy; (9) Case Review; and (10) Case Tracking [38]. Not all of these services need be provided at the CAC. For example, medical exams are frequently undertaken off-site.

In terms of forensic interviews, the National Children's Alliance requires that interviews be "conducted in a manner that is legally sound, of a neutral, fact-finding nature, and are coordinated to avoid duplicative interviewing" [38]. NCA does not endorse a particular forensic interview model or structure.

Subsequent to the emergence of NCAC, one of the earliest and most influential CACs was the CornerHouse Interagency Child Abuse Evaluation Center. Like NCAC, leadership for the development of CornerHouse came from the county attorney's office, which, in 1986, sent representatives to visit the NCAC in Huntsville [39].

5. Early Writings about Forensic Interviewing

In this section, the pioneering role of the Kempe Center, early research on forensic interviewer practices, the leadership role of the U.S. Government, and the International Interdisciplinary Consensus Statement will be described.

5.1. Kempe Center Advice

One of the earliest written guides for professionals interviewing children about sexual abuse came from the C. Henry Kempe National Center for the Prevention and Treatment of Child Abuse and Neglect [4]. In 1985, David Jones, who was Associate Director, and Mary McQuiston, who directed the therapeutic pre-school at the Kempe Center, wrote a 44 page pamphlet published by the Kempe Center entitled *Interviewing the Sexually Abused Child*. Despite its brevity, it was prescient in identifying and offering guidance about key interview and investigative issues. The pamphlet documented the extent and effects of sexual abuse, provided a summary of relevant research, laid out a framework for gathering information about the sexual abuse allegation, provided advice about the interview process, and suggested criteria to be used to "validate" the allegation. This pamphlet was revised twice, the last time in 1989 and is no longer in print [40].

The authors advised review of background information before the interview, a practice that has led to debate because of concerns that prior knowledge could bias the interviewer [41], but now is considered best practice and is incorporated into most interview protocols [23,27]. Jones and McQuiston advised against having a parent present in the interview room, but rather assuring the child knew where the caretaker was and allowing the child to check in with the parent, if needed, during the interview process. The authors favored audio and video recording but acknowledged that prosecutors might oppose taping because of potential inconsistencies in the child's disclosures and potential challenges to interview techniques.

In terms of interview structure, they advise a simple (beginning, middle, end), flexible one that could be tailored to the allegations and the child. The interviewer should begin by explaining his/her role and building rapport by asking the child about salient issues in the child's life. The middle was the abuse-related part of the interview, and the end was closure. Consistent with current guidelines related to abuse inquiry, Jones and McQuiston recommended beginning with general, open-ended questions and only using more specific questions if the general ones did not assist in resolving the allegation. Moreover, they instructed the interviewer to follow an affirmative response to a specific question with an open-ended probe. Interviewers were to endeavor to gain details about the "who", "what", "when" and "where", but avoid asking the child "why", advice that is still good today.

Areas where Jones and McQuiston's advice differed from subsequent practice were recommending more than a single interview, advising the use of media, such as anatomical dolls, drawings, free drawings, and books about good and bad touch, and allowing time in the assessment for observation of the child in free play. Finally the authors suggested many more toys in the interview room than is current practice [4].

5.2. Initial Research on Interview Practice

A pioneering study to document practices for interviewing children about possible sexual abuse was undertaken by Conte, Sorensen, Fogarty, and Dalla Rosa [42]. They endeavored to gather data from a national sample of professionals assessing children for sexual abuse. Of the 212 respondents to their survey, 40% were child protection workers, 46% mental health professionals, and 14% other professionals, including police officers and states attorneys. Seventy-nine percent were female, and on average they had 8.8 years of experience working with sexually abused children. Most documented their interviews with written notes, but approximately a third endorsed the use of both audio and videotaping.

Just under half of respondents interviewed the "non-offending" parent before interviewing the child, and about half sometimes interviewed the child in the presence of the non-offending parent.

Interview media played a prominent role in child interviews of these experts. Ninety-two percent employed anatomical dolls; half used other dolls; two-thirds used anatomical drawings; 87% used free drawings, and about half used puppets [42].

Having a parent in the room and the extensive use of media, especially anatomical dolls, during interviews are not currently considered optimal practice [27]. Nonetheless, this research documented contemporary practice among a national sample of child sexual abuse experts and is important in understanding the evolution of forensic interviewing.

5.3. Federal Leadership

Another important provision of CAPTA was the establishment of the National Center on Child Abuse and Neglect (NCCAN) within the U.S. Department of Health and Human Services' Children's Bureau [17]. NCCAN played a leadership role in both child welfare policy and practice. Among its endeavors was the development of the *Child Abuse and Neglect User Manual Series*, intended to provide guidance to child welfare professionals in all domains of child maltreatment [43]. In 1993, NCCAN published a User Manual on child sexual abuse [7]. This User Manual addresses a spectrum of issues, including: (1) The emotional impact of working in the field of sexual abuse; (2) The scope, effects, and definitions of sexual abuse; (3) A general structure for investigations; (4) Child interviews; and (5) Treatment of the victim and family. Because the manual was developed for professionals in the child welfare field, which primarily addresses intra familial maltreatment, the manual offers guidance about psycho-social interviews with the non-offending parent and the alleged offender, as well as the child.

The chapter on the child interview suggests that interviews not be limited to a single interview, provides advice about appropriate questions, suggests guidelines about the use of media or props during interviews, and outlines a strategy for deciding about the likelihood of sexual abuse. This chapter provides a continuum of 5 types of questions from open-ended to close-ended for the interviewer to employ during inquiry about possible sexual abuse: (1) General questions (about the child's well-being); (2) Focused questions (on people, body parts, and circumstance of sexual abuse); (3) Multiple-choice questions; (4) Yes/no questions; and (5) Leading questions. Further, the manual admonishes the interviewer to use the most open-ended questions first and place more confidence in information elicited from more open-ended questions and correspondingly less confidence in information from more close-ended questions [7]. It, nevertheless, advises the interviewer, if faced with the prospect of not being able to resolve the allegation or asking a close-ended question, to ask a close-ended question.

Media or props are also discussed in the child interview chapter, as are instructions for their use. Media include: (1) Anatomical dolls, citing both their disadvantages and advantages; (2) Anatomical drawings; (3) Picture drawing; and (4) The dollhouse [7].

This is the first interview publication to articulate a continuum of questions, an issue that has been addressed more extensively in subsequent guides. Extensive use of media was soon to be dropped from advice to interviewers.

5.4. The International Consensus Statement

In 1993, there was a meeting of experts on child sexual abuse from Europe, North America, and the Middle East to develop consensus about child sexual abuse assessment. The meeting resulted in a document entitled "The investigation of child sexual abuse: An international, interdisciplinary consensus statement", which was drafted by Michael Lamb, revised based upon the meeting participants' feedback, and subsequently published in three scholarly journals: *Family Law Quarterly*, *Child Abuse & Neglect: the International Journal* and *Journal of Child Sexual Abuse*. The document was co-signed by 20 of the participants in the meeting. It represented the state of knowledge about child sexual abuse, including the scope of the problem, behavioral indicators of sexual abuse, interviewing child victims, use of dolls and other props during interviews, and the medical examination [44].

Recommendations regarding interviewing included interviewing the child as soon as possible after the alleged abuse, using open-ended questions designed to elicit a narrative, but with an acknowledgement that direct and focused questions may also be needed, especially with young children, and recording of interviews, preferably video recording. With regard to the use of dolls and other props, the consensus statement notes that they can be useful with children under 5, with reluctant children, and with uncommunicative children. The consensus statement supports a wide range of props, including anatomical dolls and anatomical drawings. The statement cites the importance of training and skill for interviewers using props and warns that anatomical dolls may elicit sexualized play from non-abused children. Such play is regarded as a red flag but not conclusive of sexual abuse in most cases [44].

6. The Development of Interview Structures

In the 1990s, professionals began to appreciate that interview guidance needed to involve more than mere advice about questions and the use of media; child welfare professionals needed advice about the structure of the interview, itself. This necessity derived from the characteristics of the interviewers and the interviewees.

Most professionals charged with the responsibility of interviewing children about sexual abuse did not have extensive mental health backgrounds or knowledge about child development. This was especially true of law enforcement, but might also have been true of child protection workers because the usual requirement for the position was a bachelor's degree, which could be in criminal justice [45]. Moreover, forensic interviewers at CACs did not necessarily have mental health or child development training.

Interviewees needed guidance because they were children. For most of them, an interview about sexual abuse is an anomalous and possibly frightening experience. Children needed to know what the expectations for the interview were. Moreover, bewildering for most children was the request to provide a narrative about their abuse experience instead of responding to short answer questions.

Below I will describe the development of interview structures, variations in their flexibility, and three notable components of these structures, providing children with ground rules, truth/lie strategies, and categorizing interview questions.

6.1. The Proliferation of Forensic Interview Structures

Beginning in the 1990s, dozens of interview structures were developed [46], most with a focus on the mandated investigators—child protection and law enforcement, and on forensic interviewers at Children's Advocacy Centers. Some interview structures were developed in academic institutions, for example, the Stepwise Interview [47], the Cognitive Interview [48], and the Ten Step Investigative Interview [49]. Others were developed by agencies charged with interviewing children, for example, the National Children's Advocacy Center [50] and CornerHouse [51]. Eventually, states began developing interview protocols to be used by first responders and CAC forensic interviewers in their state. Examples are Oregon [52], Michigan [53] and Washington State Child Interview Guide [54].

6.2. Degree of Flexibility of the Interview Structure

Interview structures vary from scripted (e.g., Ten Step Investigative Interview [49], NICHD [27]), to semi-structured (e.g., RATAC [51], ChildFirst [55], Poole and Lamb's Investigative Interview [56]), to flexible (e.g., Faller's Child-Focused Flexible Interview [21], National Children's Advocacy Center Forensic Interview Protocol [50]). RADAR (Recognizing Abuse Disclosure types and Responding), which builds upon the NICHD protocol and research, is unique in that it has a scripted version for inexperienced interviewers and a semi-structured version for more experienced interviewers [57]. Moreover, RADAR provides the interviewer with a decision tree that takes into account possible barriers to disclosure, whether there has been a prior disclosure, and any prior allusion to abuse [57].

Scripted interview structures provide verbatim what the interviewer should say. During the abuse-related phase of the interview, however, when the interviewer is gathering information about the specifics of abusive experiences, the guidance is less prescriptive. Most scripted structures are linear; that is, they assume the interviewer will be able to move through the phases or stages in the order they are designated in the interview structure.

Semi-structured interview guides provide the interviewer with advice about various tasks, for example, the use of anatomical or other drawings, but indicate that the interviewer should decide whether to incorporate such components based upon the individual child, for example, the child's developmental stage, his/her comfort level, or specifics of the allegations [51].

Flexible interview structures take into consideration local community practices and state legal requirements (NCAC) [50], which may specify aspects of the interview structure. Faller points out that an interview structure is a two-edged sword [46]. It offers needed guidance to the interviewer, but the structure can also be used to challenge the interviewer who fails to follow the structure. The more prescriptive the structure, the greater the risk that the interviewer will deviate. This is because interviewers also try to follow the child's lead, and the child does not know the structure. Because of concern that the structure may be used against the interviewer, she argues for simpler structure. For example, an interview structure with a beginning, middle, and end allows for greater flexibility than one with many phases (e.g., the Step-wise Interview [47], Ten Step Investigative Interview [49]).

6.3. Interview Ground Rules

Two issues influenced the development of interview ground rules. First, research has documented that children perform better in a forensic interview if they know what the expectations are [58]. Second, professionals thought rules would assure that children provided accurate information during forensic interviews. The number of ground rules varies by interview structure (4–9 rules). Some structures have fewer rules, in part because the interview structure developers were concerned that the child would not be able to remember and apply a lot of rules. One way some protocols have addressed this problem is by having children practice the rule as it is given. For example, the NICHD Protocol [27], which only has four rules, has the child practice each one of them. The order in which the ground rules are provided to the child varies. Below are ground rules found in interview structures.

(1) "I am going to ask you a lot of questions. If you know the answer, tell me" [21]. Many protocols fail to instruct the child to tell, if they know.
(2) "If you don't know the answer, say I don't know." "Don't guess." Both the NICHD [27] and the Ten Step [49] give the child an opportunity to demonstrate this skill by asking the child, "What is my dog's name?" The Ten Step then gives the child the opportunity to demonstrate his/her ability to answer a question, "Do you have a dog?" This is information the child knows.
(3) "If I ask you a question you don't understand, tell me and I'll ask it is a better way." Both the Ten Step Protocol [49] and RADAR [57] use the example, "What is your gender?" to give the child an opportunity to say they don't understand. The child is then asked to say whether he/she is a boy or a girl, a question the child understands.
(4) "If I make a mistake, tell me." Or "If I say something that's wrong, tell me." This rule is included to give children permission to correct interviewer error [47].
(5) "Even if you think I already know something, please tell me anyway [58]." Some protocols add "I wasn't there" [48]. This rule is included both because of concerns the child might assume the interviewer already knows what happened (and often they do) and because the goal of the forensic interview is to get information directly from the child. Some interview structures add that the child should provide details, even if the child does not think they are important (e.g., Cognitive Interview [48], Achieving the Best Evidence [59]).

Some interview structures give the child permission not to answer a question if it makes him/her uncomfortable. For example, the Step-wise Interview Protocol includes the rule: "If you feel uncomfortable at any time, please tell me or show me with the stop sign" [47]. Similarly, some structures include the rule, "If I ask the same question more than once, that doesn't mean your first answer was wrong. Sometimes I forget" (Cognitive Interview [48]).

6.4. Truth/Lie Competency

One of the strategies intended to assure children tell the truth is to have a discussion of the truth and lie during the ground rules part of the interview. Informative research on children's capacity to differentiate truth-telling from lying was undertaken by Thomas Lyon and Karen Saywitz [60]. They tested 96 children, ages 4–7, under the jurisdiction of the Los Angeles County Dependency Court, on three tasks: (1) Children were asked to define the truth and a lie; (2) Children were asked to tell the difference between a truth and a lie; and (3) Children were given 4 examples and asked to tell the researcher whether each was the truth or a lie. The children did quite poorly at tasks 1 and 2, but older children did better. All children performed much better on the identification of examples of the truth and lie, especially the 6 and 7 year olds [60,61].

This research has led interview structure developers to include examples of true and false statements in the rules phase of the interview. For example, the NICHD Protocol instructs the interviewer to ask the child if the interviewer's shoes are red and whether he/she is standing up [27]. Lyon and Saywitz [62,63] have developed a series of pictured examples with accompanying text to use in truth/lie competency assessment. These are available through the University of Southern California Law School website under Thomas Lyon and can be downloaded free of charge [62]. That said, Lyon, who is the developer of the Ten Step Investigative Interview Protocol, does not include the truth/lie exercise in the Ten Step [49].

Nevertheless, analogue research has found that getting children to promise to tell the truth increases their likelihood of doing so [58] [1]. Thus, the Ten Step Protocol includes "Do you promise that you will tell the truth? Will you tell me any lies?" [49] Some protocols, for example ChildFirst [55], give the interviewer the option of including the truth or lie exercise.

6.5. Interview Questions

All interview structures provide guidance about appropriate questions/probes/prompts, and there is general agreement that open-ended questions are superior to close-ended ones [27,58]. The specific terms used to label a given type of question/probe are not consistent across interview structures, and there is not complete consensus about where on the question/probe continuum different types of interviewer utterances fall. Moreover, some interviewer structures prefer probes (e.g., tell me) rather than questions (e.g., can you tell me? do you remember?). Those preferring the probe strategy are concerned that the question strategy will give the child an out to say "no" [64]. Those that prefer a question strategy are concerned that the "tell me" approach will be experienced by the child as coercive and/or may compel the child to respond even though the child does not know the answer [64]. Below is a table (Table 1) which attempts to take into account dominant interview structure [2] terms [3] and definitions and provides a continuum, generally from most preferred to least preferred questions/probes. The continuum is structured from most open-ended to most close-ended and suggests forensic interviewers place more confidence in responses to open-ended questions/probes and correspondingly less confidence in responses to more close-ended questions/probes.

---

[1] Although some analogue studies involve children with a history of maltreatment [60], there are no field studies using the promise to tell the truth. This is because it is very difficult to develop a research sample that consists of abuse allegations that the researcher knows what happened.

[2] These terms derive from the NICHD protocol, the Ten Step Investigative Interview Guide, the NCAC Interview, RADAR, RATAC, APSAC Practice Guidelines for Psychosocial Evaluation of Suspected Sexual Abuse, the Memorandum of Good Practice and its revision, Achieving the Best Evidence, and ChildFirst.

[3] When more than one term is used for a question/probe, the Continuum will include all terms.

Table 1. Question/Probe Continuum.

Open-Ended		More Confidence
Type of Question/Probe	Definition	Examples
Rapport building question/Probe	Open-ended inquiry about the child's well-being or rapport-building issues; does not assume an abusive experience.	So how are you doing today? Tell me the things you like to do. Tell me about your last birthday.
Open, abuse-related/ Transitional question	Open-ended inquiry that assumes there may have been an abusive experience.	Tell me the reason we are talking today. I understand something may have happened to you. Tell me about it.
Invitation/Invitational probe	Probe that invites a narrative.	Tell me everything you can remember, from the beginning, the middle, and end. It is really important that I understand what happened. Tell me about it.
Follow-up strategies	Strategies that encourage continued narrative.	Anything else you remember? And then what happened? Say more about that.
Facilitative cue	Interviewer gesture or utterance aimed at encouraging more narration.	Umhum. OK. He touched you and then what?
Specific/Cued invitations/Wh question	Follow-up inquiry to gather details about the child's experience. May be a follow up on information already reported.	Where were you? You said (event, action). Tell me more about that. How old you were when the abuse started?
Focused Question/Probe	One that focuses the child on a particular topic, place, or person, but refrains from providing information about the subject.	Tell me about daycare. Tell me about your dad. What happens at bedtime?
Multiple choice/Option posing question	A question that presents the child with a number of alternative responses from which to choose.	Did the abuse happen in the daytime or nighttime or both? Did he hurt you when you were in the bedroom, kitchen, or some other room?
Externally derived Question/Probe	A question that relies on information not disclosed in the child interview.	I heard you talked to_____ Tell me what you talked about. Your mom is worried about you. Tell me why.
Yes-no/Direct/Option posing question	A direct inquiry about a person or a specific act.	Did Mr. Jones touch do something he shouldn't have? Did someone hurt your peepee?
Leading/Suggestive/ Tag question	A statement the child is asked to affirm.	Didn't Mr. Smith tell you not to tell anybody? Your brother put his hand inside your pants, didn't he?
Coercion	Use of inappropriate inducements to get cooperation or information.	You can have a break once you tell me about the abuse. When we're all done talking, we can go get some ice cream.
Close Ended		Less Confidence

This Question/Probe Continuum is an attempt to capture the state of empirical knowledge and practice, but it does not include all the definitions and advice found in interview structures. Moreover, there remains disagreement about how egregious it is to employ more close-ended questions in a forensic interview. The reality is that protocols, such as the NICHD Protocol [27] to be described below, which strongly advises against close-ended questions, are able to reduce the number of close-ended questions, but not eliminate them. This dilemma derives not only from the predisposition of adults to ask close-ended questions when gathering information from children, something interview structures are intended to counter, but also from the children. Children may not have the capacity to report events to interviewers who are using open-ended probes, such as "tell me everything that happened from the beginning to the end." Moreover, they are likely to be reluctant to talk about their sexual abuse and, as a consequence, require more close-ended inquiry.

7. Influential Interview Structures

There is such a multiplicity of interview structures that they cannot all be described in this article. Interview structures that have had a marked impact on interview practice will be described. In addition, I have attempted to select interview structures that represent different approaches and are intended for different types of interviewers. Interview structures to be covered are the APSAC Practice Guidelines for Psychosocial Evaluation of Suspected Sexual Abuse, the Memorandum of Good Practice and its revision, Achieving the Best Evidence [59], RATAC [51], and the NICHD Protocol [27]. In a description of each protocol, I will note why it was selected.

7.1. The APSAC Guidelines

The APSAC Guidelines, Practice Guidelines for Psychosocial Evaluation of Suspected Sexual Abuse, were developed in 1990 by the American Professional Society on the Abuse of Children (APSAC) [65], were selected for inclusion because they were the first set of guidelines covering interview structure, captured best practice at the time, and are an example of flexible interviewing. Moreover, they influenced subsequent forensic interview structures. These guidelines were aimed at mental health professionals, as opposed to child protection and law enforcement professionals, and encompassed both forensic and non-forensic evaluations [65]. As already noted, the guidelines allow for a lot of flexibility. They do, however, state the evaluator must have a graduate level mental health degree and indicate a preference for the evaluator having three to five years of professional experience with sexually abused children. The APSAC guidelines are intended for professionals evaluating a spectrum of aspects of an allegation, not for professionals who are only conducting forensic interviews, and hence address issues beyond the child interview. These include advising that the evaluator gather information from collateral contacts, advising against using parent-child sessions to determine the likelihood of sexual abuse, stating that the evaluator need not interview the alleged offender to determine the likelihood of sexual abuse, and indicating that the evaluator may form an opinion about the likelihood of sexual abuse [65].

In terms of the child interview, the APSAC guidelines state that it is not necessary for the evaluator to have a written protocol, but advise providing the child with ground rules for the interview, exploring positive and neutral topics before asking about abuse, and using open-ended questions first in an attempt to elicit a narrative from the child. Further, these guidelines state that the evaluation should not be limited to a single child interview, support the use of media in the interview, including anatomical dolls, and recommend the evaluator consider multiple hypotheses that might explain the sexual abuse allegation [65]. These guidelines were revised in 1997 [66] and are currently under revision.

APSAC also has forensic guidelines for first responders and CAC interviewers, Forensic Interviewing in Cases of Suspected Child Abuse [67]. These practice guidelines are in their fourth edition.

7.2. Memorandum of Good Practice & Achieving the Best Evidence

The Memorandum of Good Practice and its most recent version, Achieving the Best Evidence in Criminal Proceedings, will be described in this section. Although these interview structures were developed for law enforcement in England and Wales [59,68], they have been quite influential for the development of protocols in the United States. For example, the Memorandum of Good Practice was the first protocol to advise interviewers not to interrupt the child's narrative, as interviewers were prone to, to seek clarification. This instruction was incorporated into the NICHD Protocol, which is the model for many other protocols in both the United States and other countries. Another important instruction in the Memorandum and Achieving the Best Evidence is repeating the child's disclosures, using the child's own words. Although this instruction has not been as widely incorporated into other protocols, it is excellent advice. Using the child's own words avoids subtle distortions in the child's information.

7.2.1. Memorandum of Good Practice

The Memorandum of Good Practice was originally published in 1992, making it an early and therefore influential interview structure[4]. It is also probably the most widely known example of a flexible interview structure. Moreover, it is unique in that the Memorandum was developed to serve as a guide for law enforcement in England and Wales who were conducting interviews that were to be videotaped [68]. Policy in England and Wales differs substantially from that in the United States in that a videotaped statement from the child about his/her abuse can be entered into evidence in a criminal case in lieu of the child's *in vivo* testimony. Law enforcement also have the option of having the child produce a written statement to be used instead of live testimony. The Memorandum of Good Practice consists of four phases: (1) Rapport building; (2) Free narrative; (3) Gathering details; and (4) Closure, with additional specification about how to conduct each of these phases [68]. For example, as noted above, the Memorandum admonishes the interviewer not to interrupt the child and to allow for pauses, advice that law enforcement might especially need [68].

---

[4] Thus, the Memorandum of Good Practice preceded the International Interdisciplinary Consensus Statement, which was first published in 1994.

7.2.2. Achieving the Best Evidence in Criminal Proceedings

The Memorandum has been revised several times, and the current guide is entitled Achieving the Best Evidence in Criminal Proceedings and encompasses more than the child forensic interview [59]. It is a policy document developed to address all aspects of investigations involving sexually abused children and other vulnerable witnesses in England and Wales, and is 257 pages in length. Unlike interview structures in the U.S., which are not universal and vary depending upon the developer and by locality, *Achieving the Best Evidence* is intended to be applied in all law enforcement investigations of sexual abuse cases in England and Wales [5]. The child forensic interview retains its flexible, four phased structure: (1) Establishing Rapport; (2) Free Narrative Account; (3) Questioning; and (4) Closing the Interview, but with greater emphasis on eliciting narrative accounts than found in the original Memorandum of Good Practice.

During Rapport, after identification of the parties present, time, and date for the video, the advice is to get the child to provide a narrative about neutral events (not positive ones), but not to allow this endeavor to go on too long out of concern the child will tire or will become confused about the purpose of the interview. Following this portion of the Rapport section, ground rules are provided. This interview structure does not include the permission to say "I don't know" rule. It does include the two "misunderstand" rules, "if you don't understand my question, tell me" and "if I misunderstand, tell me". Achieving the Best Evidence also includes the "ignorant interviewer" rule. Children are told that the interviewer wasn't there, does not know what happened, and needs details. Despite the fact that the video (or written statement) may be used at trial in place of the child's live testimony, interviewers are not to ask children to take an oath. The interviewer does, however, advise the child that it is important to tell the truth and may ask the child to give examples of truths and lies or provide examples for the child to identify as true or false. Witnesses are informed they can take a break anytime, and interviewers are advised that multiple breaks may be needed.

For the Free Narrative Account phase, this interview structure does not provide probes for transitioning to discussion of the abuse, but rather appears to assume the child will know why he/she is being interviewed. As in the Memorandum, interviewers are admonished not to interrupt the child. In terms of free narrative prompts, this interview structure specifies that they be open-ended and gives examples such as "anything else you remember". It also encourages active listening, that is, narrative cues as described in the Question/Probe Continuum.

The Questioning phase assumes the child has provided some narrative about abuse and is intended to gather additional information about the abusive incident and case-specific information, such as family composition and how the child knows the abuser. With questions about both the abuse and case, the interviewer is instructed to divide the topic and systematically explore, for example, everything about a specific abusive act. Appropriate questions include Open-ended, for example, "tell me more about…" and Specific-closed, which are questions about who, when, where, and what. Interviewers are instructed not to ask why questions and are advised to avoid Forced-choice questions (multiple choice and yes/no), asking Multiple questions in one query, and Leading questions.

---

[5] Similarly, the NICHD Protocol applies to all interviews involving physical and sexual abuse allegations conducted by Israeli Youth Investigators.

During Closure, the interviewer summarizes the child's disclosure, using the child's own words, and invites correction and any additional information the child recalls. The interviewer then moves to a neutral topic, calms the child, if needed, and thanks the child [59,68].

The Achieving the Best Evidence document provides flexibility and gives the interviewer autonomy to determine the most appropriate method for gathering information about abuse. It emphasizes that there is no single best interview structure. The document also makes specific reference to the Cognitive Interview [48] and the NICHD Protocol [27] as alternative interview structures for gathering information from the child. Achieving the Best Evidence also supports the use of dolls, including anatomical dolls, drawings, and other props, and provides appropriate guidance on their use and cautionary advice [69].

7.3. The CornerHouse Forensic Interview Protocol: RATAC

RATAC stands for: (1) Rapport; (2) Anatomy Identification; (3) Touch Inquiry; (4) Abuse Scenario; and (5) Closure. The RATAC interview structure has been very influential because, in 2002, it was incorporated into the Finding Words training curriculum, sponsored by the American Prosecutors Research Institute and provided by the National Center for the Prosecution of Child Abuse [70,71]. In addition, in 2007, the National Child Protection Training Center, founded by Victor Vieth, entered into a contract with CornerHouse to continue to develop and sustain state courses using the RATAC protocol [71]. As will be discussed below, RATAC and its various iterations are among the most widely trained interview structures in the United States. Although there have been recent changes in the RATAC protocol in response to CornerHouse and other research, because so many professionals were trained on the original RATAC protocol and continue to follow its guidance, it is important to describe the original protocol. Revisions of RATAC will be described in subsequent sections.

The RATAC protocol is semi-structured, meaning that the interviewer makes choices about the use of components in the structure. It shares commonalities with other interview structures, but also is distinct [72]. The distinctions will be described in the next sub-sections.

7.3.1. Interview Ground Rules

Unlike other interview structures, RATAC, in its original form, did not give the child the ground rules at the beginning of the interview, but rather incorporated them as the need arose during the interview. The designers of RATAC decided that giving the children a list of rules at the beginning was too authoritarian and created a negative tone [51]. They acknowledged, however, that teaching interviewers the skill of knowing when to provide a rule was more challenging than providing all the rules at the beginning of the interview [73].

7.3.2. Use of Media

RATAC also makes considerable use of media [51,74]. There is an easel with newsprint, which is shared drawing and writing space for both the interviewer and the child. The interviewer may use a number of drawing tasks. During Rapport, the interviewer may draw a face picture of the child, sometimes with the child's help, and employ "family circles", ovals with eyes and a smile, which can be used to designate the people with whom the child lives. When the interviewer engages the child in Anatomy Identification, the interviewer employs anatomical drawings, selecting both male and female drawings that reflect the child's ethnicity. Anatomical drawings are also used during the Touch Inquiry phase to first identify positive touches (e.g., kisses, hugs) and then negative touches (e.g., places no one is supposed to touch) [74]. During the Abuse Scenario phase, the interviewer may use anatomical dolls to gather information about sexual abuse after the child has indicated something of an abusive nature happened [73,74].

7.3.3. Questioning Strategies

The original RATAC questioning strategy also differed from strategies in many other interview structures [74,75]. It did not rely on a strict hierarchy of most preferred (open-ended) to least preferred (close-ended) questions. Other interview structures rely heavily on invitational probes (e.g., "Tell me the reason you are here" "Tell me all about that") to elicit narrative accounts from children. The RATAC designers viewed invitational questions as not developmentally appropriate for younger children and preferred focused questions (e.g., "Where on your body were you touched?").

RATAC traditionally relied on the use of a yes/no question to introduce a topic of concern (e.g., "Are there places on your body no one should touch?"). This is known as scaffolding [75] and alerts the child to the topic to be discussed. If the child responds positively, then the interviewer would follow with "wh" questions. These would be followed by a close-ended question. For example, if the child answered yes to the yes/no question about inappropriate body touch, the interviewer would ask, "where?" The interviewer could then ask, "Has someone touched you in one of those places?"

The RATAC protocol also included invitational probes, but they were not the first abuse-related questions. The Touch Inquiry, which relies for the most part on yes/no and focused questions, was the transition to the abuse-related part of the interview. That said, one of the alternative strategies for the Touch Inquiry is the invitational question, "What do you know about coming to talk to me today?" [74].

7.3.4. The Revision of the CornerHouse Protocol

In 2013, subsequent to research conducted at CornerHouse [76] and likely some challenges to their use of media and questioning strategies, CornerHouse substantially revised their interview structure [76,77]. Added components are "orienting messages", that is interview ground rules, the use of a narrative approach, and privileging an invitation to children of all ages to tell what they know about the interview and its purpose [78]. The CornerHouse current structure is: (1) Build Rapport; (2) Seek Information; (3) Explore Statements; and (4) End Respectfully. It employs narrative practice during the Build Rapport stage and includes invitation and encouraging a narrative during the Explore Statements phase [77,78]. It does not abandon its use of media, but their use is not so prominently featured in the interview structure. Despite the revisions, the protocol remains faithful to CornerHouse's "Child First Philosophy", which is its hallmark [78]. See also the First Witness

Protocol, developed by the CAC in Duluth, Minnesota. First Witness is a modified RATAC interview structure based upon the CornerHouse research on narrative practice [79].

7.3.5. The ChildFirst Protocol

Just as CornerHouse revised its protocol, so did the National Child Protection Training Center, now called the Gundersen National Child Protection Training Center, with whom CornerHouse partnered in training. This new protocol takes into account the changes in CornerHouse Protocol, but also is based upon a review of existing protocols and training in forensic interviewing. The ChildFirst Protocol is a four phase structure: (1) Rapport; (2) Transition to the Topic of Concern; (3) Explore Details; and (4) Closure [80]. Narrative practice is an important technique during Rapport. Narratives are also encouraged during later phases of the interview structure.

The Rapport stage differentiates strategies by the child's age, under 5, 6–10, 11 and up. The five and under children are not informed of the fact they are being video-taped and that people are watching the interview, but older children are. With the five and under group, the interviewer uses the face drawing of the child and the family drawing, as found in RATAC. With older children these activities are optional, and the face drawing is not used with the oldest group. For all age groups, interviewers can choose whether or not to engage in a discussion of the truth/lie and request that the child promise to tell the truth [80].

The ChildFirst Protocol also takes into account relatively new knowledge about polyvictimization [81]. Children who experience sexual abuse are at greater risk for other types of victimization [81]. Interviewers inquire about a spectrum of types of maltreatment. [80]. In summary, despite the fact that National Child Protection Training Center has given their protocol a new name, ChildFirst, and has considered other forensic interview protocols, it retains many commonalities with the RATAC and revised CornerHouse Protocols.

7.4. The NICHD Protocol

Arguably, the most important development in forensic interviewing during the last 40 years has been the development of the NICHD Forensic Interview Protocol [27]. Michael Lamb and Kathleen Sternberg, two eminent developmental psychologists who worked for the U.S. National Institute of Health and Human Development, spear-headed the development of the NICHD Protocol. Their goals were to enhance the competence of interviewers and to enhance the ability of children to provide accurate and coherent accounts of their experiences. Reasons for the marked impact of the NICHD Protocol will be described in the next subsection. This will be followed by a description of the protocol, a discussion of distinguishing features of the NICHD Protocol, its revision, and its impact on other protocols.

7.4.1. Reasons the NICHD Protocol Has Had Such a Marked Impact

There are at least three reasons that the NICHD Protocol is the most important development in forensic interviewing. First, the NICHD team developed collaborations in other developed countries, notably Israel, Great Britain, Scotland, Canada (Quebec), and Sweden [82,83]. As a consequence the

NICHD team has access to interview data on over 40,000 forensic interviews using the NICHD Protocol and can conduct research on these cases [84]. Perhaps most significant is their collaboration in Israel. Israeli Youth Investigators, who conduct forensic interviews on all cases involving physical and sexual abuse, use the NICHD Protocol. Moreover, the Israeli Ministry of Labour and Social Affairs supports data collection. The NICHD Protocol has been translated into the following languages: Chinese, Finish (adapted version), French (Canada), Georgian, Hebrew, Italian, Japanese, Portuguese, and Spanish [83]. All language versions are available on the website [83].

Second, these partnerships enabled field research, as opposed to laboratory research on interview practices. Although laboratory or analogue studies [6] play a role in understanding how children report their experiences, these studies cannot replicate in their research designs the trauma, secrecy, and stigma associated with sexual abuse. The studies also do not reflect the challenges experienced in the field by actual forensic interviewers.

Third, the NICHD team had access to the infrastructure to study the effects of interview practices. Although administrative data are useful in evaluating interview outcomes (e.g., percent of disclosures, court outcomes), determining the utility of specific interview practices is very labor intensive. It requires recording and transcribing interviews, developing coding systems for interviewer utterances and child responses, and having the staff resources to code and analyze interview data. It also requires professionals who are motivated to write articles and books for professional consumption. To date, there are approximately 100 articles and five books describing research on the NICHD Protocol [84]. Thus, the research on the NICHD Protocol is very impressive and cannot be rivaled by research on other interview structures. Indeed, many other protocols have relied on the NICHD research and incorporated components of the NICHD Protocol into their interview structures (e.g., Ten Step Investigative Interview Protocol [49], RADAR [57], Michigan Forensic Interview Protocol [53]).

7.4.2. Description of the NICHD Protocol

The NICHD Protocol took as its starting point knowledge of child development; thus, it is built upon research conducted on normal children. The NICHD Protocol is an 11 or 12 phase protocol (the researchers are involved in ongoing efforts to improve the Protocol, based upon input from those using it and upon research findings). The phases are: (1) Introduction, during which the interviewer describes his/her role and provides ground rules for the forensic interview; (2) Rapport Building, which includes asking the child about things he/she likes to do; (3) Training in Episodic Memory, which involves asking about a recent event salient to the child and/or about everything that happened yesterday or today; (4) Transition to Substantive Issues (e.g., sexual abuse concerns); the Protocol provides nine different probes, from open-ended to more close-ended to assist the interviewer and the child in this transition; (5) Investigating the Incidents, using repeated invitational probes (e.g., "tell me everything about that", "tell me more", "and then what happened"); (6) Break, during which

---

[6] These studies involve children, primarily non-abused children, who experience events that are intended to be analogous to sexual abuse (e.g., activities involving body touch) and are asked to report these events in interviews that intend to replicate forensic interviews.

the interviewer leaves the room and formulates focused question as needed to gather additional details; (7) Eliciting Information that has not been mentioned by the child; these are the "who, what, when, and where" questions; (8) If the Child Fails to Mention Information you expected; during this phase, the interviewer uses externally derived information (e.g., a prior disclosure) in focused questions to elicit a disclosure or additional information; (9) Information about the Disclosure, queries about whether the child has told someone before coming to the forensic interview and the response of the person; (10) Closing, during which the interviewer asks if there is anything else the child has to tell and if the child has questions of the interviewer; and (11) Neutral Topic; the interviewer might ask the child what he/she will do after the child leaves [27,85]. As will be described in the next sections, the NICHD Protocol has a number of distinguishing characteristics.

7.4.3. The Importance of Narrative Accounts

At the core of the NICHD Protocol is eliciting a narrative account from the child. Although other interview structures advise strategies for eliciting narratives, NICHD has really led the field in its insistence on techniques to produce narratives. Narrative accounts are more accurate than responses to more close-ended inquiry, for example yes/no questions.

The Rapport building and Training in Episodic Memory phases are intended to "teach" the child to respond with a narrative so that this skill will be reflected in the child's description of the abuse. Early research by the NICHD team compared the typical rapport-building strategy, which consisted of short answer questions (e.g., where do you go to school? what grade are you in? what is the name of your teacher? and do you like school?) to rapport-building using invitational probes (e.g., tell me all about school, tell me all about a recent holiday) [86]. This study demonstrated that not only did the invitational probes result in longer narratives during rapport building but also during the responses to the invitation about abuse, "I understand something may have happened to you. Tell me about it from the beginning to the end." Interviewers in both conditions used this invitation.

7.4.4. Transitional Probes

Because professionals in the field were concerned that probes, such as "tell me the reason you are here" weren't sufficiently focused, Lamb and colleagues developed a total on nine transitional probes. Later versions of the NICHD Protocol used a different initial invitational probe from the one used in their 1997 research. The current probe is "Now that I know you a little better, tell me the reason you are here" [27]. This first probe now precedes the "I understand something may have happened to you…" probe, as the former is considered more open-ended. Other probes include asking the child why the transporter (mom, worker) brought the child, referencing prior disclosures, and querying whether someone is worried about the child. All probes are posed in as open-ended a manner as possible so as not to be suggestive of the specifics of the alleged abuse. The NICHD research, however, has demonstrated that, for children who disclosed, they usually did so to the first or second probe [87].

7.4.5. Taking a Break before Focused Questions

Other interview structures include a break after the interviewer has asked about abuse, during which the interviewer goes into the room where other professionals are observing. The primary purpose of the break is to obtain input about what other questions to ask, for example from the prosecutor. The NICHD Protocol break has an additional purpose, which is to assure that the interviewer is mindful as he/she moves into more close-ended questions and probes and plans these questions carefully [27].

7.4.6. Use of Media

The NICHD Protocol does not support the use of media, such as drawings or dolls, to gather information about abuse. One rationale for this is that inviting narratives accesses free recall memory, whereas media, such as anatomical dolls and drawings, rely upon recognition memory. Free recall is the more accurate than recognition memory, although often less detailed [88]. Secondly, children younger than three and a half may not be able to make the representational shift involved in having a doll or drawing represent a person [28,58]. Moreover, Lamb and colleagues point out that some analogue research demonstrates that anatomical dolls can elicit high rates of both false positives and false negatives with very young children [89,90]. Finally, Lamb and colleagues co-authored two studies that failed to find "value added" (that dolls elicited more information than verbal inquiry alone) in field interviews using anatomical dolls [91,92].

Nevertheless, the NICHD Protocol researchers have engaged in field research that has demonstrated the "value added" of a human figure drawing [93] and of asking the child to draw a picture of the abuse [94]. In both of these studies, the drawing activity was introduced after verbal inquiry and elicited substantial portions of new information.

7.4.7. The Revised NICHD Protocol

The initial focus of the NICHD Protocol was on children who disclosed sexual abuse during the forensic interview. Overall this was more than two-thirds of children interviewed [5]. Some years ago, relying primarily on the data from Israeli Youth Investigator interviews, Lamb and colleagues began to turn their attention to children who did not disclose during a single forensic interview. Examining the dynamics of interviews in high certainty cases (cases with substantial corroborating evidence) where children did and did not disclose sexual abuse, they noted that non-disclosing children were non-communicative beginning during the rapport-building phase of the interview, and interviewers were correspondingly less supportive of these children. These dynamics carried over into the abuse-related phases of the interviews [95]. They made two recommendations based upon these findings: (1) when interviewers find children not forthcoming during rapport-building, they should extend rapport-building rather than moving on to the abuse-related phases of the interview; and (2) interviewers should consider a second interview [95].

More recently, the NICHD researchers have revised their protocol to make it more child friendly [96,97]. The revised protocol changes the order of ground rules and rapport by placing building rapport before providing interview rules. Thus, after introducing him/herself and noting that the interview will be recorded, the interviewer asks the child about things he/she likes to do, seeking narratives from the child. After that, the interview ground rules are provided.

Hallmarks of the Revised NICHD protocol are instructing the interviewer to present a friendly, supportive demeanor, to use the child's name frequently during the interview, to acknowledge the child's feelings, but not to interpret them, and to provide non-contingent positive reinforcement. With regard to demeanor, Lamb and colleagues encourage smiling, leaning forward, and making eye contact. In the Revised NICHD protocol, interviewers can acknowledge the child's feeling related to the interview process. The interviewer can say, for example, "I see you are upset". The interviewer may also say, "You are really doing a good job", but take care not to provide this feedback only when the child discloses abuse [97,98].

To date, there are two published studies comparing the Revised NICHD Protocol to the Standard NICHD Protocol. Because there is substantial research documenting lower disclosure rates in intra-familial sexual abuse, these two studies involved allegations of intra-familial abuse. Both studies demonstrate increased disclosure rates using the Revised NICHD Protocol when compared to the Standard NICHD Protocol [97,98].

7.4.8. The Influence of the NICHD Protocol on Other Forensic Interview Protocols

Many interview structures have adapted or adopted all or substantial portions of the NICHD Protocol [99]. For example, many interview structures have adopted as a whole or in part the NICHD transitional probes. Similarly, most protocols now emphasize the importance of narrative accounts of abuse. Two interview structures are described as adaptations of the NICHD Protocol, but also have their own distinctive features. These are the Ten Step Investigative Interview Protocol [49] and RADAR [57].

The Ten Step Investigative Interview Protocol is labeled as an adaptation of the NICHD Protocol [49]. The Ten Step is much more succinct; it is only two pages, as compared the NICHD's 13 pages. The Ten Step only covers the allegation portion of the interview and not the rapport-building and the closure portions. It has the advantage over the NICHD of being quite user friendly. It is formatted so that the 10 steps have brief headings in larger font, followed by actual probes in smaller font. Because it is only two pages, it can easily be brought into the interview room.

RADAR (Recognizing Abuse Disclosure types and Responding) [57] is an interview structure that is described as adapted, in part, from the NICHD Protocol. It appears to have taken portions from both the Revised NICHD Protocol (placing the rapport-building before the ground rules) and from the Standard NICHD Protocol (e.g., narrative practice and the transition probes, although the latter are used later in the interview). RADAR also has elements not found in other interview structures. At the end of Rapport, the child is given an opportunity to ask the interviewer questions. Other interview structures may include such an opportunity during closure (e.g., NICHD [27]). In RADAR, after the ground rules phase, the interviewer conducts a barrier assessment. This begins with the interviewer asking the child how he/she feels about talking to the interviewer, followed by a query about whether the child is worried about talking. Whether or not the child acknowledges worries, the interview then asks the "try your best while we talk". RADAR also differentiates interview instructions based upon the child's age, something the NICHD does not do (but RATAC [51] and ChildFirst [55] do).

Finally, RADAR includes instructions about when to interview the child a second time and when to recommend an extended assessment [57].

State forensic interview protocols have also been highly influenced by the NICHD Protocol and its research. Among these are the Washington State [54] and the Michigan [53] protocols.

8. Training for Forensic Interviewers

Specialized training programs have been developed for forensic interviewers. These programs are needed for professionals with graduate mental health training, for CAC forensic interviewers, and for mandated child protection and law enforcement personnel who conduct forensic interviews. Mental health professionals are not usually taught forensic interview practices during their graduate training; indeed, they may need forensic interview training to "unlearn" the therapeutic interview skills taught in graduate and professionals schools [99]. In contrast, mandated investigators may be starting from scratch because often they have no training in child development, in children's memory and suggestibility, or in talking to children. Moreover, most of these professionals need training in defending their interviews in court.

8.1. Typical Training Programs and Topics

Currently, forensic interview training programs range from two days [100] to 40 h (one week) [101]. These are sponsored by state agencies responsible for training child protection and law enforcement [100], professional organizations (e.g., APSAC [101]), and agencies responsible for interviewing children (e.g., National Children's Advocacy Center [102], CornerHouse [103], First Witness [104]). These forensic interview training programs are often specific to a particular interview structure or protocol (e.g., NICHD [27], RADAR [57]). They also usually include information on child development and children's memory and suggestibility. Many include opportunities to conduct practice interviews of real children, of actors playing the roles of abused children, or of colleagues who are also participants in the interview training. These interviews may be critiqued by the trainers and other interview experts. Some of the longer training programs provide an opportunity for trainees to defend their mock interviews in a mock court (e.g., APSAC Forensic Interview Clinic [101]).

In addition to basic forensic interview training, there are also a number of agencies and states that provide advanced training. Topics for advanced training for forensic interviewers include: (1) Interviewing reluctant children; (2) Interviewing special needs children; (3) Interviewing sexually exploited children, (4) Interviewing pre-school children; and (5) Forensic interviewing for Spanish-speaking children (e.g., Gunderson National Child Protection Training Center [105]; National Children's Advocacy Center [102]).

8.2. Statistics on Training Programs

According to a 2013 survey with responses from 320 of the 916 CACs from which data were solicited, the training program most commonly attended was NCAC/Huntsville training (42%), followed closely by the Finding Words/ChildFirst training (39%). Thirty-two percent attended the CornerHouse Forensic Interview training and 31% the RATAC training; when combined they constituted 63% of training programs attended. Fourteen percent of respondents' staff attended an APSAC forensic interview clinic, 35% state-based training, 10% the NICHD training, and 8% other trainings [106]. The National Children's Advocacy Center conducted a survey of 247 CAC respondents in 2009 with similar results [107].

More than 54,000 child abuse professionals from all 50 states and 20 countries have been trained by the NCAC [34]. CornerHouse has provided forensic interview training to over 29,000 professionals from every state in the United States and in 18 foreign countries, including the investigators of the International Criminal Court at the Hague [103]. Children's Advocacy Center interviewers and mental health professionals who engage in forensic interviewing are likely to attend training on a number of interview structures and to continue to develop their skills by attending advanced training [106,107]. Despite the modest percentage of participants who have attended training on the NICHD protocol in the U.S., training in other countries is le, extensive. For example, all forensic interviewers in Israel are trained on the NICHD protocol [5].

8.3. Implementing Training in Forensic Interview Practice

Despite training, research on the NICHD and other protocols indicates that it is difficult for forensic interviewers to follow the advice of forensic interview trainers and to adhere to interview structures [108]. Professionals may think they are actually following the interview guidelines, but analysis of their interviews indicates that they are not [109,110]. Although forensic interviewers have been faulted for failure to follow forensic interview structures, it is important to acknowledge that they are also admonished to follow the child. They often face the dilemma of "follow the protocol or follow the child", a dilemma exacerbated by the fact the child is unfamiliar with the protocol [46].

Various strategies have developed to assist interviewers in adhering to interview structures. One is "quick guides" (Michigan [53], Washington State [54]). These are short summaries on laminated cards of the procedures for various components of the interview, for example, of transition probes and appropriate questions. The interviewer has these in the interview room and can refer to them. RADAR is actually incorporated into a laminated pocket guide, which is 12 double-sided 4 by 6 inch pages, with color-coded tabs so the interviewer can quickly find the appropriate section [57].

A second strategy is ongoing (weekly) supervisor feedback on adherence to the interview structure. This is labor intensive because it requires the supervisor to review a video or transcript of the interview [109–111]. Research indicates that supervisor feedback is effective, but it needs to be ongoing. Otherwise, interviewers begin to deviate from the interview structure.

A third strategy is peer review. In the national survey of U.S. CACs conducted by the National Children's Advocacy Center in 2009, 94% of respondents stated they participated in peer review [107]. Peer review, however, is usually not weekly, as recommended by Lamb and colleagues [111]. Rather it is most likely to be quarterly. Such peer review usually involves forensic interviewers bringing challenging cases and asking for advice from peers. Peer review does not necessarily address adherence to a forensic interview protocol.

9. Conclusions

Forensic interviewing to determine the Likelihood of child sexual abuse is a dynamic and evolving area of practice. This review has documented the remarkable progress over the last 40 years. The dynamic nature of the field is demonstrated in the constant changes and improvement in forensic interview models and structures. Especially helpful in the progress has been the research of the team advocating the NICHD Protocol [27,82,84–87,93–98].

Nevertheless, forensic interviewing continues to be characterized by a number of contested issues. These include: (1) Whether an interview structure should flexible, semi-structured, or scripted; (2) Whether, which, and how ground rules should be introduced; (3) Whether children need to complete the truth/lie exercise; (4) What the most appropriate types of questions are; (5) The relative importance of eliciting narratives; (6) Whether media should be employed in forensic interviews; and (7) Whether children should be allowed more than one interview. Moreover, the forensic interview field is still struggling with how to ensure that interviewers actually implement the training they have received and follow interview structures.

Much of the research and the practice advice has been driven by the concern that forensic interview practices might elicit false reports of sexual abuse and thereby jeopardize the lives of adults. More recently there is an appreciation that the single forensic interview, limited to open-ended questions, may jeopardize the lives of children, who are fearful of disclosing their abuse. Developing a balance between interview strategies that correctly identify sexually abused children (sensitivity) and correctly exclude children who have not been sexually abused (specificity) is enormously challenging, and the stakes are high.

There is much work to be done. Models that allow the child more than one chance to tell must be a future focus, that is, providing for more than a single interview and extended assessment for children, who are reluctant, frightened, or compromised in other ways, so they can experience safety and justice. Work is emerging that acknowledges this need [112–115].

In addition, although gender differences in both interviewers and children have received attention [116], racial and ethnic differences have hardly been studied [116,117]. There is some training for forensic interviewers who need to interview children in Spanish, but racial and ethnic issues have not been sufficiently addressed. For example, despite the fact that Israeli Youth Investigators are interviewing both Jewish and Arab children (both populations in Hebrew), the researchers have not examined how ethnicity may affect the disclosure rates.

The challenge of interviewing very young children remains. Their assessment needs have been addressed in the clinical literature [29], but they remain a highly vulnerable population. As noted earlier [28,88], children four and older have been successfully forensically interviewed, but the three and younger population cannot be reached with current forensic interview structures [29,30].

Finally, what has been learned by conducting forensic interviews of children who may have been sexually abused in the United States and other developed countries needs to lead to comparable applications in other countries. Arguably the problem of sexual abuse is as great or greater in the developing world [118]. Children in these countries deserve protection and justice, too.

Despite the work that remains, the development of forensic interviews for children alleged to have been sexually abuse is quite remarkable. This approach has inspired a new professional role, the forensic interviewer. Forensic interviews originated as a strategy to address the problem of sexual abuse. These interviews are now being employed to elicit disclosures of other types of maltreatment and endangerment of children [5,55].

Conflicts of interest

The author declares no conflict of interest.

References

1. Henry, Kempe C. "Sexual abuse: Another hidden problem." *Pediatrics* 62 (1978): 382–89.
2. Finkelhor, David. *Sexually Victimized Children.* New York: The Free Press, 1979.
3. Finkelhor, David. "Chapter 1: Sexual abuse as a social problem." In *Child Sexual Abuse: New Theory and Research.* Edited by David Finkelhor. New York: The Free Press, 1984, pp. 1–13.
4. Jones, David, and Mary McQuiston. *Interviewing the Sexually Abused Child.* Denver: Kempe National Center for the Prevention and Treatment of Child Abuse, 1986.
5. Hershkowitz, Irit, Dvora Horowtiz, and Michael Lamb. "Trends in children's disclosure of abuse in Israel: A national study." *Child Abuse & Neglect* 29 (2005): 1203–14.
6. Olafson, Erna, David L. Corwin, and Roland C. Summit. "Modern history of child sexual abuse awareness: Cycles of discovery and suppression." *Child Abuse & Neglect* 17 (1993): 7–24.
7. Faller, Kathleen Coulborn. *Child Sexual Abuse: Intervention and Treatment Issues.* Washington, D.C.: U.S. Department of Health and Human Services, 1993.
8. Everson, Mark. "Child Forensic Interviewing at Age 30: Virtuous to a Fault." Paper presented at the San Diego International Conference on Child and Family Maltreatment, San Diego, CA, USA, 26 January 2012.
9. Ceci, Stephen, and Maggie Bruck. *Jeopardy in the Courtroom.* Washington, D.C.: American Psychological Association, 1995.
10. Hechler, David. *The Battle and the Backlash: The Child Sexual Abuse War.* Lexington: Lexington Books, 1989.
11. Myers, John E. B. *The Backlash: Child Protection under Fire.* Thousand Oaks: Sage Publications, 1994.
12. Finkelhor, David, Linda Williams, and Nancy Burns. *Nursery Crimes: Sexual Abuse in Day Care.* Newbury Park: Sage Publications, 1988.
13. Butler, Edgar, Hiroshi Fukurai, Jo-Ellen Dimitrius, and Richard Krooth. *Anatomy of the McMartin Child Molestation Case.* Lanham: University Press of America, 2001.
14. Richardson, Sue, and Heather Bacon. *Child Sexual Abuse: Whose Problem? Reflections from Cleveland.* Edited by Sue Richardson and Heather Bacon. Birmingham: Venture Press, 1991.

15. Gall, Charlie. "Orkney Child Sex Abuse Scandal: 20 Years since the Ordeal that Horrified a Nation." *Daily Record*. Available Online: http://www.dailyrecord.co.uk/news/real-life/orkney-child-sex-abuse-scandal-1099361 (accessed on 10 June 2014).
16. Cheit, Ross. *The Witch-Hunt Narrative: Politics, Psychology, and the Sexual Abuse of Children*. New York: Oxford University Press, 2014.
17. "Child Abuse Prevention and Treatment Act. CAPTA Reauthorization Act of 2010 (P.L. 111–320)." *Child Welfare Information Gateway*, 2011. Available online: https://www.childwelfare.gov/systemwide/laws_policies/federal/index.cfm?event=federalLegislation.viewLegis&id=142 (accessed on 1 June 2014).
18. American Humane Association. *Official Reports of Child Abuse and Neglect 1978*. Denver: American Humane Association, 1980.
19. U.S. Department of Health and Human Services, Administration for Children and Families. "Child Maltreatment 2012." Available online: http://www.acf.hhs.gov/programs/cb/resource/child-maltreatment-2012 (accessed on 2 June 2014).
20. Nelson, Barbara. *Making and Issue of Child Abuse*. Chicago: University of Chicago Press, 1984.
21. Faller, Kathleen Coulborn. "Interviewing children who may have been abused: A historical perspective and overview of controversies." *Child Maltreatment* 1 (1996): 4–18.
22. Alexander, Randell A. "Medical advances in child sexual abuse." *Journal of Child Sexual Abuse: Research, Treatment, & Program Innovations for Victims, Survivors, & Offenders* 20 (2011): 481–85.
23. Faller, Kathleen Coulborn. "Chapter 5: Child Interviews When Sexual Abuse is Suspected." In *Understanding and Assessing Child Sexual Maltreatment*. Thousand Oaks: Sage Publications, 2003, pp. 105–40.
24. Faller, Kathleen Coulborn. "Chapter 1: Child Maltreatment and Child Protection in the United States." In *Maltreatment in Early Childhood: Tools for Research-Based Intervention*. Edited by Kathleen Coulborn Faller. New York: Haworth Press, 2000, pp. 1–12.
25. Scheuer, Suzanne. Michigan State University, East Lansing, MI, USA. Personal communication, 20 May 1980.
26. State of Michigan Child Protection Law. *Act No. 238, Public Acts of 1975, as Amended, Being Sections 722.621–722.638, Michigan Compiled Laws*. Michigan: State of Michigan Child Protection Law, 2011.
27. Lamb, Michael, Yael Orbach, Irit Hershkowitz, Phillip Esplin, and Dvora Horowitz. "A structured forensic interview protocol improves the quality and informativeness of investigative interviews with children: A review of research using the NICHD Investigative Interview Protocol." *Child Abuse & Neglect* 31 (2007): 1201–31. doi:10.1016/j.chiabu.2007.03.021.
28. DeLoache, Judy, and Diane Marzolf. "The use of dolls to interview young children: Issues of symbolic representation." *Journal of Experimental Clinical Psychology* 60 (1995): 155–73.
29. Hewitt, Sandra. *Assessing Allegations of Sexual Abuse in Preschool Children: Listening to Small Voices*. Thousand Oaks: Sage Publications, 1999.

30. Faller, Kathleen Coulborn, and Sandra Hewitt. "Chapter 10: Special Considerations for Cases Involving Young Children." In *Interviewing Children about Sexual Abuse: Controversies and Best Practice*. Edited by Kathleen Coulborn Faller. New York: Oxford University Press, 2007, pp. 142–51.
31. Bolen, Rebecca. "Chapter 6: Extra-familial Sexual Abuse." In *Child Sexual Abuse: Its Scope and Our Failure*. New York: Kluwer Academic/Plenum Publishers, 2001, pp. 91–112.
32. Faller, Kathleen Coulborn. "Chapter 3: Working with Protective Services and the Police." In *Understanding and Assessing Child Sexual Maltreatment*, 2nd ed. Thousand Oaks: SAGE Publications, 2003, pp. 55–72.
33. National Center for the Prosecution of Child Abuse. *Child Abuse and Neglect State Statute Series: Vol. 5. Crimes.* Washington, D.C.: National Center on Child Abuse and Neglect Clearinghouse, 1997.
34. National Children's Advocacy Center. "History." Available online: http://www.nationalcac.org/history/history.html# (accessed on 20 June 2014).
35. Cordisco-Steele, Linda. National Children's Advocacy Center, Huntsville, AL, USA. Email communication, 2 October 2014.
36. National Children's Advocacy Center. "About the NCAC Child Abuse Library Online (CALiO)." Available online: http://www.nationalcac.org/calio-library/about-the-ncac-child-abuse-reseach-library-calio.html (accessed on 3 October 2014).
37. National Children's Advocacy Center. Available online: http://www.nationalcac.org/history/history.html (accessed on 3 October 2014).
38. National Children's Alliance. "Standards for Accredited Members Revised 2011." Available online: http://www.nationalchildrensalliance.org/sites/default/files/download-files/NCARevisedStandardsforMembers_0.pdf (accessed on 3 October 2014).
39. CornerHouse. "Timeline." Available online: http://www.cornerhousemn.org/timeline.html (accessed on 14 June 2014).
40. Jones, David, and Mary McQuiston. *Interviewing the Sexually Abused Child*. London: Gaskell Royal College of Psychiatrists, 1989.
41. *Idaho V Wright* 116 Idaho 382, 775 P-2d 1224 (1989).
42. Conte, Jon, Erin Sorenson, Linda Fogarty, and Julie Dalla Rosa. "Evaluating Children's Reports of Sexual Abuse: Results from a Survey of Professionals." *American Journal of Orthopsychiatry* 61 (1991): 428–37.
43. Child Welfare Information Gateway. "The Child Abuse and Neglect User Manual Series." Available online: https://www.childwelfare.gov/pubs/usermanual.cfm (accessed on 1 June 2014).
44. Lamb, Michael. "The Investigation of Child Sexual Abuse: An International, Interdisciplinary Consensus Statement." *Family Law Quarterly* 28 (1994): 1021–28.
45. Faller, Kathleen Coulborn, Marguerite Grabarek, and Robert Ortega. "Commitment to Child Welfare Work: What Predicts Leaving and Staying?" *Children and Youth Services Review* 32 (2010): 840–46.

46. Faller, Kathleen Coulborn. "Chapter 7: Interview Structure, Guidelines, and Protocol." In *Interviewing Children about Sexual Abuse: Controversies and Best Practice*. New York: Oxford University Press, 2007, pp. 66–89.
47. Yuille, John. *The Step-Wise Interview: Guidelines for Interviewing Children*. Edited by John C. Yuille. Kelowna: Department of Psychology, University of British Colombia, 2002.
48. Saywitz, Karen R., Edward Geiselman, and Gail Bornstein. "The Effects of Cognitive Interviewing and Practice on Children's Recall Performance." *Journal of Applied Psychology* 77 (1992): 744–56.
49. Lyon, Thomas. "The Ten Step Investigative Interview, 2nd ed." Available Online: http://works.bepress.com/thomaslyon/5/ (accessed on 14 October 2005).
50. National Children's Advocacy Center. "Update to National Children's Advocacy Center's Forensic Interview Structure 2014." Available online: http://www.nationalcac.org/images/pdfs/TrainingandConferences/NCAC-Training/ForensicInterviewingOfChildren/TrainingMaterials-BFI/2014TrainingMaterials/Update%20to%20NCAC%20CFIS%20-3-4-14.pdf (accessed on 10 December 2014).
51. Anderson, Jennifer, Julie Ellefson, Jodi Lashley, Anne Lukas Miller, Sara Olinger, Amy Russell, Julie Stauffer, and Judy Weigman. "The Cornerhouse Forensic Interview Protocol: RATAC®." *W. M. Cooley Journal of Practice and Clinical Law* 1 (2010): 193–331.
52. Oregon Department of Justice, Crime Victims' Services Division, Child Abuse Multidisciplinary Intervention (CAMI) Program. "Oregon Interviewing Guidelines, Third Edition, 2012." Available online: http://www.doj.state.or.us/victims/pdf/oregon_interviewing_guidelines.pdf (accessed on 10 July 2014).
53. State of Michigan Governor's Task Force on Child Abuse and Neglect and Department of Human Services. "Forensic Interviewing Protocol, 3rd ed." Available online: http://www.michigan.gov/documents/dhs/DHS-PUB-0779_211637_7.pdf (accessed on 10 July 2014).
54. Harborview Center for Sexual Assault and Traumatic Stress, and WA State Criminal Justice Training Commission. "Washington State Child Interview Guide." Available online: http://depts.washington.edu/hcsats/PDF/guidelines/WA%20State%20Child%20Interview%20Guide%202009%202010.pdf (accessed on 10 July 2014).
55. National Child Protection Center. "ChildFirst Interview." Available online: http://www.gundersenhealth.org/ncptc/childfirst (accessed on 11 July 2014).
56. Poole, Debra, and Michael Lamb. *Investigative Interviews of Children*. Washington, D.C.: American Psychological Association, 1998.
57. Everson, Mark, Chris Ragsdale, and Scott Snider. *RADAR: Child Forensic Interview Pocket Guide*. Chapel Hill: North Carolina Conference of District Attorneys, 2014.
58. Lyon, Thomas. "Interviewing children." *Annual Review of Law and Social Science*, 2015, in press.
59. Ministry of Justice. "Achieving Best Evidence in Criminal Proceedings." 2011. Available online: http://www.justice.gov.uk/downloads/victims-and-witnesses/vulnerable-witnesses/achieving-best-evidence-criminal-proceedings.pdf (accessed on 8 August 2014).

60. Lyon, Thomas, and Karen Saywitz. "Reducing maltreated children's reluctance to answer hypothetical oath-taking questions." *Law and Human Behavior* 25 (1999): 81–92.
61. Lyon, Thomas. "Children's competency to take the oath." *APSAC Advisor* 1 (1995): 4–8.
62. Lyon, Thomas, and Karen Saywitz. "Qualifying Children to Take the Oath: Materials for Interviewing Professionals." Available online: http://works.bepress.com/thomaslyon/9 (accessed on 14 May 2000).
63. Lyon, Thomas D., and Angela Evans. "Young Children's Understanding That Promising Guarantees Performance: The Effects of Age and Maltreatment." *Law and Human Behavior* 38 (2014): 162–70.
64. Faller, Kathleen Coulborn. "Chapter 8, Questions." In *Interviewing Children about Sexual Abuse: Controversies and Best Practice*. New York: Oxford University Press, 2007, pp. 90–109.
65. American Professional Society on the Abuse of Children (APSAC). "Practice Guidelines: Psychosocial Evaluation of Suspected Sexual Abuse in Young Children." 1990. Available online: http://www.apsac.org/practice-guidelines (accessed on 12 May 2014).
66. American Professional Society on the Abuse of Children (APSAC). "Practice Guidelines: Psychosocial Evaluation of Suspected Sexual Abuse in Young Children, 2nd ed." 1997. Available online: http://www.apsac.org/practice-guidelines (accessed on 12 May 2014).
67. American Professional Society on the Abuse of Children (APSAC). "Practice Guidelines: Forensic Interviewing in Cases of Suspected Child Abuse." 2012. Available online: http://www.apsac.org/practice-guidelines (accessed on 12 May 2014).
68. Home Office. *Memorandum of Good Practice on Video Recorded Interviews with Child Witnesses in Criminal Proceedings*. London: Her Majesty's Stationery Office, 1992.
69. Ministry of Justice. "Achieving the Best Evidence in Criminal Proceedings 2011: Conducting Interviews with Children." Available online: http://llrscb.proceduresonline.com/chapters/g_achv_best_evid.html#conducting_interv_ch (accessed on 12 August 2014).
70. CornerHouse. "Interagency Child Abuse Evaluation Center." Available online: http://www.cornerhousemn.org/timeline.html (accessed on 13 August 2014).
71. Vieth, Victor. "Letter to the Editor." *Child Abuse & Neglect* 32 (2008): 1003–06.
72. Toth, Patti. "Comparing the NICHD and RATAC Child Forensic Interview Approaches—Do the Differences Matter?" *The Link ISPCAN Newsletter. Northern Spring/Southern Autumn* 1 (2011): 4–6.
73. Anderson, Jennifer. CornerHouse, Minneapolis, MI, USA. Email communication, 13 January 2012.
74. Rapport, Anatomy Identification, Touch Inquiry, Abuse Scenario, and Closure (RATAC). "CornerHouse/Finding Words Training Manual." Available online: http://rtmq.infosathse.com/Kansas/ratac.htm (accessed on 18 December 2014).

75. National Children's Advocacy Center. "Forensic Interviewing Training Materials." Available online: http://www.nationalcac.org/images/pdfs/TrainingandConferences/NCAC-Training/ForensicInterviewingOfChildren/TrainingMaterials-BFI/2014TrainingMaterials/NCAC%20Child%20Forensic%20Interview%20Structure%202012.pdf (accessed on 20 August 2014).
76. Anderson, Gwendolyn, Jennifer Anderson, and Jane Gilgun. "The Influence of Narrative Practice Techniques on Child Behaviors in Forensic Interviews." *Journal of Child Sexual Abuse* 23 (2014): 615–34.
77. Anderson, Jennifer. "Recent Changes to the CornerHouse Forensic Interview Protocol." *Update* 24 (2014): 1–3.
78. CornerHouse. "Forensic Interview Protocol." 2013. Available online: http://www.cornerhousemn.org/forensicinterviews.html (accessed on 13 August 2014).
79. First Witness—Child Advocacy Center. "First Witness Forensic Interview Training." Available online: http://www.firstwitness.org/child-forensic-interview-training/ (accessed on 13 August 2014).
80. Gundersen National Child Protection Training Center. "ChildFirst™ Protocol." Available online: http://www.gundersenhealth.org/ncptc/childfirst (accessed on 13 August 2014).
81. Finkelhor, David. *Childhood Victimization: Violence, Crime, and Abuse in the Lives of Young People*. New York: Oxford University Press, 2008.
82. Pipe, Margaret Ellen, Michael Lamb, Yael Orbach, and Ann-Christian Cederborg. *Child Sexual Abuse: Disclosure, Delay, and Denial*. New York: Taylor and Francis Psychology Press, 2007.
83. "NICHD Protocol and Translated Versions." Available online: http://nichdprotocol.com/the-nichd-protocol/ (accessed on 20 August 2014).
84. "NICHD Protocol Research." Available online: http://nichdprotocol.com/peer-reviewed-research/ (accessed on 20 August 2014).
85. Lamb, Michael, Irit Hershkowitz, Yael Orbach, and Phillip Esplin. *Tell Me What Happened: Structured Investigative Interviews of Child Victims and Witnesses*. West Sussex: Wiley-Blackwell, 2008.
86. Sternberg, Kathleen, Michal Lamb, Irit Hershkowitz, Liora Yudilevitch, Yael Orbach, Phillip Esplin, and Meir Hovav. "Effects of introductory style on children's abilities to describe experiences of sexual abuse." *Child Abuse and Neglect* 21 (1997): 1133–46.
87. Sternberg, Kathleen, Michael Lamb, Yael Orbach, Phillip Esplin, and Suzanne Mitchell. "Use of a structured investigative protocol enhances young children's responses to free recall prompts in the course of forensic interviews." *Journal of Applied Psychology* 86 (2001): 997–1005.
88. Faller, Kathleen Coulborn. "Chapter 9: Media for Interviewing Children." In *Interviewing Children about Sexual Abuse: Controversies and Best Practice*. Edited by Kathleen Coulborn Faller. New York: Oxford University Press, 2007, pp. 110–41.
89. Bruck, Maggie, Stephen Ceci, Emmet Francoeur, and Ashley Renick. "Anatomically detailed dolls do not facilitate preschoolers' reports of a pediatric examination involving genital touching." *Journal of Experimental Psychology: Applied* 1 (1995): 95–109.

90. Bruck, Maggie, Stephen Ceci, and Emmet Francoeur. "Children's use of anatomically detailed dolls to report genital touching in a medical examination: Developmental & gender comparisons." *Journal of Applied Experimental Psychology* 6 (2000): 74–83.
91. Lamb, Michael, Irit Hershkowitz, Kathleen Sternberg, Barbara Boat, and Mark Everson. "Investigative interviews of alleged sexual abuse victims with and without anatomical dolls." *Child Abuse and Neglect* 20 (1996): 1239–47.
92. Thierry, Karen L., Michael E. Lamb, Yael Orbach, and Margaret-Ellen Pipe. "Developmental Differences in the Function and Use of Anatomical Dolls during Interviews with Alleged Sexual Abuse Victims." *Journal of Consulting and Clinical Psychology* 73 (2005): 1125–34.
93. Aldridge, Jan, Michael Lamb, Kathleen Sternberg, Yael Orbach, Phillip Esplin, Lynn Bowler. "Using a human figure drawing to elicit information from alleged victims of child sexual abuse." *Journal of Consulting and Clinical Psychology* 72 (2004): 304–16.
94. Katz, Carmit, and Irit Hershkowitz. "The effects of drawing on children's accounts of sexual abuse." *Child Maltreatment* 15 (2010): 171–79.
95. Hershkowitz, Irit, Yael Orbach, Michael Lamb, Margaret-Ellen Pipe, Kathleen Sternberg, and Dvora Horowitz. "Dynamics of forensic interviews with suspected abuse victims who do not disclose." *Child Abuse & Neglect* 30 (2006): 753–70.
96. Lamb, Michael E., Irit Hershkowitz, and Thomas Lyon. "Interviewing victims and suspected victims who are reluctant to talk." *APSAC Advisor* 25 (2013): 16–19.
97. Hershkowitz, Irit, Michael Lamb, Carmit Katz, and Lindsey Malloy. "Does enhanced rapport-building alter the dynamics of investigative interviews with suspected victims of intrafamilial abuse?" *Journal of Police and Criminal Psychology* 10 (2013): 27–36.
98. Hershkowitz, Irit, Michael Lamb, and Carmit Katz. "Allegation Rates in Forensic Child Abuse Investigations: Comparing the Revised and Standard NICHD Protocols." *Psychology, Public Policy, and Law* 2 (2014): 336–44.
99. Poole, Debra, and Michael Lamb. "Chapter 4: A Flexible Interview Protocol." In *Investigative Interviews of Children*. Edited by Debra Poole and Michael Lamb. Washington, D.C.: American Psychological Association, 1998, pp. 105–12.
100. Child Abuse Training Service. "Prosecuting Attorneys' Association of Michigan." Available online: http://www.michiganprosecutor.org/index.php?home=cats&activitylist=Y (accessed on 9 September 2014).
101. "APSAC's Child Forensic Interview Clinic." Available online: http://www.apsac.org/mc/community/eventdetails.do?eventId=390153&orgId=apsac&recurringId=0 (accessed on 10 September 2014).
102. National Children's Advocacy Center. "Forensic Interview of Children Training." Available online: http://nationalcac.org/events/bfi-training.html (accessed on 10 September 2014).
103. CornerHouse "Training." Available online: http://www.cornerhousemn.org/training.html (accessed on 10 September 2014).
104. FirstWitness. "Training." Available online: http://www.firstwitness.org/child-forensic-interview-training/ (accessed on 10 September 2014).

105. Gunderson National Child Protection Training Center. "Training." Available online: http://www.gundersenhealth.org/ncptc/trainings (accessed on 10 September 2014).
106. Midwest Region Children's Advocacy Center. "Key Survey Findings National Multi-Site Survey of Children's Advocacy Centers." 2013. Available online: http://www.mrcac.org/content/uploads/2014/02/2013-Key-Survey-Findings.FINAL_.pdf (accessed on 10 September 2014).
107. National Children's Advocacy Center. *Forensic Interviewing Practices in Children's Advocacy Centers*. Huntsville: National Children's Advocacy Center, 2011.
108. La Rooy, David, Michael E. Lamb, and Amina Memon. "Forensic Interviews with Children in Scotland: A Survey of Interview Practices among Police." *Journal of Police and Criminal Psychology* 28 (2010): 28–34.
109. Sternberg, Kathleen, Michael Lamb, Graham Davies, and Helen Westcott. "The Memorandum of Good Practice: Theory *versus* Application." *Child Abuse and Neglect* 25 (2001): 669–81.
110. Lamb, Michael, Kathleen Sternberg, Yael Orbach, Phillip Esplin, and Suzanne Mitchell. "Is ongoing feedback necessary to maintain the quality of investigative interviews with allegedly abused children?" *Applied Developmental Science* 6 (2002): 35–41.
111. Lamb, Michael, Kathleen Sternberg, Yael Orbach, Irit Hershkowitz, Dvora Horowitz, and Phillip Esplin. "The effects of intensive training and ongoing supervision on the quality of investigative interviews with alleged sex abuse victims." *Applied Developmental Science* 6 (2002): 114–25.
112. La Rooy, David, Michael Lamb, and Margaret Ellen Pipe. "Repeated Interviewing: A critical evaluation of the risks and potential benefits." In *Child Sexual Abuse: Research, Evaluation, and Testimony for the Courts*. Edited by Kathryn Kuehnle and Mary Connell. Hoboken: John Wiley, 2008, pp. 327–64.
113. La Rooy, David, Carmit Katz, Lindsey Malloy, and Michael Lamb. "Do we need to rethink guidance on repeated interviews?" *Psychology, Public Policy & the Law* 16 (2010): 373–92.
114. Javonda Williams, Deborah Nelson-Gardell, Kathleen Coulborn Faller, Linda Cordisco-Steele, and Amy Tishelman. "Is There a Place for Extended Assessments for Evaluating Concerns about Child Sexual Abuse? Perceptions of 1294 Child Maltreatment Professionals." *Journal of Forensic Social Work* 3 (2014): 88–105.
115. Faller, Kathleen Coulborn, and Debra Nelson-Gardell, "Extended evaluations in cases of child sexual abuse: How many sessions are sufficient?" *Journal of Child Sexual Abuse: Research, Treatment, & Program Innovations for Victims, Survivors & Offenders* 19 (2010): 648–68.
116. Lamb, Michael E., and Michelle E. Garretson. "The effects of interviewer gender and child gender on the informativeness of alleged child sexual abuse victims in forensic interviews." *Law and Human Behavior* 27 (2003): 157–71.
117. Springman, Rachael E., Jeffrey N. Wherry, and Paul C. Notaro. "The Effects of Interviewer Race and Child Race on Sexual Abuse Disclosures in Forensic Interviews." *Journal of Child Sexual Abuse: Research, Treatment & Program Innovations for Victims, Survivors & Offenders* 15 (2006): 99–116.
118. Kinnear, Karen. *Child Sexual Abuse: A Reference Handbook*. Santa Barbara: ABC-CLIO, Inc., 2007.

Protecting Children and Adolescents in Uruguay: Civil Society's Role in Policy Reform

Amy Risley

Abstract: This article analyzes the advocacy efforts of civil societal actors in Uruguay who have sought to promote the rights of children. I discuss the strategies that members of non-governmental organizations (NGOs) used to achieve a greater presence in debates leading to significant policy changes in the area of child protection. Child advocates achieved relatively high levels of political mobilization and influence throughout the 1990s and early 2000s. The analysis focuses on their multi-year campaign to reform the Children's Code of 1934, which culminated in the adoption of a new Code of Childhood and Adolescence in 2004. I argue that two variables help explain their participation in policy making: effective issue framing and successful alliance building.

Reprinted from *Soc. Sci.* Cite as: Risley, A. Protecting Children and Adolescents in Uruguay: Civil Society's Role in Policy Reform. *Soc. Sci.* **2014**, *3*, 705–725.

1. Introduction

In recent years, civil societal actors in Latin America have positioned themselves at the forefront of some of the region's most dramatic policy reforms in the area of children's rights and child protection. Child advocates in Uruguay, for example, achieved high levels of political mobilization and policy influence throughout the 1990s and early 2000s. Analysts of Uruguayan politics have described this trend as "exceptional" given the broader pattern of civil society "demobilization" following the country's democratic transition ([1], p. 49)[1]. Most remarkable, perhaps, were their arduous efforts to reform the Children's Code of 1934. The long process of influencing policy "entailed interactions with the political system and a broad-based mobilization and advocacy effort," according to the leader of a non-governmental organization (NGO) [2]. Another participant observed, "The NGOs involved in children's issues played an active role during the entire process of formulating the Code…. We proposed some key provisions and contributed to the re-drafting of others. There was a presence in parliamentary committees and a strong lobby" [3]. In short, child advocates influenced the formal agenda as well as the content of legislation and also pressured members of parliament to enact reforms. Their involvement was an important factor contributing to the passage of a new Code of Childhood and Adolescence (*Código de la Niñez y la Adolescencia*, Law No. 17.823) in 2004.

These findings call into question the received wisdom on Uruguayan democracy, which suggests that such actors necessarily find themselves at a disadvantage vis-à-vis political parties and the state. No one disputes the centrality of institutions in the country's political development. Nevertheless, the time has come to nuance the discussion and challenge dichotomous approaches that pit a robust political society (or a strong state) against an enfeebled civil society. In the present article, I take a

---

[1] All translations from the original Spanish are my own.

step in this direction and highlight the vibrancy of civil society in a context where it is sometimes overlooked. In particular, I analyze civil societal involvement in policy making in the area of child protection. I explain this participation by underscoring the importance of effective collective action frames and inter-organizational cooperation. I argue that activists who join forces in alliances and frame ideas in persuasive ways are generating opportunities for greater involvement in decision making. I support these arguments with qualitative data collected through the administration of a survey to child advocates and a close examination of the groups' publications.

The analysis is organized into four sections. First, I briefly review ongoing scholarly debates concerning the political potential of civil society organizations (CSOs) in Latin American democracies. I then elaborate the article's central arguments, which highlight civil societal actors' strategic mobilization of ideas and resources while engaging in advocacy. The third section discusses the research methods I employed while analyzing these activist strategies. It also details the reasons for selecting Uruguay as the country context for this study. In the remainder of the article, I focus on the child advocates who have spent years promoting the rights and well-being of children in Uruguay. Particular emphasis is placed on their campaign to create a new Code of Childhood and Adolescence. This case demonstrates that alliance building was a primary means by which advocates achieved policy influence. Additionally, their framing strategies simultaneously emphasized pressing social issues such as poverty and inequality and rights-based discourses that resonated with cherished cultural and political values and reinforced characteristics of Uruguayan national identity.

2. The State of the Debate

For years accounts of civil society advocacy were strangely absent from the literature on Latin American politics. Although few studies published in the 1990s and early 2000s addressed the subject directly, the scholarship often led one to expect limited civil society involvement in policy debates and decisions. A number of institutional, structural, and social factors seemed to conspire against meaningful citizen participation and policy engagement. Foremost among these were the concentration of authority in the executive branch and exclusionary, technocratic policy-making processes [4–6]. Traditional representative and intermediary institutions had declined, leaving few stable channels for the articulation of interests [7,8]. Meanwhile, a majority of Latin American specialists advanced the structuralist argument that social and economic transformations had weakened the popular sectors. The demobilization of organized labor and grassroots actors, the suppression of their demands, and the unequal distribution of economic and political power were products of neoliberal reforms and authoritarian experiments in "market individualism" ([9], p. 161). Mainstream parties acting merely as custodians of the neoliberal model privileged the interests of big business and industry [10,11].

Furthermore, as states' social welfare responsibilities and expenditures decreased, programs were contracted out to NGOs tasked with implementing policies. Analysts thus concluded that the state was co-opting civil societal actors and placing their expertise and labor in the service of neoliberalism [12]. They warned that organizations involved in the implementation phase risked acting as "transmission belts" for government policies and relinquishing their autonomy ([13], p. 138; see also [14]). Many scholars relying on institutionalist and structuralist approaches have overlooked the fact that CSOs can and do participate in policy making, even under seemingly inauspicious circumstances.

In summary, a remarkably diverse group of scholars focusing on different aspects of political life seemed to suggest that civil societal actors in Latin American countries generally lacked the institutional access, organizational resources or attributes, and overall strength required for policy engagement and influence. In some cases of policy making, civil society's involvement has indeed been limited. Yet in other instances, groups have been able to influence the agenda-setting, formulation, and adoption phases. The primary objective of my research, distinct from much of the existing work, is to explain these different levels of participation. In doing so, I add my voice to an emergent scholarly dialogue: in recent years, area specialists have fortunately begun to focus directly on the advocacy role of Latin American civil societal actors [15–20].

Following in the footsteps of scholars who analyze interest groups, nonprofits, and social movements in developed countries, Latin American specialists have investigated the role of organizational resources (e.g., expertise, prestige, leadership, and administrative capacity) as well as external variables that affect the likelihood of group involvement, including the presence/absence of allies in key government positions and the nature of the party system [16,18,21]. Some political scientists have investigated the recent proliferation of consultative councils and other types of participatory institutions in the region [16,22,23]. Moreover, scholars inspired by constructivist frameworks have argued that global human rights regimes have generated political opportunities for domestic advocates by strengthening their rights-based claims [20].

Explanations that privilege global norms, political opportunities, organizational resources, and similar sets of variables are not without their merits. However, I offer a more dynamic, agency-driven account of CSO involvement in countries where resources are often scarce and political elites seldom consult civil societal actors. In the following section, I discuss two important variables explaining participation: effective alliance building and successful issue framing.[2]

3. Theory and Arguments

The first proposition of this study is that groups improve their chances of policy participation markedly when they create, join, and/or sustain effective partnerships. Civil society alliances vary significantly with respect to their size, scope, internal organization, goals, and strategies. While some boast a large, diverse membership base, others are made up of a few professionalized NGOs. Alliances also differ in terms of the structure of their leadership and the frequency and intensity of their activities. On one end of the spectrum, we find informal, temporary arrangements, such as ad hoc coalitions, which tend to be motivated by concrete objectives. Certain individuals or organizations may serve as coordinators, but coalitions sometimes lack nominal leaders. More formal, permanent partnerships, which usually have their own legal status as second- or third-tier organizations (including federations and peak associations), are situated at the other end of the continuum. Networks (*redes*) and forums (*foros*) generally fall somewhere between these two ends of the spectrum. They are more likely than coalitions to be formally constituted, with a name, charter,

---

[2] These arguments are also developed in previous studies [24–26].

and identifiable membership. They frequently unite a greater number of groups and are meant to endure. In addition, their aims and activities are varied: they often seek to strengthen their members by providing services, building group capacities, and facilitating the exchange of information, for instance.

The main advantages of building alliances are threefold. First, groups pool their organizational resources, namely information, analysis, expertise, prior experience, credibility or name recognition, administrative capacity, and political and media contacts. By doing so, they marshal greater amounts of resources than any single CSO can muster and overcome the scarcity problem. Second, through alliances, activists can coordinate their advocacy efforts and avoid redundancies in their activities, which conserves precious time and resources. Third, they are better able to generate a critical mass, bolster their collective demands with greater numbers, and present a united front vis-à-vis the authorities or other civil societal actors. These combined benefits increase the likelihood that governing elites and the public will notice and listen to CSOs.

Three characteristics appear to enhance the effectiveness of alliances: an efficient division of labor, a balance between internal cohesion and diversity, and a willingness to collaborate with other alliances or broader social movements in pursuit of common objectives. Alliances function smoothly when they take advantage of their members' individual strengths and areas of expertise through the distribution of tasks and responsibilities. Furthermore, although it is beneficial for an alliance to bring together likeminded people who agree on both goals and strategies, if participating groups exemplify a range of ideological proclivities, focus areas, and organizational missions and structures, the alliance will appear more representative of larger civil society constituencies. Lastly, forging ties with other alliances or movements achieves an effect similar to that of increasing internal diversity.

Inter-organizational cooperation increases the likelihood of a civil societal presence during several phases of policy making. During the formulation phase, for instance, it is more efficient and convenient for decision makers to consult representatives of an existing alliance than to meet with dozens of separate organizations. Government officials sometimes welcome the existence of such an entity, accepting it as representative of a certain group of civil societal actors and/or a legitimate authority on a specific policy domain. NGO networks or other semi-permanent alliances can be particularly relevant during this stage. When the authorities seek civil society's input, they reach out to networks, because these include many member organizations and "can legitimately claim to represent a broader range of voices and experiences than any one organization" ([27], p. 9). Strength in numbers also helps CSOs seeking influence during policy agenda setting and adoption. Working collectively augments the capacity of groups to persuade decision makers that an issue deserves attention and pressure them to enact a certain policy. The logic of joining forces is compelling in countries where CSOs tend to lack certain resources—for instance, money and members—compared to their counterparts overseas.

In addition to mobilizing organizational resources in alliances, civil societal actors mobilize ideas and discourses. By devising creative ways of "spinning" the issues, they endeavor to shape public discourse as well as the policy agenda. Building on the concept of framing used in the literature on social movements, I submit that members of NGOs who devise persuasive collective action frames are more likely to become involved in policy agenda setting, formulation, and adoption. Social movement scholars define framing as strategic efforts to create shared understandings that "legitimate and motivate collective action" ([28], p. 6). Activists often use frames to identify perceived injustices (or other problems), to articulate grievances, and to make rights-based claims. They also help actors interpret events and their own life experiences. The targets of framing are many and can include prospective participants in social movements or protests, constituents, opponents, bystanders, and/or governing elites. Frames are said to achieve resonance when they succeed in expressing grievances in compelling ways and offering remedies to pressing problems [29]. Frames identify a problem, a responsible actor or institution, and a solution. Diagnostic framing problematizes an issue and identifies "who or what is culpable" ([30], p. 1071), whereas prognostic framing offers a potential remedy. Motivational framing, meanwhile, usually emphasizes urgency and severity and appeals to justice or morality.

Each of these framing tasks is important. However, I argue that CSO members must be especially attentive to the diagnostic and prognostic dimensions. Policy-friendly frames tend to communicate a positive, constructive, and/or hopeful message while also de-emphasizing culpability and proposing feasible solutions to problems. Frames that blame pressing problems on specific, powerful elites can threaten such actors and even provoke their active opposition to reform. Moreover, activists' demands seem more reasonable and realistic when their frames contain feasible remedies and proposals that can more easily be integrated into policies. Alternatively, frames that call for the dismantling or transformation of existing political systems or policy models are less efficacious. Even when these models are, in fact, flawed and advocates are legitimately diagnosing the problem, they still must propose workable solutions. Members of CSOs who include these characteristics in their diagnostic and prognostic framing increase the likelihood of being involved in policy and decrease the likelihood that they will be politically marginalized.

Stated briefly, civil societal actors often rely on the persuasiveness of their ideas and information to influence governing elites. Public-interest NGOs in particular seek to become credible purveyors of ideas and interpreters of reality. The arguments summarized here center on the strategic mobilization of ideas and resources, thus privileging the agency of civil societal actors. This approach is more illuminating than some of the rival explanations proposed in existing scholarship and helps solve the puzzle of CSO involvement in countries where formal channels for consulting such groups are often lacking.

4. Research Methods

Uruguay is widely perceived as exemplifying just such an environment. According to the conventional wisdom, the state has historically functioned as the "central engine for societal transformation" and social integration, while civil society is granted a secondary and subordinate status ([31], p. 38). Before Uruguayan democracy broke down in 1973, the country was renowned for its high levels of economic and social development, political stability, strong parties and state structures, and extensive welfare system. Civil society did play a role in challenging the repressive civil-military dictatorship, as was the case in other Southern Cone countries during the same period. Uruguayan citizens managed to recover their democratic regime in 1985, and the country was subsequently classified as a (re)consolidated democracy. However, analysts claim that most of the movements that emerged under authoritarian rule demobilized following the democratic transition, when parties reclaimed their traditional monopoly over political life. Civil societal actors were unable (or unwilling) to challenge their hegemony and play a greater role in the articulation of demands and mediation of interests. Scholars have also portrayed the sphere as weak vis-à-vis the state: civil society's capacity to organize and propose policy alternatives is limited, and a state-centric vision of politics prevails [32,33]. In light of these characterizations, Uruguay represents a difficult political context in which to test the hypotheses of the study regarding civil society participation.

This project's dependent variable of civil society involvement in policy making is defined as group members exercising some degree of influence during the agenda-setting, formulation, and adoption phases. For instance, advocates may disseminate their ideas in the media when the agenda is taking shape. They may also share analysis and information in an effort to influence the content of policy during the formulation phase. Activists then try to persuade legislators (or other decision makers) to adopt their preferred policy by meeting with policy makers, organizing demonstrations, and using additional tactics meant to communicate demands and galvanize the public. Members of NGOs can engage in direct or indirect advocacy during each of these stages: the first entails interacting with public officials in the legislative and executive branches; the second involves pressuring these power holders by mobilizing their constituencies and the broader public.

To ascertain the frequency and forms of civil society engagement with the policy process, I administered a questionnaire to members of NGOs involved in children's issue between 2012 and 2013. The survey instrument covered the most pressing problems facing Uruguayan children and the issues that NGOs have prioritized during the past decade, their advocacy strategies (especially tactics used to influence governing elites), and, more specifically, their role in the process of reforming the Code of Childhood and Adolescence. Advocates were asked to elaborate on their interactions with policy makers in the legislative and executive branches, their attempts at shaping the content of policy proposals, their actions intended to pressure decision makers, and the other dimensions of the dependent variable mentioned previously. Respondents were also asked to comment extensively on the discursive and framing strategies they used during the campaign and on opportunities for inter-organizational cooperation and alliance building. To supplement the survey responses, I consulted reports, newsletters, press releases, and additional documents authored by members of non-profit, public-interest NGOs.[3]

While conducting this research, I discovered that child advocates campaigning for policy reforms in Uruguay relied on both direct and indirect forms of advocacy. Civil societal actors sustained their efforts for more than a decade in a campaign that spanned the presidential administrations of Luis Alberto Lacalle (National Party, 1990–1995), Julio María Sanguinetti (Colorado Party, 1995–2000), and Jorge Batlle (Colorado Party, 2000–2005). The next section will analyze their persistent attempts to promote and safeguard the rights of young people.

---

[3] Six of the twelve organizations contacted completed the questionnaire, yielding a response rate of 50 percent. Recipients were selected using online NGO directories and the secondary literature on children's rights advocacy in Uruguay. In particular, I targeted groups that had the institutional memory necessary to reflect on civil society's participation in reforming the Code and still existed at the time the survey was administered.

5. Child Advocacy in Uruguay

5.1. Civil Society Organizations' Demands and Activities

NGOs in Uruguay have intervened in a number of different areas, such as juvenile justice, education, disability, child labor, sexual exploitation, and domestic abuse. Poverty, inequality, and other social issues have figured prominently in CSOs' publications and shaped their day-to-day activities to a large extent. By the mid-to-late 1990s, NGOs had assumed important responsibilities in the co-administration of social policies for the National Institute for Minors (INAME) and other state agencies; public funds represented an increasing proportion of their funding base [34]. This implementation role became a defining characteristic of government-civil society relations during that period. Additionally, the country's youth have found themselves living in more precarious economic and social circumstances in recent years. Broader economic trends—most notably changes in the labor markets that entailed a growing wage gap between skilled and unskilled workers and more precarious and unstable forms of employment—have created pockets of poverty [1]. Rising rates of school desertion and the geographic concentration of poverty in certain areas of Montevideo have led to social exclusion (and made social mobility more difficult). Accordingly, a greater number of NGOs focused their attention on the plight of street children, for example [34]. Meanwhile, neoliberal reforms had limited the state's ability to respond to these social problems: since the 1980s, government officials had endeavored to reduce public spending, to privatize the delivery of social policies and services (to an extent), and to provide targeted assistance to at-risk communities with the goal of alleviating poverty [1].

The country then experienced an economic recession beginning in 1999. Rising unemployment and decreasing real wages led to greater rates of poverty and inequality in general terms. The percentage of Uruguayans living below the poverty line increased from 15.3 percent in 1999 to 31.9 percent in 2004. The crisis affected young people dramatically: the poverty rate for children aged five and under shot up to 56.5 percent in 2004; 54 percent of children aged six to twelve were also living in poverty at that time [1][4]. Mired in these difficult circumstances, many child advocates insisted upon the interconnectedness of economic, social, political, and legal rights.

Different types of CSOs have been active in children's causes. The Peace and Justice Service (SERPAJ) and other human rights organizations (HROs) that had emerged during the authoritarian regime embraced the promotion and defense of children's rights. Indeed, the Legal and Social Studies Institute of Uruguay (IELSUR), an HRO founded in 1984, became one of the more influential groups at the national level [1]. Additional groups, including Gurises Unidos, Vida y Educación, and El Abrojo, were established in the late 1980s and the period following Uruguay's ratification of the United Nations (UN) Convention on the Rights of the Child in 1990. The Convention established that all children, regarded as rights-bearing subjects, are entitled to certain rights guaranteeing their care and protection [35]. Examples include the right to participate in the broader community, freedom of expression, the right to health, education, recreation, and an identity

---

[4] The increase was dramatic: the poverty rates for children aged five and under had been 30.7 and 32.5 percent in 1994 and 1999, respectively; the rates for children aged six to twelve were 28.8 and 28.3 percent those same years [1].

(e.g., a name and a nationality), and protection from discrimination, abuse, and exploitation. Uruguayan child advocates have prepared non-governmental reports for the UN assessing the country's compliance with the Convention. These "alternative" reports, which challenged the official (government-authored) accounts, provided CSOs with an international audience for their research and ideas regarding possible policy alternatives. In short, the global embrace of children's rights lent further legitimacy to advocates' demands for reforms.

The UN Children's Fund (UNICEF) was especially instrumental in supporting CSOs in Uruguay. The agency also encouraged the adoption of a rights-based approach to children's issues [1]. Over time, the integral protection paradigm, discussed below, gained adherents within the NGO sector. The Convention thus served to revitalize civil society in this domain and helped activists raise awareness of the problems affecting children and their status as rights-bearing individuals.

5.2. Advocating for Policy Reform

The process of aligning Uruguay's legal framework with the norms of the Convention has been gradual. Prior to the adoption of the 2004 Code of Childhood and Adolescence, extant laws and practices were contradictory and frequently at odds with a rights-based approach. The country's legal framework for addressing children's issues was based on the Convention, the constitution (which was amended in 1997), the Children's Code of 1934, the Civil Code, and the Penal Code. Taken together, these offered very different conceptualizations of the family and children. As in other Latin American democracies, paternalistic approaches toward intervening in the lives of "at-risk" children had been institutionalized in the early decades of the 20th century. The doctrine of the "irregular situation" had been applied for decades to young people accused of having committed criminal offences as well as neglected, abandoned, abused, and/or economically disadvantaged children. In cases of alleged "material" or "moral" abandonment, family courts asserted the state's right to assume legal guardianship of children, remove them from their families, and place them in public or private institutions. According to the doctrine, children were viewed paternalistically and passively as objects of protection and control. Judges enjoyed broad discretionary authority while determining the situations facing children; due process was not always guaranteed.

The Convention sought to replace this framework with the integral protection doctrine, which considers children and adolescents as rights-bearing subjects capable of becoming responsible for their actions and demanding the fulfillment of their rights. This newer doctrine is based on respect for due process and motivated by the goal of interning young people only in exceptional circumstances and as a last resort. For example, a dearth of material resources can no longer be the sole basis for a judicial decision to order separation from one's family. The integral protection doctrine also emphasizes the rehabilitation and resettlement of juvenile offenders into their families and communities. Child advocates have endeavored for years to harmonizing domestic laws and practices with these international norms; indeed, the irregular situation doctrine and its legal manifestations proved remarkably resistant to change [20,25].

Uruguay's legal system was no exception. The Children's Code of 1934, like the laws that governed children and family life in other Latin American countries, was based on the doctrine of the irregular situation and related approaches for identifying threats to the prevailing social order. Public authorities understood combating delinquency and containing other perceived social dangers as ways to protect the greater community. The state targeted young people who were poor, not attending school, sheltered in precarious housing, and/or in other situations deemed "irregular" for intervention [1]. Most child advocates in Uruguay have therefore called on the authorities (and INAME officials in particular) to change their approach toward assisting children at risk.

In 1994, special commissions established by the executive branch researched and prepared bills, which relevant legislative committees subsequently considered. None of the proposals progressed until September 1999, when one chamber of parliament actually passed a bill [1][5]. Widespread agreement exists among NGO members and outside observers that their mobilization in favor of a new Code was significant and that they achieved high levels of participation in multiple phases of policy making from 1995 onward [1]. Examples of especially influential groups include Gurises Unidos, Vida y Educación, Arco Iris, El Abrojo, and DNI (Defence for Children International). Members of IACi, a cooperative of lawyers dedicated to defending and promoting children's rights, offered specialized expertise throughout the policy-making process [36]. As noted previously, child advocates relied on a combination of direct and indirect advocacy. They met with (and lobbied) lawmakers, published research and analysis, organized workshops, seminars, and other events, and led public campaigns. Partly as a consequence of their involvement, the bill contained provisions that accorded with the integral protection paradigm.

These efforts notwithstanding, the bill did not advance. From a procedural standpoint, the proposal was probably doomed: it was introduced far too late in the legislative session for meaningful debate to take place [1]. Moreover, civil society pressure alone could not change the mindset of legislators who opposed sweeping reforms. Opponents were found within the ranks of every major political party, namely the traditional Colorado and National parties and the center-left Broad Front. Some apparently found the provisions addressing the institutionalization of young people objectionable. Members of faith-based organizations were apparently concerned about some of the proposed reforms concerning adoption and shared these reservations with sympathetic lawmakers.[6] However, in broader terms, no civil society groups organized a major campaign in opposition to the reforms and/or the principles of the Convention, a characteristic that differentiates this case from children's rights movements in neighboring countries, such as Chile [1].

The bill's demise caused significant consternation among those civil societal actors who had spent years clamoring for reform. Members of certain NGOs were so disappointed that they put their advocacy work on hold [1]. Others carried on with the goal of keeping the issue on both the public and formal agendas. Advocates with legal expertise and/or experience in human rights remained involved.

---

[5] The first such bill was prepared by a commission and then taken up by a Senate committee in May 1994. Another executive-branch commission drafted a proposal in March 1997. A third version produced by yet another commission during the same year was sent to the legislative branch and passed by one of the chambers in 1999 [1].

[6] According to Pereira and Nathán, some observers have suggested that generational differences help explain the observed patterns of opposition and support within parliament; however, their own data did not confirm or disconfirm this hypothesis [1]. Further research and interview data are needed to uncover the reasons for the legislators' hesitancy to embrace the integral protection doctrine at that time [1].

Lawmakers resumed their work in the early months of 2000.[7] Pereira and Nathán have described the ensuing legislative process as "arduous," "problematic," and even "chaotic" due to contending views on the subject, which produced competing proposals ([1], p. 29). This phase of negotiation led to a bill being introduced into the Chamber of Deputies in 2002. Because some of the more controversial provisions had been eliminated, the proposal differed considerably from previous versions. Once the bill made its way to the Senate, child advocates were fearful that it would suffer a fate similar to that of the 1999 bill. These concerns prompted a change in strategy: members of UNICEF, who had previously encouraged CSOs to mobilize, convinced some groups to retreat. The idea was to allow legislators to bargain with each other and build consensus; reform was henceforth "the responsibility of the parties" and a few individuals and groups with specialized expertise ([1], p. 29). Prioritizing intra- and inter-party bargaining over civil society advocacy was a quintessentially Uruguayan approach. Indeed, the process was marked by several characteristics associated with the country's enduring political culture, including a preference for gradualism and partial reforms and the privileged status of parties in the channeling of societal demands [31].

Pereira and Nathán conclude that this change in tactics led to the demobilization of many CSOs. According to their interpretation, a much smaller number of civil societal actors—mostly highly specialized experts—stayed involved [1]. In contrast, the informants for this study insisted that the campaign continued until the law's passage [3]. A member of El Abrojo, for example, stated that CSOs sustained "very active participation and mobilization… for almost twelve years (1992–2004)." To the best of her recollection, "there was no explicit decision to leave it in the hands of legislators" [37]. Some advocates contended further that they redoubled their efforts immediately prior to the Code's passage [3]. The extent to which NGO members left politics up to the politicians is therefore disputed.

On the other hand, everyone agrees that the Code finally adopted in September 2004 fell somewhat short of meeting the high standards of NGO members. The Code integrated the norms and language of the Convention into provisions addressing issues such as abuse and maltreatment, child labor, adoption, and due process for children and teens in trouble with the law. A leader in DNI regarded it as a "great advance" in modernizing domestic legislation [2]. A member of IACi likewise judged the Code to be a step in the right direction [38]. Nevertheless, traces of paternalistic modes of intervention in the lives of at-risk children remained. Certain provisions of the Code were entirely at odds with the Convention's principle of progressive autonomy, the right of children and teens to exercise their rights in accordance with their abilities [38].[8] The Code also established that young people should be deprived of their freedom only in exceptional circumstances and for the least amount of time

---

[7] The 1999 elections changed the composition of parliament. A number of the legislators who had previously supported a new children's code continued to pursue reform, but newly elected officials also took an interest in the issue [1].

[8] Deus was especially chagrined by the Code's mention of assigning a custodian during legal proceedings, which seemed to reflect a continuing tendency to treat minors as incapable of acting in the civil/legal realm instead of a strict adherence to the principle of progressive autonomy. The author argues further that the revised Code is merely a start: to fully enact the rights-based approach, more profound legal, institutional, and cultural transformations are necessary. "The doctrine of guardianship formed an intrinsic part of the value system of the patriarchal ideology that permeated our legislation for the past two centuries" ([38], p. 2).

possible. In practice, however, judges continued to incarcerate teens accused of crimes; the loss of freedom was not yet widely viewed as a last resort [38]. Additionally, INAME's rechristening as the Institute of the Uruguayan Child and Adolescent (INAU) did not persuade child advocates that the agency's traditional focus on assisting "abandoned or delinquent" children had changed along with its name ([39], p. 18)[9]. NGO members also found vestiges of the age-old attitudes that had objectified young people and denied them a voice and opportunities for participation.

The Code's shortcomings serve as a reminder that we must distinguish influence over policy outcomes (and outputs) from participation in the policy-making process. Civil society involvement in policy making does not automatically lead to the attainment of desired results. Most scholars of advocacy therefore avoid exaggerating the importance of outcomes and insist that actors articulate "positions or sets of demands" without "necessarily securing them" ([40], p. 297). In the case of Uruguay, child advocates could not overcome entrenched forms of resistance enough to create an ideal law. One respondent observed, "The Code that was achieved was the best that could be negotiated at that time" [3]. Yet this failing should not detract from their major achievements in this case and, in particular, their high levels of engagement and involvement throughout the policy-making process.

Moreover, some NGO members have subsequently worked to strengthen the Code. To illustrate, IACi recently proposed changes that would address cases of sexual abuse and maltreatment [36]. The Civil Association SAI (Rainbow Program) formulated a law prohibiting the use of physical punishment and humiliating treatment to discipline young people; participants then pressured parliament to adopt the reform (Law no. 18.214) [3]. Civil societal actors have also been proactive on the issues of juvenile justice, adoption, and education, among others.

The advocacy campaign in favor of a new Code should be analyzed as part of a longer-term process of bringing domestic legislation in line with the Convention, which Uruguayan scholars have deemed "one of the most constructive developments in NGO-state interactions" in recent history ([1], p. 26). Certain issues have led to especially "fruitful" forms of dialogue and cooperation between governmental and non-governmental actors ([1], p. 40). The status of Uruguay's street children is an important example. A working group comprised of NGO members and officials in INAME/INAU has analyzed the phenomenon and devised innovative, coordinated strategies for more than a decade [1]. Participants viewed it as an "important achievement and an enriching experience for state-civil society interaction" ([34], p. 49). Since 1998, representatives from the NGO sector have also contributed to the agency's consultative body (*Mesa de Diálogo INAME/ONGs*), which began functioning in 1998.

CSOs continued to engage the policy-making process during the Tabaré Vázquez administration (2005–2010). From 2006 onward, opportunities for "exchange and dialogue" between organizations,

---

[9] Members of the Comité, an alliance discussed below, also criticized the Code's limited reforms of social policies targeting children. Participants had hoped for further discussion of the state's obligations in terms of strengthening economic, social, and cultural rights through the implementation of such policies. The Code, in their estimation, "timidly" describes the state's responsibilities, focuses on problems affecting certain specific groups of children, and neglects to underscore more universal policies that extend to *all* children and teens in accordance with the Convention ([39], p. 19).

civil society alliances, and members of the Broad Front government arose in certain areas of social policy ([32], p. 4; see also [33]). Under the current administration of President José Mujica (Broad Front), high-level officials within INAU are "always willing to receive civil society [representatives]," according to one NGO leader. He described his organization's relationship with legislators representing certain Broad Front parties as "very good:" they "consult us on a permanent basis" [2].

In short, examples of NGO-government collaboration abound in this policy domain. Although these interactions vary in terms of quality and the satisfaction levels of those involved, they are suggestive of a certain amount of mutual respect between both sets of actors. What explains the child advocates' ability to link up with government officials, to exert considerable pressure on policy makers, and, more generally, to play such a prominent role in the process of reforming Uruguay's laws and policies to achieve compliance with the Convention? I submit that alliance building has been a significant factor. It is the subject of the following section.

5.3. Civil Society Alliances

Civil societal actors promoting the rights and well-being of children have created several relatively effective partnerships. The Uruguayan Committee for the Rights of the Child (Comité), founded in 1991, is one of the most important NGO networks to have emerged. Its members have served as diligent monitors of the state, prepared the non-governmental (alternative) report for the UN, and used their findings as a basis for raising awareness of problems affecting children, making demands, and promoting a rights-based perspective [1]. The Comité united more than 50 groups across the country under the leadership of some of the most influential CSOs in this issue area, IELSUR, El Abrojo, and Colegio de Abogados [34][10]. By the mid-1990s, it had achieved a strong media presence, increased its visibility, and begun to influence the government. According to the vice-president of an NGO, Comité members "worked arduously in the formulation of the Children's Code so that it would incorporate the ... integral protection doctrine" [2].

A majority of the organizations that participated in the Comité also belonged to the National Association of NGOs of Uruguay (ANONG), an umbrella group that had nearly twice as many members. Although ANONG was not comprised exclusively of children's NGOs, the alliance did bring together many of the most important groups engaged in this issue area. By the mid-to-late 1990s, it had raised its profile considerably, intensified its activities, and assumed the role of "spokesperson" for the NGO sector *vis-à-vis* the government [1]. With support and financing from UNICEF, ANONG organized a working group in the 1990s with the concrete goal of facilitating NGO involvement in policy making [34]. As lawmakers embarked on the process of reforming the Children's Code, participants in the working group were well positioned to offer suggestions. Their efforts to modify the proposal were productive: a number of their recommendations were incorporated into a draft prepared for one of the relevant committees in the lower chamber [34]. Indeed, these activities coincide with the period discussed previously, when civil societal actors

---

[10] The Comité, formerly known as the Uruguayan Committee for Monitoring the Rights of the Child, was comprised of HROs and groups specializing in children and families. Over time, the CSOs that worked directly with young people became increasingly predominant within the alliance [1].

achieved the highest levels of participation and managed to shape the content of the bill that was almost adopted in parliament.

CSOs created the even-larger Childhood Collective, a national meta-network of various alliances and federations, in 2000. The umbrella group united hundreds of organizations that worked directly with children, teens, and youth across the country. Like ANONG, it became an important interlocutor vis-à-vis governmental actors and agencies [1]. Participants in both alliances endeavored to represent the interests of their members, for instance, during the formulation of the policies and programs in which they were heavily invested and/or involved.

Yet another alliance, the Network of Childhood and Adolescence NGOs, also brought together a diverse group of CSOs that provided services to children, teens, and families in Montevideo, including daycare centers, early childhood schools, communal kitchens, and recreational facilities.[11] These groups were important sources of specialized knowledge and expertise on problems affecting young people. Many CSOs had gained legitimacy in the eyes of government officials by carrying out successful projects on their own as well as implementing public policies [34]. To illustrate, El Abrojo developed a literacy program that targeted children and mothers living in extreme poverty. Effective projects such as this one, which was recognized by the UN, "increased the level of confidence" in the NGOs' work ([34], p. 54). Furthermore, staff members of some of the more prominent groups possessed highly specialized forms of legal expertise in the areas of juvenile justice and/or human rights. They also worked closely with lawyers who did not belong to NGOs but nonetheless offered technical assistance. Their cooperation was especially welcome given that some participated in the commissions that had formulated the first proposals for a new code [1].

In summary, by forming partnerships, CSOs shared their experiences, combined their areas of competency, and pooled other resources (such as media and political contacts, legitimacy, and human resources), thereby augmenting their political influence. The Childhood Collective was a means through which many organizations earned a seat at the table within INAU on the above-mentioned *Mesa de Diálogo*. Similarly, thanks to their membership in ANONG, they gained representation on the National Advisory and Consultative Council for the Rights of Children and Adolescents, a body created by the 2004 Children's Code [37]. According to several respondents, alliances served as one of the main vehicles for engaging in advocacy. A member of El Abrojo concluded that participation in several partnerships—namely, the Network of Childhood and Adolescence NGOs and, subsequently, ANONG and the Comité—was a crucial dimension of their advocacy efforts [37][12]. Another participant in multiple alliances observed that they "allow us to mobilize and strengthen our efforts, to take advantage of each organization's capabilities, … [and] to combine the resources that increase our chances of achieving influence" [2]. Still others considered

---

[11] The Childhood Collective's diverse membership included ANONG, el Comité Departamental de Asociaciones Civiles del Plan CAIF de Montevideo, la FIPAM (Federación de Instituciones Privadas de Atención al Menor), la FIPEI (Federación de Instituciones Privadas de Educación Inicial), and AUDEC (Asociación Uruguaya de Educación Católica). The Network of Childhood and Adolescence NGOs emerged in 1983 and comprised approximately 160 groups at one time, though it began to lose momentum after 1998 [37].

[12] All but one of my informants were members of organizations that participated in both the Comité and ANONG. Most also belonged to a variety of other local, national, and international alliances.

inter-organizational cooperation to be an effective strategy for achieving influence and "demanding accountability;" it was especially necessary considering the relatively "deficient" government-created spaces for participation [3,41]. Thus, the remarks of NGO members suggest that civil societal actors do not merely wait for invitations "from above" to participate in policy making; instead, they try to create their own opportunities by joining forces.

5.4. Collective Action Frames

Effective framing strategies also generated opportunities for participation. Several patterns can be discerned. To begin with, the broad resonance of human rights discourse proved advantageous for activists defending children's rights. Citizens had experienced an acute identity crisis during Uruguay's democratic breakdown and descent into authoritarianism. These were astonishing and traumatic events for a country that had formerly been regarded as the "Switzerland of Latin America" due to its relatively high levels of economic and social development, extensive welfare system, and stable political democracy. It was henceforth known as the nation "with the highest per-capita rate of political incarceration anywhere on earth" ([42], p. 85). An estimated one in 50 citizens was detained at one time or another during the dictatorship, and one in 500 received a lengthy prison sentence for political offenses [42].

Following the democratic transition, human rights and democracy attained an unchallenged status as political goods to be cherished and hegemonic discourses that transcended political differences [34]. Over time, advocates included the problem of social exclusion—and specifically, high child poverty rates—in the larger struggle to defend and promote human rights [34]. Framed as a human rights question, childhood gained significance. Additionally, civil societal actors adapted their discourse to the language used in the Convention [1]. Normative and discursive changes at the international level therefore had a profound effect on domestic activism. Like their counterparts in other Latin American countries during this period, NGO members constantly invoked the norms of the Convention to raise awareness and underscore the gap between those norms and existing policies.

Moreover, public officials were increasingly talking "rights talk" [20]. At the "highest levels" of government, people were embracing rights-based discourses and approaches to children's issues [41]. One advocate attributed the change to sustained civil societal efforts: "The [civil society] organizations are the ones who have imposed … a language of rights. Most of the innovations that the state has incorporated into policies and programs addressing children come from discourses, practices (and individuals) from the NGO world" [37]. The methodological challenges that arise while trying to determine the true origins of "rights talk" and the direction of causality are considerable. Nevertheless, we can conclude with some certainty that this shared discourse has facilitated government-NGO interactions and CSO participation in policy making. A participant in the movement offered a concise summary of these trends when she observed, "Human rights are politically correct" in Uruguay [36].

As discussed previously, civil societal actors made a strong case for the gravity of the country's social problems. In doing so, they succeeded in communicating a sense of urgency to policy makers and the broader public, thus attending to the motivational task of framing. To illustrate, a non-governmental report assessing the country's compliance with the Convention contained a lengthy discussion of social exclusion and segregation in Montevideo [43]. A second such report likewise emphasized the disproportionate effects of poverty on the country's youngest inhabitants. Its authors concluded, the "social situation of children ... deteriorated enormously between the years of 1997 and 2004" ([39], p. 50). The poverty rate for children aged five and under was more than 50 percent by 2001. Meanwhile, the rate for people over 64 years of age was dramatically lower (18 percent) due in part to the state's more generous social spending on policies helping the elderly meet their needs. In short, the "infantilization of poverty" was a recurring theme in these documents.

Child advocates provided a powerful call to action: the country's growing "marginalization and social exclusion" is a "dramatic reality that should concern us," they asserted; yet the fact that poverty affects children and teens most, "harming their own development and injuring their future, is a reality that should deeply move us" ([43], p. 91). The trends were especially disquieting in a country that for decades was known and esteemed for its high levels of development. Compared to its neighbors, Uruguay had lower levels of income inequality, a more sizeable middle class, and an expansive welfare state, which provided social security and access to health care and education, among other benefits [1]. Although Uruguay was still one of most equal countries in Latin America in the late 1990s, the distinction was rather dubious considering the world's highest levels of income inequality were found in the region: "we must recognize that we are among the best of the worst group," the advocates lamented ([43], p. 27). Civil societal actors underscored the gap separating reality from deeply cherished middle-class values and the country's self-image as a highly equal, integrated society. The message that something important and special was slipping away resonated broadly.

The frames were also resonant because, as noted earlier, many activists viewed social problems as obstacles to the full enjoyment of human rights. They discursively linked reforms in this issue area to the defense and promotion of rights and even the preservation and strengthening of democracy. Advocates expressed concern that children were experiencing "everything that we want to leave behind: poverty, vulnerability, and social and political invisibility" ([43], p. 91). In addition, they issued a warning:

> Each child who experiences any of these situations today will very soon be a citizen who will have sufficient reasons to distrust democracy and promises of growth. To neglect children ... is to resign one's self to nearly half of all future adults having sound reasons for distrusting the political system and the development strategy ([43], p. 91).

Such rhetoric emphasized the importance of social integration for democratic citizenship, present and future. By deploying these discourses, CSO members performed the task of motivational framing while also incorporating hopeful, positive elements. Moreover, in their prognostic framing, activists proposed a feasible solution to the problems affecting children while demanding that lawmakers adopt a new Code. Although additional reforms would certainly be needed, child advocates hoped the law would pave the way for future changes.

Some advocates included a similarly constructive theme in their frames: they called for more universal social policies that would extend to *all* children and teens, not only those living in extreme poverty [37]. We must once again place this demand in its proper historical context and consider the long tradition of making claims based on economic and social rights and the extensive support for the welfare state. Furthermore, proposing universal policies amounted to an indirect criticism of neoliberalism as opposed to a full frontal assault. The idea that neoliberal policies were harming young people or violating their rights did not appear as often in their publications. CSO members instead identified poverty as the primary force causing injury, a view much less likely to provoke controversy or backlash.

NGO members did not shy away from scrutinizing the state institutions and practices that were preventing children and teens from fully exercising their rights. In particular, they voiced concerns over the culture of guardianship that still shaped child protection policies, the application of the above-mentioned doctrine of the irregular situation, and the treatment of young people in the juvenile justice system. They lamented the fact that many children and youth were detained, housed in institutions, and deprived of their freedom. To illustrate, the detention rate increased 18 percent from 1995 to 1999 [43]. Participants in CSOs noted the authorities' inclination to "punish and criminalize the poverty of families" who lacked the "basic rights" to work, an education, and health ([43], p. 32). Discourses that privileged security, with their usual emphasis on fighting crime, became more prevalent during the 1990s, and child advocates argued that these were being institutionalized in state agencies and programs. The idea that poverty was generating crime and constructions of young people as dangers to society were pervasive and contributed to the justice system's "repressive" and "severe" treatment of children and teens ([43], p. 43). Maclure and Sotelo have identified similar trends in Nicaragua, where "many people question the value of assisting youth who are deemed to be hooligans" ([35], p. 98).

These critiques notwithstanding, advocates generally used cautious language and avoided rhetoric emphasizing the most negative characteristics of state institutions and actors. Importantly, they refrained from assigning blame to judges and other powerful elites who supported the status quo. These discursive choices were not especially threatening to the policy-making establishment. Their frames can therefore be contrasted with those deployed by child advocates in neighboring Argentina. For years, Argentine activists traced the plight of children to structural and systemic factors, most notably neoliberalism, the criminalization of poverty, and "perverse" state institutions. Identifying these as the main forces harming children was key to diagnostic framing but problematic for prognostic framing. The frames did not privilege feasible, workable solutions to problems, and they mostly lacked positive messages. Members of CSOs frequently drew connections between the neoliberal model, poverty, and the lamentable state of the nation's children and underscored the precariousness of social and economic rights in the wake of structural adjustment, social spending cuts, and widespread unemployment. Additionally, child advocates were adamant that state institutions and the juvenile justice system deprived children of their rights and jeopardized their well-being. These discursive strategies complicated their ability to influence the policy-making process [25].

6. Conclusions

Numerous factors affect the likelihood that CSOs will become involved in policy debates and decisions. In this article, I have sought to underscore the importance of just two variables: effective framing and alliance building. Both were relevant in the case of child advocacy in Uruguay. By joining forces in partnerships, members of organizations combined their resources and areas of expertise and earned a greater presence in policy-making debates. As noted previously, alliance building was a primary means for engaging in advocacy and achieving influence. Moreover, child advocates directly addressed poverty, inequality, and related social problems but did so using discursive strategies that resonated with cherished cultural and political values and reinforced aspects of national identity. Social questions were tied to rights-based discourses. "Rights talk" was virtually the only game in town. CSO members also relied on discursive strategies that were comparatively more constructive, less threatening, and more careful, especially in terms of identifying the actors (and institutions) who bore responsibility for pressing problems affecting children. Taken together, these framing strategies helped advocates persuade policy makers to take action in this issue area, to include the integral protection doctrine in their proposals, and to eventually adopt legislation.

CSO members working to enhance the rights and well-being of young people have achieved relatively high levels of participation and influence in recent years. These findings challenge some of the received wisdom found in studies of Latin American politics and Uruguayan politics more specifically. As discussed throughout this article, much of the existing literature depicts Uruguay as a statist country in which the state dominates society and parties monopolize politics. Inter-elite bargaining, consensus building, and legislative gradualism represent the "Uruguayan way." Civil society, in contrast, has not always been able (or willing) to challenge the hegemony of parties: its capacity to organize social constituencies, make political demands, or propose policy alternatives is thus limited. CSOs pushing for sweeping reforms would find themselves especially disadvantaged according to such views.

Yet child advocates have played a prominent role in the process of harmonizing domestic policy with the principles and norms of the Convention. They have also collaborated with government officials on numerous occasions to promote the rights and well-being of young people. The case demonstrates that civil societal actors can become politically influential even in political environments characterized by a vibrant political society and a strong state. Indeed, a growing body of evidence collected in the region's democracies tells a story that differs from the scholarly narrative that predominated for years. Time and again, participants in CSOs have demonstrated their capacity for mobilization and commitment to engaging the political system in their quest for change. Furthermore, this engagement has generated meaningful policy reforms that have helped protect and promote human rights.

Acknowledgments

The Faculty Development Endowment at Rhodes College provided support for this research.

Abbreviations

ANONG: National Association of NGOs of Uruguay; CSO: Civil society organization; DNI: Defence for Children International; HRO: Human rights organization; IELSUR: Legal and Social Studies Institute of Uruguay; INAME: National Institute for Minors; INAU: Institute of the Uruguayan Child and Adolescent; NGO: Non-governmental organization; SERPAJ: Peace and Justice Service; UN: United Nations; UNICEF: United Nations Children's Fund.

Conflicts of Interest

The author declares no conflict of interest.

References

1. Javier Pereira, and Mathias Nathán. "Acción pública no gubernamental y Convención sobre los Derechos del Niño." In *Intercambios: Serie de Documentos de Trabajo de UNICEF Uruguay*. Montevideo: UNICEF Uruguay, 2009. Available online: http://www.unicef.org/uruguay/spanish/intercambios_1.pdf (accessed on 22 March 2013).
2. Vice-president of DNI (Defence for Children International) Américas, e-mail message to author, 11 January 2013.
3. Member of Asociación Civil SAI, e-mail message to author, 8 January 2013.
4. Guillermo O'Donnell. "Delegative Democracy." *Journal of Democracy* 5, no. 1 (1994): 55–69.
5. Paul W. Posner. "Popular Representation and Political Dissatisfaction in Chile's New Democracy." *Journal of Interamerican Studies and World Affairs* 41, no. 1 (1999): 59–85.
6. Alfredo Riquelme Segovia. "¿Quiénes y por qué 'no están ni ahí'? Marginación y/o automarginación en la democracia transicional. Chile, 1988–1997." In *El modelo chileno. Democracia y desarrollo en los noventa*. Edited by Paul Drake and Iván Jaksic. Santiago: LOM Ediciones, 1999, pp. 261–80.
7. Douglas Chalmers, *et al.* eds. *The New Politics of Inequality in Latin America: Rethinking Participation and Representation*. New York and Oxford: Oxford University Press, 1997.
8. Frances Hagopian. "Democracy and Political Representation in Latin American in the 1990s: Pause, Reorganization, or Decline?" In *Fault Lines of Democracy in Post-Transition Latin America*. Edited by Felipe Agüero and Jeffrey Stark. Miami: North-South Center Press, 1998, pp. 99–143.
9. Kenneth Roberts. *Deepening Democracy? The Modern Left and Social Movements in Chile and Peru*. Stanford: Stanford University Press, 1998.
10. Paul Drake, and Iván Jaksic, eds. *El Modelo Chileno. Democracia y Desarrollo en los Noventa*. Santiago: LOM Ediciones, 1999.
11. Eduardo Silva, and Patricio Rodrigo. "Contesting Private Property Rights: The Environment and Indigenous Peoples." In *The Bachelet Government: Conflict and Consensus in Post-Pinochet Chile*. Edited by Silvia Borzutzky and Gregory B. Weeks. Gainesville: University Press of Florida, 2010, pp. 181–214.
12. Jasmine Gideon. "The politics of social service provision through NGOs: A study of Latin America." *Bulletin of Latin American Research* 17, no. 3 (1998): 303–21.
13. Brian Loveman. "Chilean NGOs: Forging a Role in the Transition to Democracy." In *New Paths to Democratic Development in Latin America: The Rise of NGO-Municipal Collaboration*. Edited by Charles Reilly. Boulder: Lynne Rienner, 1995, pp. 119–44.
14. Joe Foweraker. "Grassroots Movements and Political Activism in Latin America: A Critical Comparison of Chile and Brazil." *Journal of Latin American Studies* 33, no. 4 (2001): 839–63.

15. Carlos Acuña, and Ariana Vacchieri, eds. *La Incidencia Política de la Sociedad Civil.* Buenos Aires: Siglo XXI, 2007.
16. Jordi Díez. *Political Change and Environmental Policymaking in Mexico.* London and New York: Routledge, 2006.
17. Claudio Fuentes. *Contesting the Iron Fist: Advocacy Networks and Police Violence in Democratic Argentina and Chile.* London and New York: Routledge, 2005.
18. Adolfo Garcé, and Gerardo Uña, eds. *Think Tanks y Políticas Públicas en Latinoamérica: Dinámicas Globales y Realidades Regionales.* Buenos Aires: Prometeo Libros, 2006.
19. Inés González Bombal, and Rodrigo Villar, eds. *Organizaciones de la Sociedad Civil e Incidencia en Políticas Públicas.* Buenos Aires: Libros del Zorzal, 2003.
20. Jean Grugel, and Enrique Peruzzotti. "Grounding Global Norms in Domestic Politics: Advocacy Coalitions and the Convention on the Rights of the Child in Argentina." *Journal of Latin American Studies* 42, no. 1 (2010): 29–57.
21. Marcelo Leiras. "Observaciones para el análisis y la práctica de la incidencia." In *La Incidencia Política de la Sociedad Civil.* Edited by Carlos Acuña and Ariana Vacchieri. Buenos Aires: Siglo XXI, 2007, pp. 67–86.
22. Paul W. Posner. "Local Democracy and Popular Participation: Chile and Brazil in Comparative Perspective." *Democratization* 10, no. 3 (2003): 39–67.
23. Andrew Selee, and Enrique Peruzzotti, eds. *Participatory Innovation and Representative Democracy in Latin America.* Baltimore: The Johns Hopkins University Press, 2009.
24. Amy Risley. "It's Not Easy Being Green: Environmental Advocacy and Policy Making in Chile." *Society & Natural Resources* 27 (2014): 421–35.
25. Amy Risley. "The Power of Persuasion: Issue Framing and Advocacy in Argentina." *Journal of Latin American Studies* 43, no. 2 (2011): 663–91.
26. Amy Risley. "The Political Potential of Civil Society: Advocating for Freedom of Information in Argentina." *The Latin Americanist* 49, no. 2 (2006): 99–130.
27. Bonnie Shepard. *NGO Advocacy Networks in Latin America: Lessons from Experience in Promoting Women's and Reproductive Rights.* The North-South Agenda Paper no. 61. Miami: the North-South Center, 2003.
28. Doug McAdam, John McCarthy, and Mayer Zald, eds. *Comparative Perspectives on Social Movements: Political Opportunities, Mobilizing Structures and Cultural Framing.* New York and Cambridge: Cambridge University Press, 1996.
29. Robert Benford, and David Snow. "Framing Processes and Social Movements: An Overview and Assessment." *Annual Review of Sociology* 26 (2000): 611–39.
30. Daniel Cress, and David Snow. "The Outcomes of Homeless Mobilization: The Influence of Organization, Disruption, Political Mediation, and Framing." *American Journal of Sociology* 105, no. 4 (2000): 1063–64.
31. Eduardo Canel. *Barrio Democracy in Latin America: Participatory Decentralization and Community Activism in Montevideo.* University Park, PA: Pennsylvania State University Press, 2010.

32. Javier Pereira, and Andrés Peregalli. "Participación de la sociedad civil en políticas de infancia y adolescencia: una mirada desde las etapas del policy making." Paper Presented at the VIII Conferencia Regional de América Latina y el Caribe de la Sociedad Internacional para la Investigación del Tercer Sector (ISTR), Buenos Aires, Argentina, 12–14 July 2011. Available online: http://new.lasociedadcivil.org/softis/cv/69 (accessed on 3 January 2013).
33. Florencia Bastarrica, Mathías Nathán, Andrés Peregalli, and Javier Pereira. "Participación de la sociedad civil en las políticas de infancia: una mirada desde el proceso de policy making." Paper Presented at IX Jornadas de Investigación de la Facultad de Ciencias Sociales, UdelaR, Montevideo, 13–15 September 2010. http:// www.fcs.edu.uy/archivos/Mesa_8_Pereira%20et%20al.pdf (accessed on 28 March 2013).
34. María Elena Laurnaga. "Interacción estado – sociedad civil en el sistema de políticas públicas de infancia." Montevideo: Instituto de Comunicación y Desarrollo, 1999. Available online: http://lasociedadcivil.org/uploads/ciberteca/infancia.pdf (accessed on 1 April 2013).
35. Richard Maclure, and Melvin Sotelo. "Children's Rights and the Tenuousness of Local Coalitions: A Case Study in Nicaragua." *Journal of Latin American Studies* 36, no. 1 (2004): 85–108.
36. Member of IACi (Infancia, adolescencia ciudadana), e-mail message to author, 22 November 2012.
37. Member of El Abrojo, e-mail message to author, 15 January 2013.
38. Alicia Deus. "El acceso a la Justicia de las niñas, niños y adolescentes. El rol del defensor y el curador del artículo 8 del Código de la Niñez y la Adolescencia del Uruguay." In *Infancia y Administración de Justicia: La Importancia de la Defensa Jurídica*. Montevideo: UNICEF y Dirección Nacional de Defensorías Públicas, 2010. Available online: http://www.unicef.org/uruguay/spanish/uy_media_Infancia_y_administracion_Justicia.pdf (accessed on 1 April 2013).
39. Comité de los Derechos del Niño de Uruguay. "Informe no gubernamental de aplicación de la Convención de los Derechos del Niño." Montevideo, 2006. Available online: http://www.crin.org/docs/Uruguay_CDNU_NGO_Report_SP.pdf (accessed on 28 March 2013).
40. J. Craig Jenkins. "Nonprofit Organizations and Policy Advocacy." In *The Nonprofit Sector: A Research Handbook*. Edited by Walter W. Powell. New Haven: Yale University Press, 1987, pp. 296–320.
41. Member of Aldeas Infantiles SOS, e-mail message to author, 25 January 2013.
42. Lawrence Weschler. *A Miracle, A Universe: Settling Accounts with Torturers*. New York: Pantheon, 1990.
43. Gustavo Leal. *La incorporación de los Derechos del Niño a las Políticas Públicas en Uruguay. Informe no gubernamental de la aplicación de la Convención Internacional de los Derechos del Niño en Uruguay. Balance del Período, 1996*. Montevideo: Comité de los Derechos del Niño de Uruguay, 2000.

Regional Frameworks for Safeguarding Children: The Role of the African Committee of Experts on the Rights and Welfare of the Child

Julia Sloth-Nielsen

Abstract: This article discusses the safeguarding movement in the context of child protection. After providing it's key principles and precepts, the relevant provisions of the African Charter on the Rights and Welfare of the Child which link to safeguarding are stipulated, as well as a brief description given of the mandate of the African Committee of Experts on the Rights and Welfare of the Child. Some aspects of the practical working methods of the Committee are thereafter considered. With reference to the Committee's interface with non-governmental organisations, some proposals concerning the Committee and the safeguarding movement are put forward.

Reprinted from *Soc. Sci.* Cite as: Sloth-Nielsen, J. Regional Frameworks for Safeguarding Children: The Role of the African Committee of Experts on the Rights and Welfare of the Child. *Soc. Sci.* **2014**, *3*, 948–961.

1. Introduction

This article commences with the basic introduction to the child safeguarding movement and its core precepts and principles. It then turns to a brief elaboration of the substantive provisions of the African Charter on the Rights and Welfare of the Child (1990) and their relevance to the safeguarding movement. Thereafter, the role of the African Committee of Experts on the Rights and Welfare of the Child, the body in charge of monitoring the implementation of the Charter, is elaborated with reference to the mandate it derives from the Charter. The section which follows discusses the reporting mechanisms incurred by States Parties. It also describes some aspects of the everyday practices of the Committee insofar as they pertain to safeguarding principles. The penultimate section examines the Committee's interface with NGOs, prior to formulating some proposals for improving the Committee's response to safeguarding standards and their implementation.

2. Child Safeguarding

Child safeguarding is the responsibility that civil society organisations have to make sure their staff, operations, and programmes "do no harm" to children, that is, that they do not expose children to the risk of harm and abuse, and that any concerns the organisation has about children's safety within the communities in which they work are reported to the appropriate authorities. It, thus, concerns the activities and functionning of organisations that are in contact with children, in the first instance.

The child safeguarding movement was born out of the realisation that relief workers, development agencies, humanitarian organisations and the like, many of whom do not have children as their primary focus or mandate, can and do become involved in abuse of children, or become aware of it occurring during the course of their endeavours. As Keepingchildrensafe.org detail, in 2002, a joint report by the United Nations High Commission for Refugees and Save the Children claimed child abuse was endemic in refugee camps, highlighting allegations against 67 workers and 42 agencies involving 40 victims. In 2004, it was reported that in the Democratic Republic of Congo (DRC), many girls and women traded sex for food and other items with peacekeepers as a survival tactic. Save the Children reported from research in 2008, in Cote D'Ivoire, Sudan, and Haiti, that nearly 90% of those interviewed recalled incidents of children being sexually exploited by aid workers and peacekeepers [1]. In September 2014, Human Rights Watch released a report providing evidence that African Union (AU) soldiers, relying on Somali intermediaries, have used a range of tactics, including humanitarian aid, to coerce vulnerable women and girls into sexual activity. They have also raped or otherwise sexually assaulted women who were seeking medical assistance or water at African Union Mission in Somilia (AMISOM) bases. The report prompted AU Commission chair Dr. Nkosazana Dlamini-Zulu to appoint a commission of inquiry into the allegations on 21 October 2014.

Furthermore, when abuse of children is reported within organisations, it is often concealed and dealt with as an internal matter, as the organisations concerned (often reliant on donor funding) do not wish to air their dirty laundry in public. The safeguarding movement acknowledges that commitment to protection of children often involves challenging deep rooted cultural perceptions about children, for instance relating to the role of corporal punishment, traditional practices which can be harmful to children, early marriage, and so on. This may be especially relevant for locally recruited staff in aid and humanitarian operations, given that they are drawn from local communities.

Impunity for violations of children's rights in the context of violence against children has been identified as endemic and routine [2], with adult perpetrators seldom being held accountable. Taking steps to introduce mechanisms within organisations working in the development sector and their implementing partners to improve accountability is seen as a way of reducing the impunity of adults and mitigating risks to children. Hence, the safeguarding movement can overlap with child protection, but does not cover the same terrain, as it deals principally with intra-organisational policy and practice, rather than service delivery and programmes.

The safeguarding concept extends beyond direct actions (such as violence) against children, to include ensuring that everyone in an organisation behaves appropriately and does not abuse the position of trust that comes with being an aid or development worker (whose role can be very influential and powerful, even in difficult and conflict or emergency situations). It also entails assessing risks to children in advance that are associated with activities as diverse as where to build playgrounds (avoiding marshy spaces to minimise the risk of a child accidently drowning) to when and how cash transfers are distributed [3].

Child safeguarding members have oriented their advocacy around four central standards which seen together constitute the framework for implementation of child safeguarding strategies at a local level. These are as follows:

(1) Policy: the member organisations are encouraged to develop a policy that describes how it is committed to preventing, and responding appropriately to, harm to children;
(2) People: the member organisations are expected to place clear responsibilities and expectations on their staff and associates (including volunteers) and to support them by holding training and capacity building to understand and act in line with the child

protection policies; futhermore, organisations are required to implement "child sensitive" recruitment processes for both staff and volunteers;

(3) Procedures: the member organisations must strive to create a child-safe environment through implementing child safeguarding procedures that are applied across the organisation; these include steps to be taken when an incident of abuse or the risk of abuse is reported;

(4) Accountability: the member organisations should monitor and review their safeguarding measures, thereby also ensuring that infringements are not met with impunity [4].

The child safeguarding movement is based on the principles that: all children have equal rights to protection from harm; that everybody has a responsibility to support the protection of children even if child care and protection is not their core mandate; that further to this, organisations have a duty of care to children with whom they work, are in contact with, or who are affected by their work and operations; and that if organisations work with partners, such as community-based groups or local actors from civil society, they then have an added responsibility to help partners meet the minimum requirements for the protection of the child beneficiaries (direct or indirect) of their interventions [4].

All actions on child safeguarding are taken in the best interests of the child, which are paramount [4]. Thus, the child's best interests determine the kind of response to be initiated when a complaint is received. The adoption of a complaints procedure for following up on reports received is a core tenet of organisational practice.

The members of the safeguarding movement are a diverse array of NGOs, civic organisations, UN agencies and INGOs, and faith-based organisations. This has implications for understanding the interplay between child safeguarding and the role of the African Committee of Experts on the Rights and Welfare of the Child (ACERWC), as will be explained below. The principle contribution of the safeguarding partners to date appears to have been the creation of specific standards to be applied within organisational development processes to further child protection, as well as institutionalising child protection within organisational development, including in organisations whose principle activities do not principally concern children.

3. The Charter Mechanisms

The principle framework for addressing child protection and safety in this regional context is the text of the African Charter on the Rights and Welfare of the Child (ACRWC) itself. Two areas warrant discussion: the substantive provisions affecting the protection of children against certain rights violations, and the provisions which determine the mandate of the Committee of Experts, the body elected to oversee implementation of the Charter provisions [5].

3.1. Substantive Provisions

The principle protection against child abuse and torture (as the article is headed) is to be found in article 16 of the Charter. This sets a high bar in requiring States Parties to take specific legislative, administrative, social and educational measures to protect the child from all forms of torture, inhuman or degrading treatment and especially physical or mental injury or abuse, neglect or maltreatment including sexual abuse, while in the care of the child (sic) [6].

The article differs in one respect from article 19 of the Convention on the Rights of the Child (CRC), insofar as it adds torture, ill treatment and degrading treatment to the violence protection covered in article 19 of the CRC. However, given the extensive interpretation of violence that has taken root at the international level, inter alia through publications of the UN Secretary General's Special Representative on Violence against Children [7] and the CRC Committee's General Comment (No. 13) on Violence against Children [8], it is doubtful that inhuman or degrading treatment is not already provided for under the rubric of "all forms of violence against children". Arguably, "inhuman treatment" and "degrading treatment" are, for instance, comprehensively addressed in paragraphs 20 and 21 of the CRC Committee's General Comment referred to above, which also clarify that the concept of violence is not capable of being exhaustively determined [9]. Further, paragraph 21 of the General Comment specifically refers to inhuman and degrading treatment in the context of physical punishment, and paragraph 26 elaborates on this theme [10]. Thus the differences in the text of the ACRWC and the CRC are not material.

Article 16(2) of the ACRWC, which echoes article 19(2) of the CRC, provides for the implementation mechanism: it requires protective measures under article 16(1) to include procedures for the establishment of special monitoring units to provide the necessary support for the child and for those who have the care of the child, as well as other forms of prevention, and for identification, reporting, referral, investigation, treatment and follow up of instances of child abuse and neglect. This provision therefore appears to fall squarely within the safeguarding paradigm, especially to the extent that the safeguarding coalition is aimed at prevention of violations of children's rights in the first instance, but where this does occur, then at follow up and redress.

Mention must also be made in the African context of articles 15 and 21 of the Charter. Article 15 deals with the protection of children from all forms of economic exploitation and from performing work likely to be hazardous or harmful or to interfere with a child's physical, mental, spiritual, moral or social development. The article requires a minimum age for admission to employment, appropriate regulation of hours and conditions under which children work; and appropriate penalties and sanctions and dissemination of information on the hazards of child labour to all sectors of the community. Whilst it is possibly farfetched that the kinds of organisations who become members of child safeguarding initiatives would employ child labour directly, and especially children below the minimum age of employment, can the same be said of all their employees? The phenomenon of housemaids and young girls in domestic work is ubiquitous in some regions and contexts, and is hidden from scrutiny because it occurs at a household level. It would be desirable that member organisations require their employees, volunteers and associates to sign up to international standards in regard to the use of child labour in domestic work, and that these commitments of employees are monitored for compliance.

Similarly, the protection provided by article 21 of the ACRWC deserves to be highlighted. This article provides for comprehensive protection against harmful social and cultural practices which affect the welfare, dignity, normal growth and development of the child, and, in particular, those practices which are prejudicial to the health of the child and those which discriminate on the basis of sex or other status. Article 21 also prescribes a minimum age of marriage to be 18 years. There is growing normative consensus—internationally, as well as on the African continent—on at least the most egregious forms of harmful cultural practice, such as Female Genital Mutilation/Cutting (FGM), early marriage, killing of children with disabilities, or those accused of witchcraft. The question arises, within the context of the enormously varied contexts within which organisations committed to safeguarding operate, how they "police" associates, employees and volunteers for compliance with article 21? For instance, is taking a child bride, or allowing daughters below the minimum age to be married, proscribed for staff? In addition, what would the consequences be of associates or volunteers allowing FGM to be performed on their daughters? Admittedly, the approach of the safeguarding movement tends to blend capacity building and education of staff with more reactive approaches (ending impunity and ensuring follow up via organisational child protection protocols), but where the line is drawn on remedial action (e.g., dismissal) is not always clear cut.

Article 27 of the Charter is also relevant: it provides for protection against sexual exploitation and sexual abuse. State Parties are required in particular to take measures to prevent the inducement, coercion or encouragement of a child to engage in any sexual activity. This might extend to online behaviours undertaken by staff in both official settings and in their homes, such as inappropriate sexting, posting of sexually explicit material on social media, and so forth. Given the rapid increase in access to digital media (especially via cellphones) which is occurring in developing regions, the risk of harm to children via online activities is real rather than illusory.

Finally, article 22 of the ACRWC deals with children and armed conflict. It sets a much higher standard than the equivalent provision of the UN CRC. In addition to prohibiting the recruitment of children (aged below 18 years) into state armed forces, it requires states to ensure that they take all necessary measures to ensure that "no child takes part in hostilities". This prohibition also applies to internal armed conflicts and strife [11], which suggests that organisations in specific settings may bear some level of responsibility for children not associated with state armies, e.g., when working in camps and in disaster and relief work. This provision may additionally have a bearing on civil society and humanitarian organisations which are in contact with rebel groups, factions and gangs.

3.2. The Mandate of the African Committee of Experts on the Rights and Welfare of the Child (ACERWC)

Forty-seven of the fifty-four states of the AU have ratified the Charter at the time of writing, and the ACERWC has launched a campaign to lobby for universal ratification by the time of the 25th anniversary of the Charter in November 2015. The Committee comprises 11 experts elected by secret ballot by the AU Heads of State for a five-year term. The mandate of the ACERWC in the Charter is expansive. It is obviously premised on the State Party reporting procedure in the first instance, according to article 43 [11] and, to this end, it must be noted that there has been a dramatic increase in reports received and considered by the Committee in the last while—13 reports are currently awaiting consideration. Additional to this, the Committee has the broad mandate as prescribed by article 42 to promote and protect the rights of the child enshrined in the Charter, to collect and document information, to commission interdisciplinary assessments of the situation of children in Africa, to organise meetings on child rights, and to encourage national and local institutions concerned with the rights and welfare of the child, as well as giving its views on child rights and making recommendations to governments (Article 42(a)(i)) [11].

The Committee is empowered to formulate and lay down rules aimed at protecting the rights of children in Africa (Article 42(a)(ii)), and to cooperate with other African, international and regional institutions in connection with the promotion of children's rights and welfare. It may also interpret the Charter's provisions at the request of a State Party or an institution of the AU or "any other person or institution recognised by the AU or any State Party" (Article 42(c)). The Committee is enabled by the treaty to perform such other tasks as may be entrusted to it by the Assembly of the Heads of State of the AU, the Secretary General of the AU or any other organs of the AU or the UN (Article 42(d)). This conglomeration of capacities accorded the Committee of Experts is often referred to as the elaboration of the Committee's promotional mandate [12,13].

Article 45 concerns the investigative mandate of the Committee, which may "resort to any appropriate method of investigating any matter falling within the ambit of the Charter". The Committee, in fulfilling this assignment, may request from the State Parties any information relevant to the implementation of the Charter, and may also resort to any method of investigating the measures the State Party has adopted to implement the Charter.

The provisions of article 44 concern the Charter's communications procedure. The article is brief:

(1) The Committee may receive a communication from any person, group or nongovernmental organisation recognised by the AU, by a member state, or the UN relating to any matter covered by this Charter;

(2) Every communication to the Committee shall contain the name and address of the author and shall be treated in confidence.

However, the Committee of Experts has elaborated much more fully the requirements for the submission of a communication in its Guidelines for the Consideration of Communications [14]. From the text of article 44, it emerges that, as long as a communication relates to "any matter" covered in the Charter, there is a broad remit as to who may submit a communication and upon which issue. To date the Committee has received three communications, and the judgment on one made fully public [15,16]. None really deals with the concerns of the safeguarding movement, since all three have been brought against governments as the alleged perpetrator of rights violations.

Questions as to the interface between the protective objectives of the safeguarding alliance and the work of the Committee will be addressed further below. Suffice it to state at this point that the primary duty bearers under the Charter are State signatories, *i.e.*, governments. Whilst NGOs play a complementary role, as will be elucidated in the penultimate section, they are not primarily accountable for fulfilment of the Charter rights *vis-à-vis* the Committee.

4. Subsidiary Mechanisms: The Reporting Guidelines; Dialogue with State Parties and Award of Observer Status

4.1. Guidelines for State Parties

The first set of Guidelines that may have relevance to the issue of safeguarding of children are the Guidelines on the Form and Content of Periodic State Party Reports to be Submitted Pursuant to Article 43(1)(b) of the African Charter on the Rights and Welfare of the Child [17]. These Guidelines give some clues as to what information on safeguarding–related matters and child protection in general could be required by the Committee, or brought to Committee's attention by State Parties who are submitting reports.

First, the State Party should provide information on:

- Legislative, administrative, social and educational measures taken to protect children from all forms of torture, inhuman or degrading treatment. In particular, the State Party should indicate whether it has outlawed corporal punishment in all settings; and
- Whether it has established special monitoring units to provide necessary support for children and for those who have the care of the child ([18], para. 19(a)(f)).

Second, with regards to harmful cultural practices, the Guidelines require State Parties to provide information on:

(a) The nature, type and prevalence of harmful social and cultural practices within its jurisdiction;
(b) Measures taken to discourage and eliminate harmful social and cultural practices;
(c) Measures taken to rescue and rehabilitate children who have been subjected to or affected by harmful social and harmful practices;
(d) Where applicable, measures taken to specifically protect children with albinism from violence;
(e) Whether child marriage and the betrothal of girls and boys are prohibited under its laws.

Information should also be provided on: whether the State Party has taken effective action to specify the minimum age of marriage to be eighteen years; and whether it has made registration of all marriages in an official registry compulsory ([18], para. 23). With regard to sexual exploitation, the State Party should provide relevant and updated information on measures taken to protect the child from all forms of sexual exploitation and sexual abuse ([18], para. 22(f)).

The Guidelines do not, therefore, specifically refer to the safeguarding principles, although they could be expanded to include steps that a State Party has put in place to require non-profit organisations which it registers or licenses to comply with safeguarding principles. An example in point is South Africa. First, the Children's Act 75 of 2005 establishes a National Child Protection Register, and Part B thereof contains the names of persons found unsuitable to work with children. Amongst other duty bearers, any person managing or operating an institution, centre, facility or school must establish whether the name of any person who works with or has access to children at the institution, centre, facility or school appears in Part B of the Register; as must any designated child protection organisation [19]. In addition, it has been proposed that when amendments to the Children's Act are effected, that an insertion in the Act will enable the Minister to prescribe a code of conduct for persons or organisations involved in child protection [20]. This code of conduct will clarify how children are to be treated by non-state staff employed by organisations working with children. For instance, it has been proposed that the code should specify that staff may not sleep close to unsupervised children unless absolutely necessary in which case the staff member must obtain the manager's permission and ensure that another adult is present if possible. Further, the code should provide that staff may not use any computers, mobile phones or video or digital cameras inappropriately to exploit or harass children or to access pornography through any medium. The code should spell out that staff must refrain from physical punishment or discipline of children, as well as from hiring children for domestic or other labour which is inappropriate given their age or developmental stage and which interferes with their time available for education and recreational activities or which places them at significant risk of injury. The code should require staff to comply with all relevant legislation including labour laws in relation to child labour. Staff must be required to immediately report any concerns about or allegations of child abuse in accordance with appropriate procedures. The code should specify that non-compliance with the code would render them liable to a disciplinary hearing and a finding of unsuitability to work with children. Further, if organisations failed to implement a code of conduct (as prescribed), they could lose their accreditation to provide services to children, as also any government fiscal support. If enacted, these provisions would go some way forward to incorporate safeguarding principles in the domestic law of one African country, South Africa, at a level of detail that is probably a first on the continent.

However, licensing of non-profit organisations dealing with children is being or has been developed in a growing number of African countries, including Rwanda, Tanzania, and Kenya. This could provide a suitable base from which safeguarding principles could develop in domestic legal systems.

4.2. Dialogue with State Parties

In dialogue with States Parties having their reports considered by the Committee, the issues of child protection which interlink with the safeguarding initiatives could well be raised. However, since the frontline duty bearers under the Charter are State Parties, the exact nature of the State's obligations in respect of the activities and work methods of private sector organisations remains less obvious. However, State Parties could be required to show that there is an adequate response where children's rights are violated, either through criminal sanctions being pursued, disciplinary sanctions being imposed, or through licensing and registration legislation which penalises or disallows registration of organisations who do not react appropriately to breaches of children's rights. Furthermore, the State itself should ensure that safeguarding principles are upheld in relation to its own organs and employees who work with children—teachers, social workers, police, and so forth.

4.3. Observer Status

Committee practice permits that NGOs and INGOs concerned with children's rights in Africa may apply to the Committee for observer status. Rules for the consideration of applications for observer status have been developed [5]. To date, approximately ten such applications have been granted. Several more applications are under consideration. Similarly, organisations concerned with human rights on the continent may also acquire Observer Status before the African Commission on Human and Peoples' Rights which monitors the implementation of the African Charter on Human and Peoples' Rights (1980). Several member organisations of the safeguarding movement have applied for and received observer status before the ACERWC, which allows for a close linkage with the Committee. Observer status enables participation at Committee meetings, allows the organisations to make statements on issues that concern them, with the permission of the chairperson, and to request the inclusion of specific issues on the agenda of the Committee. Adherents to safeguarding principles therefore can forge a closer working relationship with the Committee. In future, were the criteria for the award of observer status to be amended, it is conceivable that applicants could be required to show that they have implemented safeguarding protocols internally. In this way, the ACERWC could complement the enforcement of safeguarding principles amongst organisations whose work affects children on the continent.

5. The Committee's Interface with NGOs

The Committee has a proud history of collaboration with NGOs and INGOs and since 2009, the Committee meetings have been preceded by a Civil Society Organisation Forum for the ACRWC, convened by an independent steering committee which is representative of the five geopolitical regions of Africa. Nine such meetings have to date been held, and according to the CSO Forum website, 446 affiliates from Africa are members of the Forum [21]. The event is usually attended by at least two committee members. The deliberations and conclusions are presented formally to the Committee at its opening ceremony. The CSO Forum represents an excellent opportunity for member organisations to place safeguarding formally on the agenda of likeminded civil society organisations, to use the audience present at the Forum to explore best practice amongst other organisations, and to disseminate examples of organisational child protection policies.

Civil society is also consulted by the Committee prior to the consideration of state party reports in closed pre-sessional meetings. In the majority of instances, civil society organisations in coalition compile formal complementary reports for the attention of the Committee. Hence, there is an avenue for raising safeguarding concerns to the extent that a State Party can be encouraged to adopt improved or different policies which affect the issue.

The Committee has from time to time held themed discussion sessions, for instance on harmful cultural practices and on birth registration. These have been characterised by wide participation from civil society as well as policy makers. The principles of safeguarding might be useful to profile, especially in the context of the diverse programmes and initiatives that the AU itself undertakes, including its peacekeeping operations, its staff recruitment policies and its internal channels for receiving complaints about child rights violations committed by staff or those allied to AU institutions.

It is true that exposing intra-organisational child rights violations may give rise to enormous reputational risk for those structures and NGOs which institute serious efforts to curb violations and end impunity. For organisations which purport to be furthering children's rights, or which are involved directly in child protection, exposure of such behaviours could be catastrophic from a donor angle.

However, the obverse is also the case. The recent Human Rights Watch report exposing sexual exploitation and rape by peacekeeping soldiers (chiefly from Burundi and Uganda) in AMISOM bases illustrates that abuse which is hidden from public scrutiny may in any event surface via other means or sources. This could be seen as a powerful incentive for civil society organisations to engage with safeguarding, as a preventive tool. It does, however, require the upfront acknowledgement that child rights violations are pervasive, that cultural beliefs which are found at community level also manifest amongst staff, associated partners and their staff and volunteers, and that a "not in my back yard" attitude prevents educational efforts to change behaviours.

6. Proposals for Improving the Response to Safeguarding in Regional Context and the Role of the ACERWC

There is considerable guidance to be sought in the CRC Committee's General Comment No. 13, the Right of the Child to Freedom from all Forms of Violence [8], on essential measures to combat violence against children in its many forms. The General Comment's Paragraph 49, for instance, requires that in every country, professionals who work directly with children should be required to report instances of violence or risk of violence against children. The ACERWC could include in the list of questions it puts to States Parties questions relating to the legal framework for the reporting of child abuse and neglect, if the State Party in its report has not spelt out in sufficient detail what legal mechanisms are in place.

Similarly, paragraph 53 [8] of the General Comment describes the necessity of follow up when a report is made. The paragraph continues:

> The following must always be clear: (a) who has responsibility for the child and family from reporting and referral all the way through to follow-up; (b) the aims of any course of action taken—which must be fully discussed with the child and other relevant stakeholders; (c) the details, deadlines for implementation and proposed duration of any interventions; and (d) mechanisms and dates for the review, monitoring and evaluation of actions. Continuity between stages of intervention is essential and this may best be achieved through a case management process.

Paragraph 55 deals with a range of interventions to ensure that violence against children is not met with impunity. Thus, States must ensure (amongst others) that disciplinary or administrative proceedings are taken against professionals for neglectful or inappropriate behaviour in dealing with suspected cases of child maltreatment (either via internal proceedings in the context of professional bodies for breaches of codes of ethics or standards of care, or through external proceedings ([8], paragraph 55(d) of the General Comment). Again, the ACERWC could usefully explore in dialogue with States Parties whether disciplinary and administrative proceedings are in fact utilised when breaches occur.

Finally, and also taken from the General Comment, is the suggestion of a National Coordinating Framework on Violence against Children. According to paragraph 69 of the General Comment [8] "[t]his coordinating framework can provide a common frame of reference and a mechanism for communication among Government ministries and also for State and civil society actors at all levels with regard to needed measures, across the range of measures and at each stage of intervention identified in Article 19. It can promote flexibility and creativity and allow for the development and implementation of initiatives led simultaneously by both Government and community, but which are nonetheless contained within an overall cohesive and coordinated framework". Together with civil society partners, the ACERWC can champion the development of such National Coordinating Frameworks at country level to ensure an improved response to violence perpetrated upon children, and to take account of some of the initiatives furthered by the safeguarding movement.

7. Limits and Contributions of the Safeguarding Endeavour

At the risk of repetition, it is worth stressing that safeguarding (as discussed here) and the development and implementation of child protection systems are not co-terminous [22]. There may be some overlap, such as where formal child protection measures are invoked as a result of safeguarding policies (reporting to the police, criminal justice action against perpetrators of violations), but the child safeguarding movement is primarily aimed at organisational development amongst non-state actors. It targets all staff (who may or may not be professionals), including drivers, cleaners, receptionists, fieldworkers and volunteers. It is intended to hold organisations to account through periodic auditing, monitoring and review. This provides at once one limitation of safeguarding and, at the same time, a strength. The limitation is that it is consciously introspective, and it does not deal at all with the (formal) external environment: is there a functioning child protection system? Are cases appropriately pursued once reported? Additionally, are state and community child protection structures functioning appropriately? These are not questions that the safeguarding movement seeks to answer. However, the narrow intra-organisational lens also lays the basis for a truly practical and preventive approach to combatting harm to children.

It has been acknowledged that safeguarding is a journey—"no organisation can claim that all children it connects with are entirely safe all the time" [3]. Once this reality is conceded, another important point emerges: namely that changing behaviour involves complex engagements about attitudes, values and beliefs. Much in the same way as current initiatives to stop FGM/C are bearing some fruit because they engage at village and community level with deeply held tenets of culture, safeguarding adherents recognise that a conscious effort to change hearts and minds is required to end exploitation in its many guises. This is challenging in a development context where many staff and partners are themselves part of communities whose cultural norms are at odds with commitments to "do no harm". It means confronting issues like early marriage, child labour, exploitative practices and corporal punishment deliberately, rather than denying that they impact within the aid and development sector much as they do in the community at large.

It is discernible that the safeguarding movement is premised on both a "top down" and a "bottom up" approach. Little progress will be made unless there is an endorsement at the highest level of an organisation of a commitment to develop the necessary policies and to implement them with rigour (a "zero tolerance approach", [3]). At the same time, the standards have to take root in the day-to-day lives of staff and associates throughout the organisation, which implies ongoing education, sensitization and capacity building at all levels from the bottom up. It, thus, is evident that inculcating safeguarding principles in practice is not, and cannot be, a "quick fix", but that it will require investments which are sustained over time.

8. Conclusions

The safeguarding initiative is a useful contribution to end impunity for violations of children's rights. It is particularly appropriate insofar as it moves the agenda from a national level and away from the realm of the state, to engage with local organisations, their partners, and the people actually working with children on a daily basis. It is also especially relevant to the African context, where the vast majority of services to children, and indeed welfare services generally, are not undertaken by government functionaries but by civil society and community-based groups, and by religious organisations.

Further to this, the safeguarding movement has as its basis the practicalities of child protection, including requiring child sensitive recruitment and screening procedures, complaints mechanisms which are monitored and reviewed for effectiveness, and codes of conduct which are supportive of children's rights. It requires a conscious assessment of risks to children, including inadvertent ones. It requires organisations to engage deliberately with difficult questions of culture and tradition amongst their staff and affiliates, and to shift values and attitudes. This deserves support.

Finally, although State signatories are the primary duty bearers for the implementation of children's rights under the ACRWC, there is considerable room for complementary dialogue between the members of the movement, individually and collectively, and the ACERWC. Some suggestions in this regard have been proffered.

Acknowledgments

The author would like to thank the organisers of the "Child Safeguarding" conference held in Cape Town, South Africa, 3–5 September 2014, for inspiring this paper, and the member organisations whose websites and publications have yielded useful information to underpin this article.

Abbreviations

ACRWC: African Charter on the Rights and Welfare of the Child;
ACERWC: African Committee of Experts on the Rights and Welfare of the Child;
AU: African Union;
CRC: Convention on the Rights of the Child;
INGOs: International Non-Governmental Organisations;
NGOs: Non-Governmental Organisations;
UN: United Nations.

Conflicts of Interest

The author declares no conflict of interest.

References

1. See for further information: Keeping Children Safe. Available online: http://www.keepingchildrensafe.org.uk/faq (accessed on 28 August 2014) and sources cited there.

2. See for instance, Centre for Applied Legal Studies, University of the Witwatersrand School of Law, and Cornell Law School's Avon Global Center for Women and Justice and International Human Rights Clinic. *Sexual Violence by Educators in South Africa's Schools: Gaps in Accountability*. Johannesburg: Centre for Applied Legal Studies, 2014. Despite a prohibition in law on corporal punishment by educators having been on the statute book in South Africa since 1996, studies estimated that 2 million children were subjected to corporal punishment in schools in 2012.
3. Examples from a presentation by the Richard Powell, International head of Child Safeguarding for Save the Children International. "Progress and Challenges of Child Safeguarding in the Aid and Development Sector." Paper presented at the Child Safeguarding Conference, Cape Town, South Africa, 2–5 September 2014.
4. Keeping Children Safe. "Child Safeguarding standards and how to implement them." 2014. Available online: http://www.keepingchildrensafe.org.uk/resources/child-safeguarding-standards-and-how-implement-them (accessed on 28 August 2014).
5. See in general the website of the ACERWC. Available online: http://www.acerwc.org (accessed on 10 September 2014).
6. The text of article 19 of the CRC reads that the protection applies against parents, legal guardians and other having the care of the child. Some words appeared to have been omitted from this phrase in Article 16 of the Charter.
7. UN Secretary General's Special Representative. Available online: http://www.srsg.violenceagainstchildren.com (accessed on 10 September 2014) and various thematic reports available there.
8. Convention on the Rights of the Child. "The rights of the child to freedom from all forms of violence." Available online: http://www2.ohchr.org/english/bodies/crc/docs/CRC.C.GC.13_en.pdf (accessed on 24 November 2014).
9. "Mental violence", as referred to in the Convention, is often described as psychological maltreatment, mental abuse, verbal abuse and emotional abuse or neglect and this can include: (a) All forms of persistent harmful interactions with the child, for example, conveying to children that they are worthless, unloved, unwanted, endangered or only of value in meeting another's needs; (b) Scaring, terrorizing and threatening; exploiting and corrupting; spurning and rejecting; isolating, ignoring and favouritism; (c) Denying emotional responsiveness; neglecting mental health, medical and educational needs; (d) Insults, name-calling, humiliation, belittling, ridiculing and hurting a child's feelings; (e) Exposure to domestic violence; (f) Placement in solitary confinement, isolation or humiliating or degrading conditions of detention; and (g) Psychological bullying and hazing by adults or other children, including via information and communication technologies (ICTs) such as mobile phones and the Internet (known as "cyberbullying").
10. This defines "physical violence includes: (a) All corporal punishment and all other forms of torture, cruel, inhuman or degrading treatment or punishment…"

11. See Article 22(2) and 22(3). African Committee of Experts on the Rights and Welfare of the Child (ACERWC). "African Charter on the Rights and Welfare of the Child." Available online: http://acerwc.org/the-african-charter-on-the-rights-and-welfare-of-the-child-acrwc/acrwc-en/ (accessed on 24 November 2014).
12. See for instance, Frances Shehan. *Advancing Children's Rights: A Guide for Civil Society Organisations on How to Engage with the African Committee of Experts on the Rights and Welfare of the Child*. London: Plan International and Save the Children, 2011.
13. Amanda Lloyd. "The African Committee of Experts on the Rights and Welfare of the Child." In *Children's Rights in Africa: A Legal Perspective*. Edited by Julia Sloth-Nielsen. Dartmouth: Ashgate, 2008, pp. 33–53.
14. A summary of these Guidelines will be available on the website of the Committee. The Guidelines were approved at the Committee meeting of October 2014.
15. This is the so-called Nubian Children decision (against the Government of Kenya). Available online: http://www.acerwc.org/wp-content/uploads/2011/09/002-09-IHRDA-OSJI-Nubian-children-v-Kenya-Eng (accessed on 10 September 2014).
16. See Julia Sloth-Nielsen. "Chapter 15: Children's rights in litigation before the African Committee of Experts on the Rights and Welfare of the Child." In *Litigating the Rights of the Child*. Edited by Ton Liefaard and Jaap Doek. Dordrecht: Springer Publishers, 2014.
17. These were adopted at the 23nd Ordinary Session of the Committee in April 2014.
18. African Committee of Experts on the Rights and Welfare of the Child. *Guidelines on the Form and Content of Periodic State Party Reports*. Addis Ababa: ACERWC, 2015, forthcoming.
19. Government of the Republic of South Africa. "Section 123 of the Children's Act." Available online: http://www.justice.gov.za/legislation/acts/2005-038%20childrensact.pdf (accessed 24 November 2014).
20. These submissions were made at various workshops convened by the National Department of Social Development with civil society organisations during 2011 and 2012 to debate amendments to the Children's Act. The proceedings were captured and incorporated in an as yet unpublished report (copy on file with the author).
21. Civil Society Forum. Available online: http://www.csoforum.info (accessed on 10 September 2014).
22. For a different use of the term "safeguarding" to theorize emerging approaches to child abuse and neglect, see Nigel Parton. *Safeguarding Childhood: Early Intervention and Surveillance in a Late Modern Society*. Basingstoke: Palgrave MacMillan, 2006.